DALTON GANG DAYS

To Uncle Boyd,
I know you will enjoy reading this. We are all just a bunch of outlaws anyway! I love you.
Sis
7/2005

"Gene" Kay

Taken at the Tulare home of Frank and Jean Latta in 1932.
Photo by Frank F. Latta and now in Bear State Library.

DALTON GANG DAYS
From California to Coffeeville

By: FRANK F. LATTA

Bear State Books
Exeter, California

2001

Printed in the United States of America

Dalton Gang Days
Frank Forrest Latta

Published by
Bear State Books
Post Office Box 96
Exeter, California 93221

ISBN: 1-892622-14-9

California History
Copyright © Latta Family Trust, 1977

All rights reserved. **Published by express permission of the Trustees of the Latta Family Trust.** No part of this publication may be reproduced, distributed, performed, or displayed, in any form **or** by any means, without the prior express written permission of the **Trustees**.

First Edition Copyright 1976, Frank F. Latta
Edition Copyright © 2001 by Chris Brewer

Edition Printing, November, 2001

COVER:
The image on the cover shows a number of Dalton related artifacts, including the famous Grat Dalton shotgun. Beneath all is Latta's hand drawing of Coffeeville on October 5, 1892, with the names of the Dalton Gang placed where they were shot. A copy of the signed Littleton Dalton interview is on the left side of the map. Littleton Dalton's photograph is seen on the lower left. Tulare County Sheriff Eugene Kay's photograph is located under the butt of the Dalton Shotgun, on the right. The Dalton Shotgun was a Greener twelve-gauge double-barrel sawed-off shotgun carried to California in a suitcase by Grat Dalton in 1891. These artifacts are now in the collection of Bear State Library.

BEAR STATE BOOKS
Post Office Box 96
Exeter, California 93221
(559) 592-6576
(559) 592-5779 fax
k1718@earthlink.net

Table of Contents

INTRODUCTION
    "The Daltons Did It" xi

CHAPTER ONE
    The Dalton Clan 1

CHAPTER TWO
    The Mussel Slough Tragedy 21

CHAPTER THREE
    Playing with Fire 39

CHAPTER FOUR
    The Alila Robbery 57

CHAPTER FIVE
    The Andy Neff Special 77

CHAPTER SIX
    Six Thousand Mile Manhunt 101

CHAPTER SEVEN
    Grat Dalton's Trial 121

CHAPTER EIGHT
    Grat Dalton's Escape 133

CHAPTER NINE
    Captured: Bill Dalton, Beck, and Smith . . . 147

CHAPTER TEN
    Dalton Mountain Battle 161

CHAPTER ELEVEN
    Grat Dalton's Ride 179

CHAPTER TWELVE
    Oklahoma Train Robberies 185

Table of Contents

CHAPTER THIRTEEN
  The Battle Of The Banks 207

CHAPTER FOURTEEN
  Bill Dalton's Gang 231

CHAPTER FIFTEEN
  Holing Up 255

INDEX 279

AUTHOR'S PROFILE 292

ARTIST'S PROFILE 293

List of Illustrations

COFFEYVILLE RAID SITE	END SHEETS
"GENE" KAY	FRONTISPIECE
LITTLETON DALTON	xx
LITTLETON DALTON, TIPTON GRAIN WAREHOUSE	7
DALTON HOME, BELTON, MISSOURI, 1889	10
LITTLETON DALTON, BENEDICT RANCH, HANFORD, 1938	15
LITTLETON DALTON, BENEDICT BARN	16
FRANK DALTON, DEPUTY U.S. MARSHAL	25
FRANK DALTON GRAVE, COFFEYVILLE, KANSAS	26
GRAT DALTON, AGE 24	35
MUSSEL SLOUGH BATTLE SURVIVORS	37
PASSENGER TRAIN	40
GRAT DALTON, AGE 20	42
DALTON HOME, 1920	43
FEDERAL COURT HOUSE, FORT SMITH, ARKANSAS	50
LITTLETON DALTON, 1888	52
FRANK HALTER	55
LONGLINE PLOW TEAM	60
SOUTHERN PACIFIC PAY CAR, 1895	61
FIRST SAN JOAQUIN VALLEY TRAIN WRECK	75
GENE KAY, 1931	76
DAN OVERALL, SHERIFF OF TULARE COUNTY	78
THE "LITTLE DINKEY TRAIN."	80
GENE KAY, 1891	83
SOUTHERN PACIFIC ROUNDHOUSE, TULARE, 1889	85
POT-BELLIED LOCOMOTIVE	86

List of Illustrations

JAMES HUME, WELLS FARGO & COMPANY DETECTIVE	90
"ANDY" NEFF	91
SOUTHERN PACIFIC PAY CAR, KERN CITY	100
TOM FOWLER, LAKE HOUSE, 1938	104
EMMETT DALTON, 1907	107
TELEGRAM, EMMETT DALTON TO FRANK LATTA	108
COALINGA STATION	120
FRANK HALTER, 1949	127
GRAT DALTON'S SHOTGUN	132
COL. JACOB YOES, U.S. DEP. MARSHAL, FT. SMITH	140
BILL AND BOB DALTON, ROGUE'S GALLERY PHOTOS	153
LERDO STATION	160
ISAAC C. PARKER, THE "HANGING JUDGE."	178
BOB DALTON, 1889	191
CONDON BANK, COFFEYVILLE, 1892	209
DALTON HORSES IN DALTON ALLEY, COFFEYVILLE, 1892	211
DALTON ALLEY, COFFEYVILLE, 1892	214
CONDON BANK AND ISHAM HARDWARE, BATTLE AREA	216
DEATH, OR DALTON ALLEY, 1938	218
JOHN KLOHER, COFFEYVILLE LIVERYMAN	219
EX-DEPUTY U.S. MARSHAL GEORGE YOES	225
CHARLES GUMP	227
HEADSTONES OF DALTON GRAVES	228
TURNER RANCH BRICK BUNKHOUSE	230
BILL DALTON	233
WINCHESTER RIFLES	245
BLIVEN HOME, LIVINGSTON, CAL.	251
LITTLETON DALTON AND CLOVIS COLE, 1938	254
LITTLETON DALTON, 1896	259
LITTLETON DALTON, 1938	267

List of Illustrations

Bill Doolin, Leader Of The Doolin Gang	268
Bill Dalton, in Death	269
Bob Dalton, Just Before Burial	270
Grat Dalton, Just Before Burial	271
Bob And Grat Dalton, In Death	272
Dick Broadwell, Just Before Burial	273
Bill Powers, Just Before Burial	274
Bill Powers, Bob and Grat Dalton, Dick Broadwell, In Death	275
Emmett Dalton In Dr. Well's Office	276
Author	292
Artist	293

INTRODUCTION

"The Daltons Did It"

Probably no characters in American history have been so fictionized as have the train and bank robbers known as the Dalton Outlaw Gang. They held my earliest interest, as that of millions of other young Americans. When I was seven years of age, I had a more vivid mental picture of Bob and Grat Dalton than I had of George Washington. To my young imagination they were the most terrible monsters possible, having six-shooters instead of hands growing out of their wrists. I gained this childish impression when I heard father say that he had no use for people such as the Daltons, who always went about with a six-shooter in each coat sleeve.

A little later I hid out and studied the paper-backed, blood-and-thunder dime-novel Dalton tales that some of the ranch mule-skinners had been reading. To tell the truth, I didn't rate them very high. As I closely examined the lurid illustrations, I couldn't find one that showed six-shooters growing out of wrists.

Still later, I was permitted to glimpse two of the Daltons, probably Cole and Ben. They were working for a neighbor, hauling fire wood from the San Joaquin river. My elder brother drove our team close by where they were working. He nudged me with his elbow and said, "Those are the Daltons." My disillusionment was complete. Although they wore gloves, I could see they had common, ordinary hands. I saw not a single six-shooter anywhere.

Not only did at least five of the Dalton brothers work for our neighbor, one of them was arrested and charged with trying to rob a train in the county where we lived. Father later pointed out to me the site of the attempted robbery. They also made an attempt to rob another train in the San Joaquin Valley of California and two of them were arrested and tried for it.

After a battle with officers in Fresno County, one of the Daltons fled to our neighbor's ranch and was hidden there while the officers searched for him. Father showed me the old two-story house with the cupola from which Grat Dalton scanned the surrounding plains with a telescope, watching for inquisitive officers.

We mentioned the Daltons guardedly even ten years after all of them had left our section of California. They spoke the language of the six-gun and had many loyal friends in our community. They still have.

Undoubtedly a number of San Joaquin Valley train robberies were not performed by the Daltons, but there were few people who believed this.

Always the cry was, *"The Daltons did it!"*

From 1889 to 1898 seven train robberies were attempted between Ceres, Stanislaus County, California, and Alila, Tulare County. From the viewpoint of the robbers, five were successful and two were failures.

It is impossible to exaggerate the wildness of the stories circulated concerning those robberies. Loot was reported up to one hundred thousand dollars and at almost every figure below, generally specified as being in twenty-dollar gold pieces. In these days of soap-coupon currency, one who never has known the heavy, yellow money and the substantial feeling it brought, will miss much of the thrill of imagining himself in the robber's boots.

One story relates that fifty thousand in twenties was taken at Pixley, February 22, 1889, the first train robbery in the San Joaquin Valley; the only unpleasant feature of which was that an officer was wounded and a tramp was killed, opening a season on such gentry that was not to close for ten years.

The improvident robbers had brought along only a single grain sack in which to carry their loot. Fifty thousand dollars in twenties weighed a hundred and eighty-four pounds. The grain sack wouldn't stand the strain. One of the robbers took off his overalls and wired shut the bottoms of the legs. Setting them across the saddle in front of him, he dumped three five-thousand-dollar bags of double eagles into each leg, rode in his underwear in the dead of winter twenty miles to Porterville, and lived there happily ever after.

The above probably is not true, but, just the same, it is a wonderfully stimulating story.

Tales of buried loot were without end. From information confidentially furnished me by numerous persons, there must be at least seven hundred thousand dollars (all in twenty-dollar gold pieces) buried by trees, under fireplaces, and at measured distances from various landmarks up and down the length of the Joaquin. I never have turned a shovel full of dirt looking for them.

Half of the sky farmers in the Joaquin expected to plow up a cache of loot (more twenties), quit farming, pay off the mortgages on their ranches, and spend twenties the rest of their lives.

The stories did not end with mere possibilities. It is still whispered that at least one farmer *did* plow up a cache of loot (still more twenties), *did* pay all his bills, and spent twenties the rest of his life. According to U.S. Marshalls he never had a dollar of legitimate income during all of that time, sold no crops or cattle, and received no checks or currency through the mail or express.

Almost a year after Pixley came the Goshen job — more loot, the killing of another tramp, and more stories, twenty thousand dollars in twenties being the most popular figure.

Next, February 6, 1891, came Alila, a little village on the Southern Pacific route, now called Earlimart. The Alila attempt was a fizzle. After the fireman had been mortally wounded, the robbers were driven off.

After Alila, for the first time, came the cry, *"The Daltons did it!"* Then came grand jury indictments and arrests. Grat, Bill, Bob, and Emmett Dalton were indicted. Bob and Emmett skipped to Indian Territory. Grat and Bill were arrested and tried; Grat was convicted, Bill acquitted.

Before Grat was sentenced came another robbery, this time at Ceres, land of the goddess of plenty. But the goddess refused to smile. After battling with an officer, again the robbers were beaten off, and with no take. The officer was wounded.

Again, *"The Daltons did it!"*

So Bill Dalton was re-arrested, and, with him, Riley Dean. But Bill was terribly unfortunate in the Ceres affair and was as upset over the robbery as were the railroad detectives and officials. He soon proved himself innocent of Ceres. In fact, the Ceres robbery had been pulled by competitors of Bill, for at the very time when that robbery was being attempted, poor Bill and his friend, Dean, undoubtedly were laying plans of their own.

Not only the train robbers, but the officers, too, were so thick that they were beginning to get in the way of each other.

It is impossible to give an exaggerated idea of the state of excitement into which the San Joaquin Valley was thrown by these train robberies. For five years probably no fewer than five hundred gum-shoe sleuths of all kinds hung about the towns of Fresno, Hanford, Visalia, Tulare, Delano, and Bakersfield.

United States Deputy Marshal Guard had twenty-five deputies and secret service men in the field most of the time. Detectives and special officers, hired by the Southern Pacific and Wells Fargo, totalled at least as many more. For six years almost every passenger train through the San Joaquin Valley carried from one to three special officers.

Sheriffs of Tulare, Fresno, and Kern Counties constantly kept large forces in the field. To these may be added the constables, city marshals, police, and night watchmen of the various cities, towns, and villages and a swarm of unattached amateur detectives, gum-shoe sleuths, and reward hunters. There were so many of them that they spent much of their time watching each other.

If a farmer or business man hired a strange laborer or clerk, within a few weeks he almost was certain to be revealed as a detective. At the first news of a robbery, or at the formation of a posse, he would take to the trail without waiting to collect his pay. When news came of the Collis robbery, the entire clerical force of Linder's Tulare business firm proved to be detectives. They jumped up and joined the chase, leaving the store open and unattended.

By the time of the Collis affair the Daltons were blamed for almost every train robbery that had occurred on the Pacific Coast or in the Middle West after 1881. The reason for this was that the ethics and procedures of professional train robbers were highly standardized. An account of a robbery done in the late '70s or early '80s could have been reprinted twenty years later with only a change of date line, without furnishing a single clue as to the deception.

Here is a typical case:

In 1881 three robbers, beardless boys, except that the leader had a small, dark moustache, held up a train between the stations of Hope and Emmett, in Arkansas, northeast of Texarkana, Texas. They left their horses three miles from Hope, walked into town, and waited in a saloon, leaving the place only as the train pulled out. The third robber had to run in order to catch the train.

The robbers drank from a bottle as they prepared to stop the train. They took fifteen thousand dollars. As much more was overlooked. As the robbers left the train near their horses, they fired a volley at the train crew and profanely ordered them on their way.

After the Alila job the cry actually went up that *"The Daltons did it!"* in Arkansas in '81. It was claimed that Grat, Bill, and Bob *"did it."*

And small wonder.

In '81 the Daltons lived not far from Arkansas. They answered very closely the descriptions given of the Arkansas robbers. At Alila in '91 the three boys were about ten years older. One had a small moustache, dyed black. They drank from a bottle. Two of them tied their horses out of town and walked to the station. They ran for the train. The train was stopped near the horses. As the robbers left the train they fired a volley at the train crew and made pointed references to their probable canine ancestry. The principal discrepancy was that at Alila fifteen thousand dollars was *not* taken.

The principal details were the same at Pixley, Goshen, and at all the others to follow, the only notable refinement being the introduction of dynamite

INTRODUCTION

bombs to "open up" the express cars when express agents became stubborn. The train bandits had developed a system.

But the train crews were developing a system, too. Note the two successive failures, Alila and Ceres.

When arrests were made after Alila and it was known that *"The Daltons did it,"* the long-excited citizenry prepared to settle back into the tedious humdrum of life in the Joaquin, always with the mental reservation, of course, that it might happen again, because two of the Dalton Gang still were on the loose.

Ceres prodded the public awake and when Bill Dalton was arrested, they said, "Sure, we knew it. *The Daltons did it!"* True, Bill soon was cleared of the Ceres affair, but few people remembered or wanted to remember that unpopular fact.

The cry *"The Daltons did it"*, kept ringing for almost another year when on August 3, 1892, a train was robbed at Collis, now known as Kerman. The robbers were determined that Collis would be no such fizzle as had been Alila and Ceres. When the express messenger refused to open up, no less than eight heavy dynamite bombs were exploded and the express car was badly wrecked. Twenty thousand dollars (in twenties) was the story.

Again went up the cry, *"The Daltons— — — — !"*

But before the cry was well under way the truth broke with the bang of shotguns and six-guns at the residence of Chris Evans in the northern outskirts of Visalia. Bill Smith, railroad detective, and George Witty, Tulare County deputy sheriff, were wounded, deputy sheriff Oscar Beaver was killed, and most of the Tulare county citizenry were startled or badly scared.

In 1896 came Tagus Switch. Two special officers were badly wounded and a bandit was literally blown from the tender by four charges of buckshot fired simultaneously from below at a distance of three feet. Dan McCall thus was accorded the distinction of being the first California train bandit to die in action.

For the Tagus Switch job, Si Lovern went to San Quentin for life. Charlie Ardel turned state's evidence and later went crazy from fear of retribution, aided by large doses of cocaine and whiskey.

By the time of the Tagus Switch affair all four of the Dalton Gang had been liquidated or jailed, but there were still four brothers left. Two of these, Cole and Littleton, were working on ranches in Fresno County, and Ben in Madera County, California. Again went up the cry, *"The Daltons did it!"* At least they must have been behind it.

Although none of the Daltons was arrested, this cry was the last straw for Littleton and Cole. Both left the San Joaquin Valley. Lit hid so well that many relatives and life-long friends never knew what had become of him. Forty-five years later some of them were astounded to learn that he still was living.

Sketchy, colored, and even facetious as may seem the foregoing pages, actually they are as nearly accurate and revealing as anything that has been written about the Dalton Gang. A half dozen prominent writers have turned out page after page about the Daltons, depending for their sources on lurid, paper-back books of yarns and wild tales, common throughout the land.

Emmett Dalton, only survivor of the Dalton Gang, wrote two books, one a paper-back, titled *Beyond the Law,* published in 1918, and the other a more legitimate-appearing volume, titled *When the Daltons Rode,* published in 1930. Neither book agrees completely with known records and facts, nor with each other. Of course, Emmett had been tried for only one crime, but he admitted participation in many. It is easy to understand how, as Emmett stated to me, "I can't put the finger of the law on myself."

For more than seventy-five years the truth about the Dalton Gang and other California bandits has been hidden from all writers of legitimate history, who have waded about in a maze of mystifying yarns and tales, hopelessly mingling some possible fact with much proven fiction.

True, there were some records. Grat and Bill Dalton had been tried for train robbery. But the testimony of most of the witnesses was known to be unreliable, and the rest was suspected of being the same. The trial records did prove, however, that neither Grat nor Bill had been at the scene of the Alila robbery. Otherwise the records were worthless.

Little by little, here and there, fragments of authentic history were brought to light by this author. First of these came from Ben Maddox and Harry Charters, Visalia and Tulare newspaper editors of Dalton Gang Days. Others came from the McDonald brothers of Estrella, neighbors of Bill Dalton when the Alila job was done, and from Arch Turner, who furnished Grat Dalton with the horse upon which he made his famous ride from Merced County to Indian Territory. But their stories were fragments. It was impossible ever to complete an historical account of Dalton Gang Days from the material at hand.

Then came the important discovery that Eugene W. Kay, Dalton Days Sheriff of Tulare county, still was living. Nothing had been known of Kay since 1894, when he left office. He was discovered in San Francisco, where he

INTRODUCTION

had hidden away for more than thirty years. For more than thirty-five years Kay had refused to speak a word about his experiences as sheriff. When I first approached him, he said, "I don't want ever to hear another word about the Dalton Gang or anything connected with my service as sheriff of Tulare County. My work there cost me more than eighteen thousand dollars, every cent I had in the world, and made tramps of me and my family. Since I left there I have never discussed the Tulare County bandits and never have read one word about them."

It required five hours of constant work on my part to induce Kay to talk. It was only after he had heard most of what already had been collected that he gradually began to warm to the subject. The result was that during a period of more than five years he furnished me with all he could remember about the days when the Dalton Gang was running rampant over the southern half of California and particularly about the famous manhunt, when he and a deputy ran Bob and Emmett Dalton more than six thousand miles over the western United States and a portion of Old Mexico.

But valuable as were the thrilling accounts furnished by Kay, they told only of the activity of officers. The inside story of the robberies and of the activity of the Dalton Gang still was a secret.

In February of 1932, Kay appeared at the Tulare Adult School during a weekend study of Dalton Gang Days. I attempted to secure Emmett Dalton as a companion speaker. Emmett would not appear, but my contact with him resulted in an association that lasted until his death.

But Emmett wouldn't "sing." He was willing to write a companion story to that of Kay's 6,000 mile manhunt, but it could not conflict with his *When the Daltons Rode*, and the story would have to reveal Kay as a "relentless bull-dog nemesis," driving the Daltons into banditry. The deal was not made.

Littleton Dalton was living. I located him near Sacramento, but Lit had not talked for forty-five years and would not talk while Emmett lived. There was little prospect of Lit's ever talking, for he was seventy-nine and Emmett was about sixty-five.

But Emmett died first, victim of the old arm wound received in the Battle of the Banks at Coffeyville, Kansas. I lost no time in contacting Littleton, but he surely was a hard old nut to crack. It makes me weary yet to remember the seemingly futile effort it took to get Lit to "sing".

The fortunate result of the work with both Lit and Kay was that finally I was able to secure the complete story of Dalton Gang Days.

Much as I should like to bring to the reader the thrill of nearness and reality experienced in interviewing these and other pioneers, much is lost in the presentation. To see and know them, to hear the story from their own lips, with their own interpretation and expression of feeling grown out of years of bitterness or pleasant recollection, is a treat possible only to the one who collects the material at its source. By presenting the original, unvarnished stories of these pioneers I hope to share with the reader these thrilling eye-witness narratives of *Dalton Gang Days*, beginning with an intimate account by Littleton Dalton.

SEPTEMBER 18, 1975

FRANK F. LATTA
304 HIGH STREET
SANTA CRUZ
CALIFORNIA

DALTON GANG DAYS

LITTLETON DALTON

Photo taken in 1938, from an unretouched negative by Dorman and now in Bear State Library.

CHAPTER ONE

THE DALTON CLAN

Yes, I am the last of the Dalton brothers, ten of us. Four were known as the Dalton Gang of Outlaws. To me those outlaws were always just ornery kids, even to that October day in Coffeyville in '92, when the winchester and shotgun smoke cleared away and left two of them dead and the third crippled for life.

What was the matter with the Dalton Gang? I believe I know. A number of things were wrong. They were raised in a lawless country and grew up among violent companions, but so did I and four others of their brothers. Most of the trouble was that they were not spanked for holding their breath when they were little.

When I was seven years old, Father sold old Liddy, our colored servant, and I helped Mother with the housework. I held the nursing bottles for those bandits-to-be, walked the floor with them, and changed diapers on them. Kids, just headstrong, willful, reckless kids. Emmett was only twenty-one and Grat was thirty when their career was over.

Those little rascals squalled and held their breath until they were blue in the face. Mother talked to them and babied them, but it only made them worse. When she wasn't around, I paddled them good, and they sure came out of it, too. Mother gave me hell when she caught me and promised to paddle me for paddling them.

Mother wasn't very tall, but she was a heavy, strong woman. She had very dark red hair and blue eyes. She managed the family and was really a good manager, in spite of what I have said. But she had no chance. She was married at the age of sixteen, bore fifteen children, and lived to be ninety-two years of age.

Why did Mother baby my brothers? I don't know. Maybe she was tired of the old paddling system. She paddled me until I was about ten years old. I sure as hell needed it, too. But little Mason and Grat and Bobbie and Emmett could not be paddled. They were bound to do everything you didn't want them to do. They got to be damned badly spoiled kids.

Almost every yarn that has been published about the Dalton Gang of bank and train robbers has done damage to the old respectable Dalton family and to younger generations of readers as well. None of those yarns is the whole truth about the Dalton Gang. Most of them have been full of lies. I could never read more than two or three pages of any one of them without throwing it on the floor or in the fire.

From 1892 until 1938 I held my tongue about the work of the Dalton Gang in California. For forty-five years I would never admit I was any relation to the gang. I left central California, where we were known, and went to Lassen and Glenn counties. Many men who knew me there for more than forty years didn't know that I was a brother to Grat, Mason, Bob, and Emmett. As long as Emmett lived, I wouldn't put the finger of the law on him. But he had a chance to tell the true story and didn't do it. Now he is gone. I am past eighty years of age and surely have only a short time to tell what I know to be the facts about the Daltons, including the "Gang".

As I said, there were fifteen of us children. Ben, Louis, and Cole were older than I. Frank, Mason, Grat, Bob, Emmett, and Simon were younger.

We will leave our sisters out of this. . . . .

It was Littleton Dalton speaking. I got in touch with Lit before Emmett died, but Lit wouldn't "sing", as he called it, as long as Emmett was living. He used to say, "Let Emmett talk. He knows more about the robberies than I do."

When I read in the papers of Emmett's death, I drove to Broderick, across the river from Sacramento.

Arriving after dark, I located Lit's cabin, but no one answered the knock. A man in a cabin nearby assured me that Lit was at home, but never would answer the door during the night unless the caller identified himself. So I rented a place and turned in.

The next morning I knocked on the door as Lit was laying a fire in his little wood stove.

"Come in!"

The voice had the clarity and command of that of a long-line mule skinner.

I stepped inside and unconsciously came to attention. You felt like doing that when you met Lit. A strong forceful character showed in every line of his face and in every angle of his posture. He would have made a fine old-school regular army captain.

I saw I was on the spot. I decided not to question.

I "sang". I talked for two hours, telling Lit all I had done in my study of the San Joaquin Valley train robberies. At the end of two hours Lit spoke for the first time.

"I didn't suppose anyone knew that much about those robberies. I have heard nothing but bunk about them for more than forty-five years. Let's have some breakfast and then talk it over."

I suggested breakfast downtown; and Lit went for it, but not in his every-day clothes. A row of perfectly blocked 1880 model Stetson hats hung on the side of the cabin. Under them, covered with curtains, were three fine, tailored blue serge suits. Below these were three pairs of vici-kid shoes, shined so that they reflected everything in the place. Lit washed and changed clothes in less than ten minutes, and we were off, but not to any cheap and greasy restaurant. "If you figure the doctor bills", Lit said, "it don't cost any more to eat good grub than it does to eat junk, and your stomach appreciates the difference."

It was a good breakfast and Lit warmed to our subject. Before we had finished eating, he had agreed to accompany me to Kern County and to aid me in every way possible to straighten out the story of the Dalton Gang in California. He was as enthusiastic as a child as we loaded his suitcase in the car and drove down the Sacramento Valley toward the San Joaquin.

Knowing that from childhood Lit habitually had been as close-mouthed as a human can be, I found it a thrilling experience to hear him talk continually, telling the interesting story of his early life and of the migrations of the Dalton family. I laid my notebook on the seat between us and made notes with my eyes on the road.

Mother used to tell me that I was born October 2, 1857, at the Blue Cut, near Independence, Missouri. The Blue Cut was an excavation on a pass on the old stage road from Independence to Harrisonville. The cut had been made into blue soil or rock, and the banks were about thirty feet high. During the Civil War the Quantrill guerrillas trapped some Union soldiers in the Blue Cut and massacred them. After the railroad was built through the cut, Jesse James and his gang robbed a train there.

Father didn't stay at the Blue Cut very long. In fact, he never stayed anywhere very long. He ran around the country in a covered wagon, looking for something, I don't know what. It wasn't good land, because he was traveling over that all the time, and it wasn't anything else I ever knew of.

My first three years were spent in a covered wagon. I can remember them as if they were yesterday. In 1860 Father was given two hundred acres of good land about a mile and a half below Denver, Colorado. He got this land from a gambler and race horse man, who had won it on a horse race. Father stopped a few months on the land and then got in his covered wagon and drove off and left it. He wouldn't have stayed in Heaven much longer.

When the family moved out of the covered wagon and into a log house at Denver, I wouldn't go to sleep at night. I would squall until Father put me in the wagon and sat on the tongue until I went to sleep. When I got to sleep, Father would move me into a bed in the house. In the morning I would be mad as hell because I wasn't in the wagon.

I remember that the last time I visited with Mother she and I talked about my covered wagon days, and she asked me if I could remember why I didn't want to sleep in the house. I sure could. Sometimes I still feel that a house is going to fall in and crush me. . . . .

Thinking that Lit would be tired by the long ride to Kern County, I decided to make it by easy stages, stopping at the Court House Park in Stockton, and at Roeding Park in Fresno. Lit sat on a park bench beside the Court House in Stockton with his Stetson hat in his lap and continued his story. His first remark after we had settled back in our seat was, "You know, for many years Tom Cunningham was sheriff of San Joaquin County. I saw him up in Stanislaus and Tulare counties many times."

I had an excellent opportunity to study Lit as he talked. The old fellow surely exhibited every supposed mark of character strength, most noticeable of all a square jaw that could be clamped shut as final as judgment day. Later on, when we visited Arch Turner on the Merced River where Lit and his brothers had worked in the '80s, Arch said to me, "Latta, whenever Lit used to say *no*, his jaws stuck out farther than his ears."

Lit had small, sharp, straight-forward grey eyes that seemed to pass over everything lightly and frankly, but which missed nothing. This last is no simple flight of speech. Continually I was to be surprised at the many things he observed at times when he was talking busily and seemed to be seeing nothing.

The thing that amused me most at Stockton was the way Lit clicked his store teeth when he was most interested in our conversation. Later Arch Turner said, "Don't it beat hell the way he can click them damn teeth — play Yankee Doodle on 'em without miss'n a word." I laugh yet when I think of Arch's observation.

Later Lit saw that I was observing his tooth accompaniment, so he explained his trouble. The upper plate would lose suction when he was talking and drop down into his mouth. In order to keep it up he had to snap his teeth together about twice a second. He had developed a coordination beyond anything of the kind I have seen. He told me, "When I get back to Sac'to I'm going to throw the darn things in the river and get some new ones. They never bothered me before because I never did any talking."

I found I didn't need to stop in order to rest Lit. He kept talking and was as alert to our route through the Joaquin as though he had been traveling it every day. He recognized almost every town and landmark when we came to it, including Alila; and when we crossed the Tulare-Kern county line he was more alert than I.

It was in April of 1938 that Lit visited our home, and we sat in front of the fireplace in the adobe study and talked by the hour. He was perfectly at home. I am sure it was the first time he had visited in a home and had eaten family cooking in about thirty years. The children were fascinated with him, and he liked them, too. Generally rough in his language, I never knew a person so alert to his surroundings. As our association continued I found that always he seated himself in a position so that he could see or hear anyone approaching. Both his sight and hearing were perfect. If he was using profanity, he always corrected himself before Mrs. Latta or any of the children who were in hearing. In fact, I learned to know that someone was approaching by the change in his vocabulary. But I never heard him utter an indecency of any kind at any time. This is one of the things I also remember about Emmett. Even in talking freely while walking alone with me on the street, Emmett was as clean in his speech as when in his parlor. Theirs had been a decent home training.

An interesting thing happened almost at the beginning of our discussions. In checking his statements Lit observed that I was taking down his exact words and that a few rough expressions were being recorded. In a second he was on guard against this and such expressions were not uttered again.

When a man is eighty years of age and has spent his entire adult life among mule skinners, sheepherders, horse racers, and cattlemen it is almost beyond a possibility that he would maintain such a sense of fitness. I once mentioned this to Lit. He almost fired his philosophy back at me.

You know, Latta, habits are the most important part of a man's life. Most of my regular habits are in relation to eating and sleeping. From the time I was seven I could recognize the bad effect of careless habits.

For a while, before he was married, Father ran a saloon. But he was a teetotaler. He took three drinks of whisky in his life, in each case to treat a cold. Never heard him swear in my life, and the last time I saw him he corrected me for swearing. I never saw him gamble on a card game. But Father *would* gamble on race horses. He was raised in Kentucky where horserace gambling was not considered a bad habit. But it sure was a bad habit with Father. He gambled away almost every cent he ever had. Mother's father, old Charles Younger, did most of the providing for Father's family. He gave Mother old Liddy, our colored house servant; at another time he gave each of his children fifteen thousand dollars. With part of this money Father bought the old home near Belton, Missouri, and some race horses. Then he gambled away both the home and the remainder of the money on that string of moth-eaten, bang-tailed nags.

I decided very early that I wasn't going to do any gambling of any kind. I have seen at least a million dollars change hands in gambling games of one kind or another, and I have never bet one red cent on anything in my life. I saw lots of gambling on card games, so I decided I would lay off cards. And I did. I have never played a game of cards in my life. When some of the fellows used to ask me to sit in a card game, Cole would say, "That damned fool don't know the jack of diamonds from the deuce of spades." It was even worse than that. I didn't even know the jack of diamonds *or* the deuce of spades when I saw them, and I don't yet. But I haven't fretted about it.

Almost as early, I got some fixed ideas about profanity and liquor. I decided to swear when I wanted to and to do without it when I wanted to. I never swear by habit. I always know when I am swearing.

For many years I never drank any kind of alcoholic liquor. I believe I was at least twenty-six years old before I ever tasted it. Then I decided to take a drink when I thought I needed it. I have never taken more than one drink of hard liquor in a day and I have never asked anyone to *take* a drink. I have always asked him if he *wanted* a drink. I seldom ever let anyone treat me. In spite of all this I ran saloons of my own for more than eight years.

And tobacco? I used to smoke occasionally and take a chew when I felt I

Littleton Dalton in front of the old Tipton grain warehouse where Grat Dalton and another train bandit, Chris Evans, worked together.
  Photo by Frank F. Latta and now in Bear State Library.

wanted one. And I still do — occasionally. The last occasion was, I believe, about forty years ago. . . . .

Lit never boasted or preached about anything in his life. From his obvious embarassment and heated attitude when he told me these things I had the feeling that never before had he put them into words. He never ran with anyone or confided in anyone. He lived to himself and kept his own counsel.

One of the first historical excursions that we took together was a visit to Hanford, where, in 1878, Lit and his two brothers, Ben and Frank, had worked for Ed Benedict. They skinned strings of ten mules, breaking new land to the plow. You might imagine the dramatic effect of listening to Lit's description of the old board and batten cabin and barn where they had eaten and had kept their teams; and then the effect of visiting the old place to find both still in existence and in use, even to the old cast iron tea kettle from which they had used hot water more than sixty years before.

On our first trip we went north through Delano, where Grat, Bob, and Emmett had stopped overnight before attempting the Alila (now Earlimart) train robbery, and through Earlimart to Pixley and Tipton, where Grat had worked in the now demolished, old, battered grain warehouse with the later train bandit, Chris Evans, and where together they probably had weighed the chances of successful train robbery in the Joaquin.

It was a fascinating excursion. We stopped in each place and talked, while I took pictures. Sometimes we met a pioneer who had been nearby when the train was stopped. On the road Lit talked, while I drove and made notes. Here is what he told me while we were on the road:

I suppose it's necessary to bring the family tree into this thing, Latta. There has been a dictionary full of wild stories told about the Daltons and Youngers and James boys, their relationships and their reported robberies together. I want that all straightened out.

Grandfather Charles Younger was born in Kentucky and came to Missouri horseback in the very early days. In Missouri he owned at least one hundred and eighty slaves. He was wealthy when he left Kentucky, and he became wealthier in Missouri. As I have said before, he once gave all of his children fifteen thousand dollars apiece. He had a number of children, ten that I knew of. When he died he left several widows. Of the final estate Mother received the colored servant that we called Aunt Liddy, and a piano. Mother didn't feel like going to court to recover the remainder of her just share of the estate; so she never received any more of it.

Charles Younger was a peculiar person, but he was very crafty. He made big money as long as he lived. He used to loan money to the merchants at Independence and at one time had more than a hundred thousand dollars loaned to them.

Few people knew that Grandfather had *any* money. Often he'd send a colored man to several of the neighbors to borrow twenty or thirty dollars from each of them. He did this to make the people around him think he had no money around the place. Then he'd get on his horse, tie a bag of ten thousand dollars on the saddle, go to Independence and loan it to the merchants. The neighbors thought that it had been necessary for him to borrow money in order to purchase supplies in Independence. I don't believe any man ever made as much money as he did and kept it so well covered up.

I don't know the degree of relationship of all the Younger children, but my Mother was Adeline Lee Younger. She was related to General Robert E. Lee. She was born in Cass County, Missouri, in 1825, but lived most of her early life in Jackson County, and married my Father in 1841. Sofronia was the youngest child. She married a man named Kirkpatrick. Littleton Younger was the oldest boy. Thomas Jefferson Younger was one of the older boys. Henry, Frank, and Bruce were other boys. Sophia, a sister, married a man named Ragan. Mary married a Gibbons. Martha married a Morgan.

Henry Younger was at least fifteen and maybe twenty years older than his sister, my Mother. Some of his children were more than that much older than we were. I believe Cole Younger was thirty years older than I. No, the Dalton Gang never ran with the Youngers, and the Youngers had nothing to do with the Dalton boys going bad. Laziness, bad company, bad habits, and bad whisky did that, regardless of any stories you may hear.

The James boys were no relation I ever knew of to either the Youngers or the Daltons. The four Younger brothers ran with the guerrilla, Quantrill, during the Civil War and raided back and forth through our country for several years. Cole Younger was a sort of headman or lieutenant under Quantrill. Cole and Jim Younger helped sack and burn Lawrence, Kansas, near where we lived for about a year, and where Grat was born.

None of this experience did the Younger boys any good. Mother tried hard to get them to quit Quantrill and join the Confederate Army. But they wouldn't do it. They would only run around with Quantrill and rob, murder,

The old Dalton home near Belton, Missouri, about 1889, as it appeared when the Dalton family lived there. The names of the parties in the photo are unknown.
Photo courtesy Mr. Leo Aldridge and now in Bear State Library.

and butcher. They did the south more damage than they did the north. After the Civil War was over they thought they could keep on robbing and killing, but it didn't work out any too well for them.

Coleman Younger was with the Quantrill band when I first saw him. Grat was about a year old, and we were moving from Lawrence, Kansas, up to Liberty, Missouri. The band stopped our covered wagon. They fully intended to rob us, I am sure, and would have killed us if necessary to their success. It wouldn't have made any difference whether we were northerners or southerners. Father was not with us, but Mother was. Ben was driving our bull team. He was about sixteen years old. The band rode their horses in front and on both sides of our team, boxing us in. Mother was in the middle of the wagon. She told all of us to keep quiet. "That is Quantrill's band", she said, "and I see Cole Younger among them."

Ben stopped and the leader of the band ordered everyone out of the wagon. By this time Cole had ridden close to the driver's seat, where Ben was sitting. He looked at Ben as though he thought he had seen Ben before. Mother climbed over our bedding and household goods to the driver's seat. For at least a half minute she knelt there looking Cole in the eye.

Cole flushed.

"Aunt Addie!" he said, taking off his hat.

"Cole, what are you trying to do?"

"Nothing, Auntie, except that we are on the lookout for Yankee spies."

"Well, you won't find any in here, Cole."

"I know that. Let the team go on, boys."

The wagon passed on without another word being said.

I will never forget Cole Younger. He was very fair and had big, baby-blue pop eyes. He and my brother, Henry Coleman Dalton, were both named for some grandfather of Mother's. I do not know how far back this Coleman came into the family.

Just before Aunt Sofronia Kirkpatrick's husband was killed, Mother, Ben, and I drove from Belton down to see them. This was the second and last time I ever saw Cole Younger. Ben was driving this time, the same as he had been the first time we met Cole. John and Cole Younger were riding together. They were about fifty yards from the road and were riding away at an angle to the direction we were traveling. They had seen our outfit and were trying to avoid us.

Mother recognized Cole and John and told Ben to stop the team. Ben called to Cole and John, and they both wheeled their horses and drew their six-shooters. They didn't recognize Ben. Cole Younger asked Ben who he was. Ben told them to put up their guns and come over and shake hands.

Cole got off his horse, and Mother introduced him to Ben and me. He shook hands with us. John wasn't certain about us and was not so friendly. He didn't get off his horse and he didn't shake hands. This happened on the old road on Deep Water, thirty or forty miles below Harrisonville. I never saw Cole or John Younger again.

In Missouri, Kansas, and Indian Territory, where we lived, there was lots of game. Both at Lawrence and Belton Father used to go out on horseback, ride up alongside a buffalo, and shoot it down. I have helped him skin and cut up many a one. We boys used to kill wild turkey, ducks, geese, quail, racoon, rabbits, possum, bear, deer, and a number of fur-bearing animals. There was lots of wild fruit. We had plums, persimmons, choke-cherries, walnuts, hazel nuts, hickory nuts, gooseberries, huckleberries, blueberries, paw-paws, and haws. With a little corn, beans, and bacon, for use in a pinch, a person could live well off the wild products of the country.

The first gun I owned was a double-barreled, muzzle-loading shot gun. It was about a ten gauge. I could use light loads in it and kill small game with no trouble. But I was always ambitious to kill big game. I kept it loaded so that it would kill a grizzly bear and then had to fire it at rabbits or quail. Some of the time my right shoulder was pounded up so badly that I had to shoot left handed. Later I used the old cap and ball revolver Father had carried in the Mexican War.

I have carried a six-shooter most of the time since I was fourteen years old, and I am as good a shot with one as any of my brothers ever were. But I always carried it purely for self-protection, and I have never had to use it. Most of this wonderfully good shooting that you have heard of famous badmen doing was done when everything was going their way, and it was like shooting fish in a barrel. When the going got tough, most of them wasted lots of ammunition and some of them couldn't hit the broad side of a barn.

At the Belton home I herded cattle from the time I was seven years old. Ben and Cole were away at school, or with Father and his race horses part of the time and I had to take over their work, in addition to helping Mother in the house. I used a light Kentucky saddle, not much like the California stock saddles. They were not so good a saddle as the cattlemen used out here. Part of the time I used a Confederate Army saddle.

The territory around Belton was all open when we went there — wild, unbroken prairie and timber. Hickory, oak, and walnut grew along the creeks. The upland was bare prairie. It was settled rapidly after the Civil War. The farmers liked to have a piece of prairie to farm and a wood lot along the river for firewood and lumber. Hickory, the finest hardwood we had, was first used for firewood and to make wagons. It was soon gone, and then oak was used for firewood.

Until I was fourteen years old, Mother did all of her cooking in fireplaces. A big cast iron teakettle for hot water and two or three large cast iron cooking pots hung on a crane. She cooked potatoes and yams in the ashes. She baked hoe cake beside the coals, and cooked the rest of our bread in dutch ovens. She broiled our meat over the coals. A griddle and a grill hung beside the fireplace.

I was ten years old before I saw my first matches, and they sure were a curiosity: gave off sulphur and phosphorus fumes that made you choke six feet away. Until we got matches, we had to keep a fire going all the time. Sometimes the fire would go out. If we had near neighbors we could borrow a kettle of coals. If not we had to get out the old steel, flint, tinder, and punk and go to work on our knees on the hearth. Sometimes it took an hour to start a fire with steel and flint.

In 1871 I hauled Mother's first stove out to the Belton home. I was still Mother's helper in the house and I believe I was more interested in that stove than she was. I thought it was one of the most wonderful pieces of cooking equipment in existence. Mother paid forty dollars for it. It was a little, cast iron, four legged firepot, as I now remember it — not as good as the one I now have in my cabin at Broderick.

One of my Father's sisters, Aunt Tillie Louis, got a wood stove at the same time Mother did. She cooked on it just one day and was so disgusted with it that she had it taken down and went back to cooking in the fireplace with a griddle, a dutch oven, and a coffee pot. I guess she was too old to learn new tricks. But this was not true of Mother and me. We were sure tickled with our stove.

Just after the Civil War, wheat flour was six and seven dollars a fifty-pound sack, when you could get it. We had wheat flour biscuits on Sunday mornings only. We were sure glad to see Sunday roll around. The rest of the time it was corn-pone, hoe-cake, and johnny-cake.

Our beds were high, four-poster affairs of walnut and cherry. They had linen covers over them and could be completely enclosed with curtains. There were no springs. The bottoms of the beds were made of ropes, running in opposite directions. The ropes had to be tightened about every month or six weeks or the middle would sag down like a bag. On these was a big, thick tick filled with corn husks, and on top of that was a feather tick a foot thick. We slept between a pair of blankets. Another feather tick was used over the blankets. When we lay down on one of those old beds, we sank out of sight. In that cold climate we couldn't sleep any other way. . . . .

By this time we had reached Tulare and stopped to visit Cicero Zumwalt, who had been in business there since before Dalton Gang Days. Lit and "Cis" had a wonderful time discussing old times in Tulare County. I hated to separate them, but finally we had to say goodbye and drive on to Hanford, Lit still dictating while I drove with one hand and made notes with the other.

Why did I never go back home to stay?
The Missouri country was sure cold; snowy and blizzardy, and, in those days we didn't have any means of preparing for it. We used to put in five months of hot, rainy, sultry weather preparing for seven months of snow, freeze, and thaw. It was no better in Indian Territory — worse, because there was little wood for fuel or trees to break the force of the wind. We used to tie a rope between the barn and the house so that we wouldn't get lost going back and forth.

The snow would fall so thick you couldn't see six feet, and the wind would drive it like number-eight shot out of a gun. The mercury went to fifteen and twenty below. You had to have a *good* sod house or you would actually freeze to death in the house, sitting by a fire. Frame houses were double walled and plastered inside. After I put in two years at Hanford, I decided I had left nothing back there that needed looking after. . . . .

In Hanford we called on Joe Richmond, editor of the *Hanford Sentinel*. Yes, Joe had known both Ed Benedict and his wife, he said; but both had passed away. They had a son living, but he was out of town. And the old barn still was standing, just outside the city limits on the Goshen road.

So we climbed back in the car and drove east. Lit recognized the barn before I began looking for it. We drove in a short distance north and found not only the barn, but also the old homestead cabin.

Nothing could have occurred to please Lit more than the finding of the cabin where he landed in 1878 to begin a stay of more than sixty years in California. I never knew a fourteen year old boy to be more enthusiastic. With a flood of feeling I realized how much our expedition was meaning to Lit. It was undoubtedly the only time since he had left the Benedict ranch, more than sixty years before, that he had smiled pleasantly or laughed joyously at anything. The taut jawed, tight lipped habits were falling away in the very locality where he had acquired them.

Littleton Dalton at the old Benedict homestead cabin near Hanford, California in 1938.
Photo by Frank F. Latta and now in Bear State Library.

Littleton Dalton at the old Benedict barn where he had "skinned mules" in 1878. Photo by Frank F. Latta and now in Bear State Library.

He was a different man during the remainder of his visit.

I photographed the cabin with Lit in front of it. We then turned our attention to the barn. There we found the old cast-iron tea-kettle, which the owner of the place presented to me for my historical collection in Bear State Museum.

We sat in the shade with our backs against the barn while Lit talked for more than three and a half hours about early days at Hanford and the events which led to his coming to California.

You see, most of my brothers had been to California from one to three times already. I hadn't because I had begun quite young as Mother's helper in the house and had sort of worked into the position of general home manager.

I told you Grandfather Charles Younger had given Mother a colored woman houseservant, Aunt Liddy. She was my nurse. But when I was seven Father sold old Aunt Liddy to a traveler for eight hundred dollars—sold her to finance a trip with his moth-eaten race horses. Before she left she gathered me into her arms and hugged and kissed me and said, "Goodby, honey!" She was gone, just as quick as that. Cole, Ben, and I thought as much of Aunt Liddy as we did of Mother. I had to take over as much of her work as I was able to do.

Well, Father made those excursions with his broken-down plugs every year. He never made a dollar betting on them, and he had too much Kentucky pride to bet on any horses but his own. After I was seven I don't believe he was home on an average of more than two months of the year. As early as 1870, as soon as there was a railroad to travel on, he came to California with the horses, running them at Sacramento, Oakland, Stockton, and Visalia. Later he took in the smaller places, including Fresno, Modesto, Hanford, and Bakersfield.

From the first, Father took one or two of the oldest boys with him, and kept this up until he had taken all but Simon and me. In 1877, when he made the Joaquin circuit, he had with him Ben, Cole, and Frank.

When they were making the Visalia stand, Ed Benedict took quite a liking to Ben and Frank. You know, this country was then in Tulare County, and Visalia was the county seat. Everyone went to the horse races there. Ed told the boys how foolish they were to follow a string of race horses around the country. He offered them a steady job at his place. He had homesteaded here in the Mussel Slough country, west of Visalia. Ed had been married not long before and wanted Ben and Frank to skin mules for him, breaking up his new land. The boys liked Ed, but they didn't like to leave Father; so they went on with him.

That fall Ben got to thinking about Benedict's offer. He talked with Mother about it, and then wrote to Benedict, asking if the job was still open. It was, so Ben took the train to California, and soon learned to skin a long-line string of mules. His pay was thirty-five dollars a month. In Missouri, ten dollars a month was good pay for ranch work.

Well, in a few months Frank had a letter from Ben. Benedict needed more skinners, and he would give Cole and Frank jobs if they would come out. Frank was anxious to go, but Cole was not. So Frank proposed that I go with him. As soon as I could see that Mother would have enough help without me, I agreed to go. I was as happy as could be to travel and work with Frank. He was our favorite brother, the flower of our family. We all worshiped him. If he had lived, I don't believe any of our brothers would have gone wrong.

Frank and I started to Kansas City with a bull team. There were about twenty of us in the party, all bound for California. I paid a hundred and fifty dollars for a ticket from Kansas City to Hanford. The middle west was then overrun with Indians. Cavalry was stationed at Cheyenne to keep the trains moving.

On the plains we ran through a big band of antelope. The passengers got out at least a hundred pistols and began shooting from the car windows. One man had a winchester repeating rifle. He could reach the antelope, but he couldn't hit the Rocky Mountains with it.

Frank and I landed here at the Benedict ranch in April of 1878, almost sixty years ago to a day. Here we learned for the first time of the custom in California of laborers carrying their blankets with them. Where we had been raised, farmers always gave their hired man a room in the house.

Ed and his wife occupied the little cabin. There they lived and there we ate the meals Mrs. Benedict prepared on a little cast iron cook stove. Ben was bunking in the southeast corner of the barn, where he and Ed had partitioned off a small room. Ed took Frank and me to Visalia to buy blankets, quilts, and a canvas to roll them in. We bunked with Ben.

Skinning a long-line string of mules was certainly a novelty to me. I had never seen anything like it. Frank had seen many long-line teams in the Joaquin, but he had never driven one.

Most of my teaming had been done with bulls. In fact, I could have qualified as a bull whacker by the time I was ten years of age. In 1866 Father put me to breaking sod with two yoke of bulls, hitched to an old sod plow. I was nine years old and just as high as the plow handles.

Let me tell you, it took better bull whacking for me to plow with that outfit than it did a grown man. Father was particular as could be about farming. I couldn't drive a bull team for him and make skips, even at the corners. I walked along on the land and held to the left plow handle with both hands. I was stocky and strong, but it was all I could do to manage that old plow. Sod breaking was a good job for a husky man, and a better one for *two* husky men.

That old Missouri sod rolled over sometimes for thirty feet before it broke. At the corners I had to stop the team within a few inches of the furrow, or I'd make a skip. Then I dug my bare heels into the ground and braced myself against that old plow handle, so that the plow wouldn't fall over in turning. I yelled "Haw!", and those bulls came lumbering around into the furrow. If the plow fell over and got wedged into the sod, I went to the house for help. Mother or Grandmother Nancy Dalton came out and helped me get started again. They also helped me yoke and unyoke the bulls. When I drove the bulls there was never anyone else there to help. Father was always away with his race horses, and Ben and Cole were either with him or away at school. Louis Kossuth, the other brother older than I, had died when he was about seven years old, so I was alone.

By the time I was ten I didn't need any help. I was a full fledged bull whacker.

Finally Father needed money to finance an expedition with his mangy racehorses, so he sold the four bulls and the plow to a neighbor to break sod. I sure jumped up and down and yelled for joy when Father sold those bulls.

The next job I had was plowing to plant corn, also with a bull team. We plowed furrows one way and marked it with a sled cross ways. Frank walked behind me with an apron full of corn and threw it by pinches where the sled marks crossed the furrows.

It was sure a long way from our Missouri way of farming to the long-line teams and farming machinery used in the Joaquin. We were all three as pleased as could be.

You know, this was a wonderful country in those days — lots of water, sycamores, willows, and oak trees. Those oaks were the finest trees I ever saw. Some of them were eight feet through and would shade two barns this size. I never saw a tree in Missouri that would anywhere near equal them. Tulare Lake was only about eight miles from the Benedict ranch. We used to drive to the lake on Sundays and fish and shoot ducks and geese, curlew, sandhill cranes, coyotes, antelope, elk, and wild hogs. I saw more wild game on Tulare Lake in one day than I had supposed existed in the world. Those were the happiest days of my life. . . . .

At this point Lit was deeply moved and we sat in silence for several minutes. It was easy to appreciate his description of the Hanford country in the '70s for we could see many beautiful oaks that still dotted the nearby fields. When he continued he launched into a thrilling account of the Mussel Slough battle, one of the most tragic and bloody battles of western history.

CHAPTER TWO

THE MUSSEL SLOUGH TRAGEDY

Ben, Frank, and I worked for Benedict until 1880. We saved our money, and by the spring of 1880 each had more than five hundred dollars in gold coin. Benedict tried to get us to buy a half section of land near his. It was for sale for a thousand dollars. As I look back on it now, it seems a shame we didn't buy it. But at that time the S.P. railroad claimed almost all the good land in this country, and there was a battle brewing between the settlers and the railroad agents. It broke only about a month after I left Benedict's. . . . .

Knowing that Lit had been acquainted with most of those involved in the famous Mussel Slough Tragedy of May 11, 1880, I listened with intense anticipation. Obviously, Lit's mind was perfectly clear about those affairs of more than sixty years before. I could see that I was due for a long audience. At ten o'clock we arrived at Benedict's old place, and we left at one-thirty. But time was gone before we realized it. It was pleasantly cool on the west side of the barn, and we settled our backs comfortably against the old, weatherbeaten boards. Lit sat with his legs stretched in front of him, broad-brimmed Stetson hat on his lap, cane poked down against the toe of one shoe; grey hair, and rugged, florid face contrasting with the grey-black boards; teeth clicking an accompaniment to his story.

At that time I just couldn't stay here in the face of a battle. I wasn't afraid. I could handle a gun as well as anyone. I had a good six-shooter. Ben had a 45-60 winchester rifle. Frank and I had brought a 44-40 winchester between us. We used the rifles for hunting antelope, elk, and wild hogs in the swamps around Tulare Lake.

But I had heard and had known nothing but fighting all my life, and I knew there was nothing in it. Father had served in the Mexican War and had taken part in the battle of Buena Vista as a fifer under General Taylor. He had seen enough fighting to last him three life-times, so he used to say. He often told his boys that a war was coming between the North and the South. But it came when his oldest boy was only fifteen, and none of us served in the army.

The Civil War caught us at Lawrence, Kansas. We knew almost all of the people there who were killed when Lawrence was raided by Quantrill's guerrillas. Grat was born at Lawrence, March 30, 1861. About November of 1862 we moved to Liberty, Missouri, so as to be out of the fighting zone. Father stayed near Liberty with an old man named Mason Frakes. My brother, Mason Frakes Dalton, was born there in 1863 and was named for that old southern farmer. Mason was the brother commonly called "Bill" Dalton. Bill was simply a nickname. We older brothers have always called him Mason.

While I'm at it, maybe I'd better straighten out the names of the rest of my brothers.

Cole's name and mine were old family names. Henry Coleman Dalton was named for one of Mother's brothers and also for Father's brother, who died in Kentucky. I was named for an uncle, Littleton Younger, who went to Oregon in the very early settlement of that state. I never saw him. He was Grandfather Charles Younger's oldest child by his first wife. He had also been named for some earlier ancestor; so I don't know the origin of the name, Littleton, in our family.

Robert Rennick Dalton was born near Belton, in Cass County, Missouri, in 1870 and was named for an old Methodist minister who served as a chaplain under General Jo Shelby of the Confederate Army.

Emmett Dalton was also born at the old Belton home, in 1872 and was named for the Irish orator, Robert Emmett.

Louis Kossuth Dalton was named for the famous Austrian patriot who was popular about the time my brother was born.

Grat's full name was Gratton Hanley Dalton. My grandmother, Nancy Dalton, named him for an old Kentucky neighbor, who, I believe, was some kind of a relative of ours.

Father actually never did provide for his family. His mother, Nancy Dalton, lived with us for years and tried to make up for his shortcomings. She did much to help Mother, but she could do little to manage ten boys. She was sitting in a little rocking chair when she kissed Frank and me goodbye in 1878 as we left for California. We never saw her again.

From the time we left Denver in 1860, before we went to Lawrence, I can remember nothing but fight, fight, fight until 1880, when I got up and left Hanford here for Lassen and Glenn counties, where no one knew me.

At Lawrence the guerrillas fought all around us. Lawrence had been raided before I was born and was raided again less than a year after we left there.

Uncle Henry Younger was killed near his store at Harrisonville, Missouri, by a couple of Union soldiers. His son, Cole Younger, killed one of the soldiers, so I was told.

There were booze and bottleggers and whisky runners and prostitutes by the hundreds. The old Whisky Trail, also called the old Border Ruffian Trail, which ran by our Belton home through Kansas down into the Indian Territory, was strung with graves. I believe there was an average of a murder a night between Kansas City and Red River.

We were living about twenty miles away from Jesse James when detectives threw a bomb into the James home and blew an arm off the mother of Jesse and Frank James and killed their half-brother. The detective rode the train to a place near the house, where the conductor let him off. Later Jesse helped rob the train and shot the same conductor full of lead.

John Younger, Mother's nephew, was killed at Chalk Level, St. Clair County, Missouri, and killed both of the officers who attacked him. Jim and John met two strange men on the road. All were horseback. John suspected that the strangers were officers and wanted to kill both of them as soon as he saw them. But Jim said, "No, let them go by." When opposite, one of the officers whipped out a little derringer and shot John through the nape of the neck. John put spurs to his horse, ran both men about two hundred yards, and shot both of them dead. Then he got off his horse and bled to death.

My uncle by marriage, Kirkpatrick, was killed below the Montegaw Springs, which belonged to grandfather Charles Younger. Kirkpatrick was out with the Younger boys on some kind of a raid and ran out of ammunition. When the officers attacked him, he ran his horse home and got more ammunition just as the officers came into the yard. His wife stood in the door facing the officers and Kirkpatrick laid his rifle across her shoulder and killed several of them. Then his ammunition again gave out and he ran out the back of the house. He was killed at a neighbor's. The officers brought back some of his personal effects for his wife to identify.

There was fighting and shooting and killing all of the time. Few of the people we knew escaped death by shooting. I don't want to see any more of it. I don't want even to have to read the news from another war. I can see one coming, and I hope I don't live long enough to meet it.

Well, Mother got fifteen thousand dollars from her father, and our father bought two hundred and forty acres of land in Cass county, Missouri, a few miles southwest of Belton and less than a half mile from the Kansas line. This land was clear of all debt. Father bought a string of scrubby race horses with some of the remaining money. Mother tried to hold onto the rest of the money. There was a good house on the Belton place. Part of it is still standing, but was shot full of holes during the Civil War when most of the homes in our neighborhood were burned. When peace came, the country was dotted with solitary stone chimneys.

Father furnished land and some money for a school on a corner of our farm. It was called the Dalton School. It was the only school I ever attended. During, and for several years after the Civil War, there were no schools in many parts of the south, and it was impossible to get an education there.

Both guerrillas and soldiers fought all around us at Belton, too. Brush Creek Hill was between us and Kansas City. We saw General Price go into the country between us and Kansas City with twenty thousand men. A federal army came over Brush Creek Hill, met him and drove him back. They drove Price's army between stone fences for a mile where they couldn't get out and killed thousands of them. We saw it. For a mile the space between those stone walls was so filled with dead horses and dead men you couldn't walk on the ground for twenty feet at a time.

When Quantrill's guerrillas massacred the Lawrence, Kansas, citizens, they went into Kansas from Missouri only a short distance from our Belton home. When they came out of Kansas after the massacre, Cole Dalton brought a party of about twenty guerrillas to our home to get powder and something to eat. We were all hid out in the brush and expected our place to be robbed and burned. Father was the only one who saw Cole at that time.

So, you see, before my brothers began to get into trouble, I was sick of fighting. I talked and reasoned and argued with them and threatened them for years, but couldn't keep them out of trouble. They were never satisfied with anything else.

The settlers around here organized a protective league to work against the railroad company. They met at a number of places. I attended a number of meetings, several on Kings River under the oak trees. I could see they were getting closer to bloodshed all the time.

About January of 1880 while we three were still at Benedict's, Frank got a letter telling him he could have a job in the Indian Territory, near home. Mother wanted him near her, so he went. In 1884 he was appointed Deputy U.S. Marshal to work out of Fort Smith, Arkansas. I hated to see Frank go into that kind of work. It meant more fighting. But he was enthusiastic about it and accepted; to be killed by a gang of bootleggers in the Arkansas river bottoms.

Frank Dalton, age 28, when he was Deputy U.S. Marshal. He was killed Nov. 27, 1887, while making an arrest.

Photo courtesy N.H. Rose, San Antonio, Texas and now in Bear State Library.

The grave of Franklin Dalton is about thirty yards from those of Bob and Grat in Elmwood Cemetery, Coffeyville, Kansas.
Photo courtesy Frank F. Latta, 1938 and now in Bear State Library.

Maybe we had better dispose of Frank right here, because I never saw him after the day I saw him on the train at Goshen. He took a deputy, Jim Cole, with him to arrest three whisky-running bootleggers across the river from Fort Smith. They went up to a tent house and the bootleggers, one after the other, came out shooting. Frank shot and killed two of them, Smith and Dixon, as fast as they ran out of the door. Cole was shot in the shoulder and ran away.

While he was killing Smith and Dixon, Frank was hit twice and was knocked down. Smith's wife ran out and grabbed a winchester from the ground and was going to shoot Frank again, but he killed her first. Then, as he lay on the ground bleeding to death, a young fellow named Towerly ran up to him and killed him. Frank's gun had jammed, or he would of killed Towerly, too. Towerly was afterward traced to his home and was killed by two deputies while he killed one of them.

Frank is buried in Elmwood Cemetery, at Coffeyville, Kansas. The family was then living at Robbins Corners about six miles west of Coffeyville. They had moved there so that the children could be near a good school. This all took place after I was in California. I was never on the place at Robbins Corners. So you can see why the boys were so easily recognized in 1892 when they attempted to rob the two Coffeyville banks at one time.

Mother spent the last of her savings to erect a fine marble headstone at Frank's grave. I heard that the government gave Frank a military funeral and erected a monument to him. Some of his marshal friends attended his funeral. That was all the military there was to it. His grave is about sixty yards from the graves of Grat and Bob, who were killed at Coffeyville in '92.

When we boys came to California we knew that we had an uncle, Coleman Younger, in San Jose. I would have enjoyed visiting him when I first came to California, but after the boys got into trouble I had no desire to see him. But Ben and Mason did visit with Uncle Coleman. They told me of their visits. What they told me is all I know about our San Jose relatives.

In Fresno Ben bought a fine suit of clothes and everything to go with it and had left more than four hundred dollars in twenty dollar gold pieces. After going to San Jose by train, Ben hired a livery stable saddle horse, ate breakfast, and rode out to Uncle Cole's place. The family was just getting up for breakfast. Ben went to the door and was met by his uncle, who seemed as pleased as could be to see him, and invited him in to breakfast.

Ben sat in the dining room and talked to them while they ate, answering their questions about the Dalton family and the other eastern relatives. When Uncle Cole had finished his breakfast, he went to a pair of large double doors between the dining room and the parlor, pulled them open and pointed to an enlarged picture on the wall. He said, "There is a picture of Charles Younger, my father and your grandfather." None of us had ever seen a picture of grandfather Younger.

When Ben and Uncle Cole went outside after breakfast, Uncle Cole was anxious to see Ben's horse, and walked around through the front yard where he could get a close look at it. As soon as he saw that it was a fresh livery outfit he lost all interest in it. Ben always thought that Uncle Cole wanted to see if he had a ridden-down horse which would indicate that he was making a getaway from some place.

Leaving Uncle Cole Younger's, Ben went to Nicholaus, on the Sacramento river above Sacramento about forty miles, to visit our father's sister and her husband. This was Aunt Nancy Emaline Noel and her husband, Robert Noel. They married in Kentucky and came to California in the '50s with a bull team. Both have been dead for a number of years. There was less than two weeks difference in their ages and both lived to be a little more than eighty years of age. They are both buried at Lincoln near Nicholaus. I also visited them at Nicholaus. They were about the finest people I ever knew. Aunt Nancy was a large woman, almost as large as Father, and looked very much like him.

When my brother Mason, or Bill Dalton, visited Uncle Cole Younger at San Jose, about 1886, he was also well dressed and had about three hundred dollars in gold in a buckskin money bag. Mason stayed overnight and slept with one of the Younger boys. Mason was always talking and showing off. When he was dressing in the morning, he purposely dropped his money bag on the floor and the boy who slept with him looked at it as suspiciously as could be.

At the time Ben visited the Youngers, none of the Dalton boys had gone bad. But Uncle Harry Younger's boys, nephews of Uncle Cole Younger, had a bad reputation from their guerrilla work under Quantrill during the Civil War and from their bank robbing afterward. Cole, Jim, and Bob Younger were then in the Minnesota state prison as a result of their attempt to rob the bank at Northfield, Minnesota. So Uncle Cole Younger was prepared for anything from any of us.

Cole and Grat came to California to stay, in January of '80. They went to work for the Turners and Stevinsons on the Merced river a few miles east of Hills Ferry. They hauled four foot oak wood to Livingston to ship to Merced on the train. The wood furnished steam power to pump water for the city of Merced. I decided to go north and see them.

I went to Visalia and bought a good Visalia stock saddle and riding rig. Then I bought a horse from Perry Phillips of Kings river, and rode horseback to the Merced. This was about the first of February, 1880. I stopped at Turner's about a week. After that time, none of us boys, except Cole and Ben, worked very long for Turner.

Both Cole and I wanted to get jobs skinning mules on a large grain ranch. Turner said to me, "If you fellows want to get onto a big grain ranch, go up to the Glenn Ranch at Willows, in Colusa County. Old Doc Glenn has the biggest grain ranch in the world." So Cole and I rode to Willows.

I think you should know something about Doc Glenn. He told me many things about himself. He was a Missourian and a fine man. He was educated to practice medicine, but came to California in '49 and mined at Murderer's Bar on the American River near Coloma, where gold was first discovered in California.

Doc left the mines and freighted out of Sacramento for a time. He said to me, "It looked to me like the livery stable and feed-yard men where I put up made more money than I did, so I gave up teaming and bought a livery stable in Sacramento."

Glenn soon gave up the livery stable business and made several trips between California and the east. The second trip west he brought out his family and also a large band of cattle. Then, disgusted with California, he took the family back to Missouri, intending to stay there. He told me, "You know, I had forgotten all about those Missouri winters, so I traded my Missouri property for a big band of horses and cattle and lit out for California again. In Utah the Indians almost got away with all my stock and me, too, but I ran the Indians down, recovered all of the stock, and finally got into California to stay."

Doc made so much money from the sale of his stock in California that he repeated his trip, making at least four trips west with stock, the last time with about six hundred head of fine draft horses. He drove these horses to Yolo County and decided to try farming. He went into partnership with Major Biggs. They made big money from the first and Doc sold out to Biggs and started out for himself at a little place called Jacinto on the west bank of the Sacramento River. There he began grain farming on the largest scale ever attempted with teams in this state, if not in the world.

The Glenn Ranch was five miles wide and more than sixteen miles long, a total of more than eighty square miles. In '80, when I went there, it was all farmed to wheat, and Doc personally supervised all of it from the back of a saddle mule. He also owned a 70,000 acre ranch in Oregon and another larger cattle ranch in Nevada. On the ranch at Willows at one time he had a hundred mule skinners and a hundred ten mule teams. It was just the place Cole and I were looking for.

I could have been fixed for life if I had stayed with Doc Glenn. He wanted to make me his straw boss. But I didn't like the idea, principally because of the class of labor he had to hire. They were almost all periodic drunks and it was a continual fight all the time to keep the teams in the field. Doc was finally killed by a drunken man who kept books for him. This man had made a mess of the books. Doc fired him and he came back with a shotgun loaded with buckshot and murdered Doc, shot him in the back of the head at short range.

It was while we were at the Glenn Ranch that Cole began drinking so much. He was older than I was, and I didn't want to have to be around him; so I left him there and went back to Turner's on the Joaquin.

Well, as I have said, Cole and I got jobs on the Glenn Ranch. We had been there only a few weeks when the Mussel Slough battle was fought. I still had about five hundred dollars, all in twenty dollar gold pieces, and I still wanted to buy land at Mussel Slough if I could hold it without having to fight a war. So, in a few weeks, I rode back to Benedict's to see if the war was over. I talked with everyone who knew anything about the battle and came to the conclusion that the S.P. had won. I bought no land, but rode my horse back to the Glenn Ranch, where I stayed until '82. But I did learn all the details of the Mussel Slough battle. . . . .

I had an intense interest in the Mussel Slough Tragedy, as we called it; so I was anxious to hear Lit tell what he knew about it. Possibly he could clear the tangled story that had grown up since 1880 about the part Walter Crow had played in the battle.

Walter was one of the finest rifle shots in California. He did most of the shooting at Mussel Slough. And certainly Mussel Slough was a tragedy.

Eight men lost their lives as a result of the battle, which lasted less then three quarters of a minute. Five men were killed instantly and three died soon afterward.

Every man died who was shot or who was armed and, with one exception, every man died who fired a shot. For length of time and percentage of casualties, it was one of the bloodiest battles of human history. Because of my own wide acquaintance with the Crow family and my admiration for many of its members, even yet it is a difficult subject for me to approach.

Having studied the Mussel Slough battle for more than fifty years, I am as well prepared to appreciate the accuracy of Lit's statement as anyone who has written of that affair. His is the only story that checks with the records, the inquest reports, which describe how each man was shot. Lit's story is an accurate, unvarnished account. While manuscript for this publication was being prepared, a wild story of the Mussel Slough battle was published in the San Joaquin Valley newspaper of largest circulation. Among other impossibilities, it portrayed the noted train bandit, Chris Evans, as taking an active part in the shooting.

We looked at Lit's fine old gold hunting case watch. It was noon. Even though I hated to break the spirit of reminiscence Lit had fallen into, I proposed that we go back to Hanford for dinner. But he decided the matter himself.

"Let's get that Mussel Slough battle off our chest and then go over to Visalia. We can eat any time. I want to show you where Grat broke jail."

So we again settled back against the barn, and the shadow crept to our feet and up our legs until, when the story was done, it was gone, and for an hour we had been basking in a mellow, afternoon April sun.

First of all, there is one thing I want to make clear about the Mussel Slough trouble. Chris Evans had nothing to do with it. He never lived in the Mussel Slough country and never owned or claimed any land there. He never attended a meeting of the Settlers' League. Every story you hear about Mussel Slough has Chris Evans' name connected with it. Any stories about Chris having been dispossessed of land there are pure fiction. Besides my own observation, I have the best authority in the world for my statements. Chris Evans attended Grat's trial every day court was in session and I knew him far better than I know you. He told me that when he first came to California he settled in eastern Tulare County and had lived there ever since. He hung around me during all of Grat's trial. He told me how he and Grat had worked together in the grain warehouses at Tulare, Tipton, and Pixley. He talked about himself by the hour, and I never heard him mention Mussel Slough.

The S.P. had begun selling land to settlers at Mussel Slough several years before I went to Benedict's. I received several of their advertising circulars. They quoted timber land at five dollars an acre and valley land at two-fifty, a quarter down and seven years in which to complete payment. I didn't buy because everyone told me the railroad title was no good, and I believed them. I don't believe yet that it was good. I'll tell you why.

The land grant to the S.P. was made with the understanding that by July of 1878 they would complete a railroad from San Francisco to Los Angeles. They were to get every odd numbered section of land for a distance of ten miles on each side of the completed road. Everybody expected the road to be built down the coast.

But the coast route didn't look good to the railroad men. Half of their land would be in the Pacific Ocean and the other half was already given away in Spanish Land Grants. They fooled around for several years and finally began connecting the end of the railroad to Gilroy with the railroad at Goshen, in Tulare County. They began at each end and built as far as Tres Pinos and Huron. Then they quit. They haven't *yet* completed the road.

During this time and for years afterward, the S.P. encouraged settlers to go on the land, with the understanding that it would sell for the same price as the open government land. Several years after settlers had moved on the land, and while I was at Benedict's, the railroad company sent land graders in to put a price on each separate piece of land. The prices established ranged from fifty dollars an acre down to ten. There wasn't an acre graded under ten dollars. The government land sold for a dollar and a quarter an acre. The settlers were being made to pay for their own improvements.

While the S.P. was delaying, homes were built and other improvements were made. Dan Rhoades built an irrigation ditch to his place, and when I arrived, many of the ranches were irrigated by three large ditches. Then the railroad began demanding a share of the crops.

The Settlers' League sent representatives to Governor Stanford and to Washington, but got a glassy-eyed brush-off. You can imagine how those settlers felt. They were the most desperate people I have ever seen. If one of them tried to borrow my rifle or Ben's, there must have been a hundred.

After I left Benedict's, things moved fast. Judge Terry, of San Francisco, wrote an opinion concerning the Mussel Slough trouble and made arrangements to come to Hanford to deliver it. The date was set for May 11, 1880, and the settlers planned a picnic where they would listen to Terry read his opinion.

On the same day, the United States Deputy Marshal, A.W. Poole, began to dispossess settlers and put buyers in possession. One of the buyers was M.J. Hart, who had for some time been Southern Pacific station agent at Goshen. Another was Walter Crow. I knew both Hart and Crow well.

Walter Crow had been raised on the east side of the San Joaquin River, west of Modesto. His father was a brother to the Crows after whom the town of Crows Landing was named. He was one of the most expert rifle shots in

California, or anywhere else, for that matter. When a young man he used to bring in bags of wild ducks and geese, shot on the wing with a thirty-two calibre single-shot rim-fire rifle. In addition, he was a quiet man, was absolutely fearless and could not be bluffed or imposed upon.

Marshal Poole and land-grader Clark took Crow and Hart to the Braden place. Braden was not at home and they hauled his furniture out and put it in the road. Hart was put in possession. Then they drove on to the next place, which Brewer and Storer held in partnership. Poole and Clarke were traveling in a buggy and Crow and Hart in a wagon. On the way the party met several people who carried to the picnic the news of what was going on. About a dozen men, some armed with revolvers, rode as fast as they could to the Brewer and Storer place. They arrived just as the marshal and his party had entered the premises.

Poole met Storer and talked with him. Storer rode out into the field where his partner, Brewer, was plowing, in order to talk the matter over with him. They stopped at the far side of the field, diagonally across from the house. While Poole was waiting for Storer and Brewer to come in from the field, the settlers rode up and met the party. Poole stood about fifty yards from the wagon where Hart and Crow were sitting. Part of the settlers surrounded Hart and Crow and began to abuse them for buying land and helping dispossess the settlers.

There has been a lot of talk about who started the fight and who fired the first shot. I can answer those questions. It was Jim Harris. I knew him well. He was a hot headed, ignorant, overbearing fellow and a coward to boot. He was always pulling a gun and threatening to shoot someone. Once, in Hanford, I saw him pull a gun on Cornelius Patrick. Patrick was unarmed, but he walked up to Harris and told him to put the gun up or he would beat him to death. Harris did put the gun up, and he left the place, too.

Harris rode to the marshal, pulled his gun and demanded that the marshal give up his gun. The marshal said nothing, but he looked Harris over and didn't give up his gun. At this time Poole was talking to some of the settlers about fifty yards away from Crow and Hart. Jim Patterson asked Archibald McGregor to guard Poole and let Poole keep his gun.

Harris rode over to where Crow and Hart were sitting in the wagon. He was mad because he saw he had made a fool of himself trying to bluff the marshal, so he began to curse Crow and Hart. Crow was a man who would stand just about so much abuse and no more. He challenged Harris to shoot, telling him he should keep the front sight filed off his gun. Harris still had his revolver out, and he threw it down on Crow and fired. He overshot and hit

Hart in the groin. There was never one of the witnesses of the battle that I talked to who disagreed with the account which I have just given you about how the first shot was fired. Jim Harris started the shooting, but Crow finished it, all but killing himself. Things happened fast and furious, for it was over in less than three quarters of a minute, all but the killing of Crow.

Crow had a revolver strapped on him, but didn't use it at first. He jumped from the wagon, grabbed his shotgun from the back of the wagon, and blew Harris off his horse.

As soon as Crow emptied the shotgun, he yelled to Hart to bring him the rifle. In his wounded condition, Hart was having a hard time to control the team. He was suffering too much to know what he was doing, but he did manage to get out of the wagon and hand Crow another gun. During this time he held to the lines and kept the team from running away.

When Crow tried to use the second gun, he saw it was not his rifle, but another shotgun and it was empty. By this time there was a terrible uproar and several of the settlers were shooting at Crow. But he held his ground and stood there facing the crowd as cool as if he was at a turkey shoot. He broke the shotgun open, reached in his pocket, took out two shells, loaded the gun, and shot Ivar Knudsen off his horse.

The killing of Knudsen was an entire mistake. I never heard anyone who was there say anything different. In the excitement of the moment Crow didn't recognize him. Knudsen was a friend of Crow, he was unarmed and had a large family of children. Crow thought that Knudsen was Mike White. White was a deadly enemy of Crow. White and Knudsen were the same size, wore the same kind of beard and looked so much alike that few persons could tell them apart a few yards away.

Next Crow shot Kelley. By then the shotgun was empty and Crow held it in his left hand while he drew his revolver and shot Haymaker, Henderson, and McGregor, who were still about fifty yards away, guarding Marshal Poole.

By this time Hart gave up trying to hold the team and collapsed on the ground. The team started to run away. Crow still wanted his rifle, so he ran after the team. But they had too much of a start and were traveling too fast for him to catch them. He did get to the rear of the wagon and actually put his hand on the stock of his winchester, but at that moment he lost his footing and fell.

I have heard it said that Crow ran from the scene of the shooting and hid as soon as it was over. That is all pure fiction. Crow never ran from anything in

Grat Dalton, age 24. He was killed at Coffeyville, Kan., Oct. 5, 1892.
Photo courtesy N.H. Rose and now in Bear State Library.

his life. In fact, he did just the opposite. He got up from the ground, picked up his shotgun, loaded it and walked back to the crowd.

By this time everyone who had been armed was lying on the ground and the marshal ran to Crow, asking him to get on a horse and make a run for it. The marshal knew that Crow had been attacked and had only shot to defend himself. Crow refused to take a horse and started afoot to walk across the fields to his father-in-law's place, where there was a [bullet-proof] brick house and where he had plenty more guns and ammunition.

In the meantime, more of the settlers were coming up to the scene of the shooting and one of these, Caleb Flewelling, caught Crow's team, took Crow's own rifle and shot him with it. Flewelling was too far away for Crow to use either the shotgun or the revolver on him. Crow still had both of these guns and they were both loaded when his body was picked up.

Well, Crow, Henderson, Harris, and Knudsen had all been killed instantly. Kelly and Hart died during the night and McGregor next morning. Haymaker lingered some time. But when Haymaker died, Caleb Flewelling was the only man left who had fired a shot that day. . . . .

> When Lit finished his story I was sunk so deeply in the tragedy of the Mussel Slough battle that I was startled to find that I still was leaning against the old Benedict barn and writing in my notebook.
>
> We brushed off our clothes, got in the car and drove to Visalia. Stopping first at the Tulare County Court House, we climbed the stairs and entered the old walnut furnished courtroom where the trial of Grat Dalton had continued for twenty-three days, at that time the longest and most expensive criminal trial in the history of Tulare County. The room was vacant when we entered and we both stood silent, imagining the drama which had been enacted there more than forty-seven years before. Then we drove to the Tulare County Jail, about two blocks distant. Here, for the one and only time, Lit was lost, and in a place in which he had expected to be entirely at home.
>
> The jail had been remodeled and it took Lit at least thirty minutes to get his bearings. In the days when Grat Dalton was there the front steps led up from the west and the Jailor's office was on the east. When we were there the steps led up from the south and the Jailor's office was in the southwest corner of the building. But, worst of all, the old cell tier from which Grat had escaped had been removed. As we talked, John Hazen came in. I introduced him to Lit. "Seems to me I have seen you before," said Lit. "Guess you have", said John, "I was working for

Five settlers, survivors of the Mussel Slough battle, who were indicted for murder and confined in prison at San Jose, California, for more than eight months. Standing, left to right: J.J. Doyle and W.L. Pryor. Seated, left to right: J.D. Purcell, James N. Patterson and William Braden.

Photo courtesy of Attorney John F. Pryor, son of the above W.L. Pryor and now in Bear State Library.

Sheriff Eugene Kay when Grat's trial was going on over in the Court House, and I went out and bought a pair of shoes which Kay gave Grat, just a few days before he escaped. After Grat escaped I told Kay I had heard of sheriffs looking the other way while their prisoners walked away, but I never heard of them giving the prisoners new shoes to walk away in. But I was only kidding about Kay helping Grat escape. It cost Kay more than six thousand dollars in chasing Grat over California, Arizona, and Oklahoma."

CHAPTER THREE

Playing With Fire

On the drive back to Kern County, Lit again became reminiscent and I let him talk on, making notes all the while in the notebook on the seat between us.

We decided to stop at Tulare for dinner. Lit mentioned that in 1878, when he first visited Tulare, then just a small village, that the best eating place in town was a Chinese restaurant, which had been established there when the railroad reached the place. "I used to buy a good meal there for two bits: 'Loast beef, loast port, beefa stew spaniś, boi' tongue. You likee beef stew, maybe?'"

Lit surely was surprised when I told him that the Chinese he had known in 1878 was Ling Jo, one of the most respected merchants ever to conduct a business in Tulare, and that his widow, Mary Jo, still operated one of the best eating places in town, one of the oldest continuously operated family businesses in the Joaquin. I had expected to stop at a restaurant uptown, but I took my foot off the clutch, stepped on the throttle and we rolled south to Mary Jo's.

"By George, it sure is a neat and clean little place, isn't it? Look at all those truck drivers eating. The grub's always good where you see truck drivers."

I agreed with Lit, but was sorry that Mary Jo was not in at the time. Lit had never seen her. She had come to America after he had left Tulare County.

The Chinese boy who took our order spoke excellent English, and there was a typed menu; so we were not treated to a rehearsal of the old pidgin English.

"It was with Father that I first ate a meal in Ling Jo's place. He came into Visalia with his darned old race horses, and I went from Hanford to visit him. He brought me to Tulare, where he looked at a race horse he was thinking of buying."

When we had given our orders and were waiting to be served, I settled myself into the chair and made some of the most interesting notes of

Train similar to the ones held up by the Daltons. This one has three too many passenger cars.

Photo courtesy of the Southern Pacific, and now in the Bear State Library.

the entire trip. Lit was again in a reminiscent mood and I didn't need to say a word.

It's a tragedy to have to blame your father for the failure of four of your brothers, but I just can't get around it. He trailed the boys around with him after a string of race horses, associating them with the worst riff-raff in the country. The example in gambling that he set them offset all the other good habits he held up to them. Why, the day he and I ate here in Tulare at Ling Jo's, Bob and Grat got into a bar room brawl uptown, here, over a poker game. Bob was in trouble enough when he was alone, but when he was with Grat he was worse. But Grat was worst of all. He was impossible. If he couldn't win in a poker game, he would start a quarrel, grab stakes, including most of the money in sight, kick over the table and start a fight. By 1888 he had fought in saloons in every good sized town in the San Joaquin Valley.

But I don't want to leave Father without giving you something of his family and his ending. Then we don't talk about him any more.

James Louis Dalton was born in 1824 near a little crossroads called Lobergrub, in Kentucky. Aunt Nancy Noel and Aunt Tilly Louis, Father's sisters, and all the rest of their brothers and sisters were born at Lobergrub. I have no idea where the place was located in Kentucky, or even how you would spell it. But I believe that it must have been near McGee College. Father attended McGee for a while before he went to the Mexican War. He apparently got there what I have always called a race horse education.

In 1850 Father came to Missouri and located in Jackson County on a piece of land almost adjoining the farm of his later father-in-law, Charles Younger.

When my oldest brother, Charles Benjamin Dalton, was about sixteen, Father sent him to McGee. He was there some time, probably a couple of years. When he came home he couldn't count out a hundred eggs for you in four hours. He couldn't ever figure for you what a dozen eggs would be worth at a dollar apiece.

Father also sent the next boy, Henry Coleman Dalton, to McGee. All he got was a whisky and poker education and not a very good one, either. He gambled away every dollar he ever made, except what he drank up, and died of stomach ulcers from trying to put the saloon keepers out of business by drinking up all their liquor.

The next boy, Louis Kossuth Dalton, was probably the brightest of all Mother's children. At least, she always claimed so. He died when he was about six and I was about four. I remember that I had the most fun of my life playing with him.

Grat Dalton at the age of about twenty years. This is as Grat appeared when he was beginning his career as a race horse hostler and bar room fighter up and down the length of the San Joaquin valley.

Photo courtesy Wells Fargo Bank and Union Trust Company and now in Bear State Library.

What remained of the old Dalton home near Belton, Missouri, about 1920. Photo courtesy Mrs. Lee Aldrich and now in Bear State Library.

By the time I came along, Father's old racing nags had run away with all the school money; so I never got any education, except about three short terms in the little Dalton School on our old farm near Belton. The rest of my education I got at Turlock, California. I went to work there for Mrs. Allen and her son, Stony, in '82, in their combination store, hotel, and saloon. Mrs. Allen asked me what kind of work I would like to do. I told her I wanted to work where I would have to learn to read, write, and figure. So Stony put me to work on the accounts. I had to look up the prices of butter, eggs, cheese, and grain in the newspaper and write them on a slate which hung behind the counter. While a crowd of bums played poker and drank whisky, I figured up what each one owed the store and hotel.

Mason, or Bill, as he was commonly called, came to California to stay in '84. He was then about twenty years old. When he first visited California with father he was not yet seventeen. I was working at Turlock when he came to stay. Mason and Ben rode in to visit me. They had been in Montana. They brought me news that Mother had been sick for some time. Soon after they left me I went home to see her.

From Turlock, Ben and Mason went down to the Turner Ranch where the other boys were and worked there a short while. Then Ben got a job over near Madera and Mason went to work for Bliven at Livingston. Mason later married one of the Bliven girls. Grat tended bar in Livingston when I was working for Mrs. Allen and Stony in Turlock.

Of the ten Dalton brothers, only Mason, or Bill, raised a family. His son, Charles Coleman Dalton, is my only nephew who has carried the Dalton name from my Father's family. He is a fine fellow and a hard worker. Charles has several boys and a girl, all good children.

When Mason was killed by the U.S. Marshals in Oklahoma, his body was returned to California and was buried at the corner of the old Bliven home at Livingston. When Bliven lost the old Livingston place, Mason's body was moved to the Turlock Cemetery.

Father was six-feet-one-inch barefoot, and, in his prime, weighed two hundred and twenty pounds. He was a fine looking man: black eyes, clear, rosy complexion and curling, coal-black hair. Emmett looked most like him of all the children. I looked most like Mother, stocky, with blue eyes, florid complexion and dark, almost red hair. I am five feet seven inches tall and a few days ago weighed one hundred and sixty pounds. Bob was the only other child that resembled Mother. He was about six feet tall and had blue eyes and sandy hair and beard.

As I have said before, Father never drank at all. Nor did he use tobacco in any form. He didn't use profanity at any time. Gambling was his one fault, and that was plenty. Father gambled the Belton home away on his ten-cent race horses. Then in '89, when Oklahoma Territory was opened for settlement, Mother obtained a piece of Indian land down on Kingfisher Creek, near the town of Kingfisher, Oklahoma.

At Kingfisher the home Father patched up was nothing compared with the old Belton place he lost after I left home. It was a typical Indian Territory dugout. When I went home in '86 and saw it for the first time, I was as disgusted as could be. It was surely a come-down from what Mother had started out with. Everything had been invested in horse races. It is true that Mother later built a frame house on the prairie land, above the dugout, but it was not the home she deserved.

The Kingfisher house was dug part way into the bank of Kingfisher Creek. It was of heavy timber with sod walls and roof. There was no fireplace in it. Mother's cook stove heated the kitchen and another woodstove heated the front room.

The bunk house, where the older boys slept when at home, was about a hundred yards east of the house. It was also a half dugout, dug into the creek bank, and with sod walls and roof.

The horses were kept in a big dugout barn west of the house.

The well was dug near the house. It had a wooden frame and pulley over it. The boys let the wheel run dry so that it would squeak when anyone drew water from the well.

There was a low, sod-roofed shelter for wood near the house and a woodpile and chopping block beside it.

The country between the place and the town of Kingfisher was as barren and level as a floor. You could see a man afoot for a mile or more.

This Oklahoma dugout into which Father's old moth-eaten bang-tails had driven Mother always stuck in my craw.

Early in '87 Father was stranded in Fresno with Emmett, who was then almost fifteen. Father was broke and had two or three broken-down race horses in a stable at Fresno. He came to me for money. I was working for Charlie Owen at the time, for thirty-five dollars a month, skinning a long-line team of mules. Prior to this time I had given Father at least two hundred dollars in cash, most of it the year before, when he was in the same kind of fix. I was sick and tired of the whole business. I told him I was going to buy him a ticket home and, that in the future, if I had any money to spare, I was going to send it to Mother, so that she could get out of that dugout in the bank of Kingfisher Creek.

I went to Owen and drew sixty dollars. This, with forty dollars I had in my pocket, I gave to Father.

When he left, I said, "Father, I am going to send you home. I am sick and tired of your damned horses and gambling. They've made a tramp of you and of the whole family. Go home. Let those bang-tailed plugs rot there in the Fresno stables. I never want to see you again." He went, and I *never did* see him again.

But Father scraped up more money from some of his associates, and took the old racing plugs east with him

When I sent Father home I was mad and I swore a good deal. He took me to task for it. He could stand everything but the swearing. He said, "You don't need to swear. Quit using such language. Don't use it around me, anyway." He was right, of course, but I was half crazy and wanted some relief from paying race horse expenses.

That was the hardest thing I ever had to do in my life, but I was completely out of patience with Father and I knew that the whole family could never earn enough money to keep him in the horse racing business.

Father continued to run around with a ten-cent race horse or two. But he never came back to California. He died away from home at Dearing, Kansas, a few years later. He was with his horses. Mother had him buried in the old Robbins Cemetery, west of Coffeyville, Kansas. She got the race horses and what equipment was with them. The curry combs and brushes were worth more than the horses. . . . .

When Lit finished, our meal was eaten and we sat for a few moments, fingering our water glasses. I thought of Emmett's rosy description of the fine stable of thoroughbred racing horses his father had owned. Neither of us could find anything to say. So we walked out in silence. It was the only uncomfortable moment we experienced together. We climbed into the car and drove to Elk Bayou before anything more was said. It was Lit who broke the silence.

You know, Latta, there are two things that must be clear before you can understand the facts about the work the Dalton Gang did here in California. In his book Emmett claimed that he was not in California at all when the Alila robbery was staged, that a man named William McElhanie was then traveling here with Bob.

Of course Emmett needed an alibi. No one can blame him for not putting the finger of the law on himself. But Bob and Emmett were in plenty of trouble before they came to California, and they drew Grat and Mason into their trouble after they got here. The William McElhanie that Emmett wrote about was no one in the world but Emmett Dalton himself.

Well, the trouble began after Frank was killed, when Bob was made Deputy United States Marshal. A number of things led up to the trouble, and it is only fair to Bob to put them on record. I had all of these facts from both Bob and Emmett two or three times and also from people who had witnessed them in Indian Territory.

Grat was really the one who got Frank's job. Then he had Bob appointed. Bob hired Emmett to work under him, guarding prisoners. They got along fine until after Bob killed a man. This killing was in self defense, but Bob took it to heart and never got over it.

At Timber Hills, Indian Territory, Bob went out to arrest Charlie Montgomery. I knew Charlie well when I was at home. He was a no-good scamp, a bootlegger, gambler, road agent, and pimp. Al Landers was a deputy with Bob. Montgomery fired at Al Landers and then ran around a house. Just at a corner of the house he ran almost square into Bob. Both fired at once. Bob's face was actually burned by the powder from Charlie's gun. He had just time to throw up his shotgun and fire both barrels into the middle of Charlie. He tried to recover Charlie's horse, but was never successful.

Bob always worried about killing Charlie Montgomery. If he told me once about it, he must have told me a dozen time. From that day on Bob went bad. He drank more and became more restless all the time. He didn't seem to care what became of him. I believe he was the final cause of Mason, Emmett, and Grat going bad.

About this time Grat was separated from the other two boys. Bob was given the job of organizing the Indian Police in the Osage Nation. He took Emmett along as a deputy. Bob gathered under him about twenty picked Indians and half-breeds, all mounted and well armed.

During this time Emmett helped Deputy U.S. Marshal Floyd Wilson arrest Carroll Collier and Bud Maxwell, two of the most dangerous bad-men in the Nations, and was well started toward becoming a good officer.

Grat stayed in the south and worked out of Fort Smith. They didn't see each other again until after Bob and Emmett were in trouble. Grat told me much of this himself. I heard some of it from Bob after he and Emmett skipped to California.

Emmett and Bob both had good reputations in the Nations until about July of 1890. Up to this time they had been getting by all right, skating a little closer to the cracks in the ice all the time, but still keeping on the side of the law. But they were tired of the law and decided to land a stake in the Nations and then skip to California.

In June of 1890, Bob and Emmett drew their last pay as officers and planned to come to California. I know this to be a fact, because Bob wrote me, telling me they had drawn their pay and wanted to come. I wrote back for them to come on, that I had arranged for them to work for Charlie Owen and Clovis Cole. But they didn't come until they got into trouble. And the pay that Emmett worried about never getting was for time when they were rustling horses and when the officers were chasing them around the Nations. The only other money that they could have had coming from the government might have been some expense claims that were sometimes slow in coming through.

First Bob and Emmett stole a band of about twenty horses and a span of mules in the Osage Nation. They drove the stock to Waggoner, Indian Territory, and tried to sell them to a man from Fort Smith. They couldn't do business with the Fort Smith man; so they went on toward Kansas. They sold the mules in the Cherokee Nation to a rancher named Emmett Vann. Vann told me about the affair when I took Cole home a number of years later. They sold the horses in Kansas.

Bob and Emmett found this business venture so profitable that they rounded up about forty head of stock near Claremore, Indian Territory. They stole these animals from Bob Rogers and Frank Musgrove. I had known both Rogers and Musgrove when I was a boy and they told me all about it just before the Coffeyville raid, while I was at home near Kingfisher.

A horse trader named Scott, who had known Father well, bought this second batch of stock at Columbus, Kansas, giving a check for about seven hundred and fifty dollars for the band. The boys used their correct names in making this sale; so Scott wasn't suspicious of them. Later the endorsed check was dead evidence against them. Scott ran his stock around Baxter Springs, Kansas, a few miles east of Coffeyville.

Immediately after selling the stock to Scott, Bob and Emmett rounded up another band of horses down in the Osage Nation and ran them over to Baxter Springs, expecting to sell them to Scott before he found that the first band was stolen, and then skip out to California ahead of the law. But the law was beginning to move a little faster than they were. They arrived at Baxter Springs just as the owners of the first band had proved ownership to Scott and were preparing to drive their reclaimed animals away. Scott and Rogers and Musgrove were as mad as men can get. They had six or eight cow punchers with them. In those days a horse thief was entitled to be shot or hung on sight by the first person who caught him. Bob and Emmett had sure ridden right into a hornet's nest without suspecting it. They soon found out where they were.

While the stockmen were organizing to capture them, Bob and Emmett made a quick getaway, and it wasn't any too quick, either. Both of their horses were tired from the forced drive with the last band of stolen animals. So they roped and saddled fresh mounts out of the loose stock and started north. The stockmen were right on their heels.

Emmett's horse soon winded and the stockmen almost caught him. He and Bob met a man with a team, stopped him, cut loose one of his horses and started on as hard as the horse could go. Emmett picked a fine horse and they got clear away, although the posse sent fifty or more bullets around them as they rode. Emmett had to leave his entire riding rig on the winded horse, including his winchester rifle and his coat. That was one time he and Bob didn't stand and fight. Funny he [Emmett] never told you about *that* horse race of his. He won, all right, but he didn't wait to collect any bets.

After the Baxter Springs affair, Bob and Emmett hid out in the mountains and sent to Grat for help. This was the very beginning of Grat's downfall. He left his work and tried to get grub, horses, guns, and ammunition to them. He was watched, trailed, captured, and thrown into jail at Fort Smith in the very cell where he had placed a dozen prisoners. They kept Grat about two weeks and then decided to turn him loose, expecting that he would again try to get help to Bob and Emmett and they would then grab all three of them.

In the meantime, Bob and Emmett had hidden for a month or so in a dugout they had made, high up on the bluffs on the Canadian river about seventy miles southwest of Kingfisher. Getting tired of this, they took the train to California. They went to our brother Mason's, or Bill's ranch, on the Estrella River, east of San Miguel, in San Luis Obispo County. Mason had rented land there in '87 and was living a short distance from his wife's brother, Clark Bliven.

The place that Mason farmed adjoined what was known as the Cotton Ranch. It was owned by a man named Barnett. Clark Bliven and Mason were in partnership. They lived about a half mile apart. These places were about thirteen miles southeast of San Miguel. For about a year, starting when Mason first moved to the Estrella country, I ran a saloon in San Miguel, and knew all about what went on at Mason's ranch.

I don't want to get you mixed up about where I was living during all of this trouble. Probably I had better do some explaining.

The Federal Court House at Fort Smith, Arkansas. Photo was taken during the era of Judge Parker, Colonel Jacob and his son, George, Yoes. Grat Dalton was placed in the same cell in this building where he had placed men he had arrested when he was Deputy U.S. Marshal in the Indian Territory.

Photo courtesy George Yoes of Greenland, Arkansas and now in the Bear State Library.

I worked on the Glenn Ranch from '80 until '82. Then I went to Turlock and worked for Mrs. Allen. In '84 I came back to Fresno county and went to work for Charlie Owen. Charlie was a farmer and race horse man. He was a brother-in-law to Clovis Cole, after whom the town of Clovis was named. Mrs. Owen was a sister to Clovis.

For almost three years I hauled lumber over the Toll House grade into Fresno for Owen. He had a fine team, but it was a mean job. To team successfully over that grade a man had to have a good outfit, good wagons, harness, team, and brakes, and he had really to know his business. I didn't like lumber teaming. I rode my near wheeler. It was a hot, dusty ride over the dirt roads into Fresno. This work caused me to quit Owen and go on a visit to San Miguel, where an old friend from Indian Territory had located. He had just purchased a saloon in San Miguel. While I was visiting him he received a telegram telling him of the death of his father in Indian Territory. He wanted to go east immediately; so, to accommodate him, I bought his saloon. I had the place about a year and a half.

This was from some time in '88 to late '89. During this time, Cole, Grat, Bob, and Emmett all four visited with Mason from time to time. I know that Bob, Emmett, and Grat were marshals at the time and were supposed to be on duty in Indian Territory. But they visited Mason at least twice during '88 and '89 for several weeks at a time. One of them used to ride to my place to get whisky for the rest. He never wanted less than a gallon demijohn full. I wouldn't sell them that much, generally a quart and once in a while a half gallon. They were drinking too much, and I continually tried to get them to stop it. I finally gave up in disgust, sold my saloon, and went to work for Clovis Cole. I worked within a mile of the present town of Clovis.

Bob and Emmett visited me in San Miguel and at Clovis Cole's and told me about all of their escapades. They thought their escape from the stockmen at Baxter Springs as funny as could be. Some of it was funny, all right, to hear them tell it, but I sure burned them up about it. I told them it was only the beginning for them, that they would end by stretching rope or by stopping a winchester bullet apiece. I was not guessing very much, and I was not surprised when they did just that at Coffeyville, little more than a year later.

About a week after Bob and Emmett had visited me at Clovis Cole's, my brother Mason, or Bill as you have heard him called, came over to talk to me about them. We talked the biggest part of two days. Mason told me what the boys had been telling him. The story they had told me was the same. Mason was just as worried as I was. Later, when I was in the Indian Territory, I heard all about their horse stealing a dozen times. So I know what I have told to be the truth.

LITTLETON DALTON ABOUT 1888.

Photo courtesy Mrs. Martha Bolton (daughter of Charles Owen) and now in Bear State Library.

Finally I told Mason that the only thing to do was to shut down on the boys completely — to tell them that he would turn them in to the local officers as soon as they made a break of any kind. I said, "Mason, there is no use going any farther with them. In a short time they'll kill somebody, and then they'll get the rope." But Mason thought he'd better play along with them.

That was the worst mistake Mason ever made. He had never been in any trouble. He was a well-respected farmer and politician. He was then Democratic central committee chairman in Merced county and also a political committeeman near Estrella.

At this time I wasn't the only one who advised Mason to cut loose from Bob and Emmett. Cole and Ben told him almost the same things I did. But Mason said, "You fellows are all wrong. As long as I don't break with the boys I can do something with them."

Mason never broke with the boys, but they sure broke him. When Bob and Emmett and Grat finally finished with him he was a bum; his stock and farming equipment were gone, he was broke; and he was finally killed running an outlaw band of his own.

One thing I want understood, before we go any farther, is that Eugene Kay, sheriff of Tulare County, and his deputies didn't hound the boys into banditry. Nothing is farther from the truth. It is true that Kay gave Bob and Emmett the hardest runs they ever got. But the story that they were persecuted by Kay is all poppycock. They were in plenty of trouble when they arrived in California and they immediately proceeded to get into more trouble here.

Contrary to Emmett's story, Sheriff Kay was the most friendly and fair to the boys of all the officers ever on their trail. Kay knew from evidence he had gathered that Bob and Emmett were guilty of the Alila robbery. When he set out on their trail, he meant business and he kept close on their heels every minute. Kay gave the boys the hardest and longest run they or any other outlaws ever had at one stretch, a hundred and twenty days through the states of California, Arizona, Nevada, Utah, Nex Mexico, Indian Territory, Kansas, Texas, and Old Mexico; and they robbed a train at Whorton, Oklahoma, within two weeks after he quit chasing them. After this chase was over the boys told me all about it and I heard Grat say that Eugene Kay was the whitest man ever to wear a sheriff's star. Bob and Emmett were sitting within ten feet of us at the time and neither had a word to say to the contrary. I have also heard Mason make almost the same statements. We all liked Kay and always spoke well of him, even if we did curse the railroad detectives.

Another story I have heard a number of times was that Grat, Bob, and Emmett held up the train at Pixley in '89. There is no truth to this. I was in California at the time and heard a great deal about it. Neither Bob, Emmett, nor Grat was in the state of California at the time. They were on active duty as deputy U.S. marshals in Indian Territory. Besides, Pixley was a dynamite and shotgun job and the Daltons never used dynamite or shotguns to hold up a train. They knew nothing about how to use dynamite.

When Grat was released from jail at Fort Smith he quit marshaling for good and went up to Mother's at Kingfisher for a few weeks. Mother insisted on his following the boys and looking out for them. So Grat bought a ticket and came to California on the train. He came to see me at Charlie Owen's. I was driving a long-line mule team and he followed me beside the plow for three days. We talked all that time and part of two nights about the trouble Bob and Emmett were in. I told him the same things I had told Mason. But there was really no use in talking to Grat. He was almost as reckless then as they were. But he said nothing to me about any plans to rob trains.

It is now hard to understand how from the start, the boys ever figured on getting away with their outlaw program. At first, they hoped to make a good haul and then come to California. When they got here broke they did more figuring and hoped to accumulate at least twenty thousand dollars apiece by robbing trains and skip to South America. In exchange a United States dollar was then equal to three or four pesos and they expected to be rolling in wealth on their South American ranches.

Of course, this was not impossible if they had been smart enough to rob trains successfully. But people who are smart enough don't start out to rob trains. Haswell, the express messenger on the train that Bob and Emmett tried to rob, hung around Visalia during the most of Grat's trail. He told me that he often carried more than a hundred thousand dollars at a time. He said that on the trip before Bob and Emmett stopped him he had for some Arizona banks a mine payroll that totalled more than a hundred thousand dollars, all in gold coin. Even with all their dreams of South America, with a jackpot like that in their hands, I don't believe they would ever have left the States. They would have felt equal to fighting the whole United States Army.

When Grat left me he went to Mason's, over on the Estrella, where, by that time our brother Cole had arrived for a visit. Cole was trying to hold the boys down, the same as Mason and I had tried. At this time Grat, Bob, Emmett, Cole, and Mason were all there together. Cole and Mason would have nothing to do with any plans to rob a train. It was Bob who planned the robbery and who took Emmett and Grat in with him. I believe that Bob per-

Frank Halter, who loaned Bill Dalton the saddle ridden by Emmett Dalton at the time of the Alila train robbery. Photo made at the time of Grat Dalton's trial.
Photo courtesy Frank Halter and now in Bear State Library.

sonally planned and dictated the details of every robbery they ever did. Bob and Emmett were close together in age and had always run together from childhood. It was their decision at Mason's to run their course together and to take Grat with them that doomed all three. Although I didn't quit trying, there was no stopping them in anything after they came to California in 1890.

Both Mason and Cole worked with the boys for about a month, trying to get them to settle down and to go to work. Part of the time they drove mule teams for Mason and Bliven, but for only a few days at a time. The rest of the time they spent in poker games in San Miguel, Paso Robles, and San Luis Obispo, getting into a dozen or more fist fights and also getting rid of what was left of the seven hundred and fifty dollars they got from Scott for the stolen horses at Baxter Springs.

A band of Miller & Lux cattle went by Mason's on the way to the Peach Tree Ranch. Mason asked the vaquero boss if there was any chance of his brothers getting work on one of the Miller & Lux ranches. The boss said that there was and told him to try the Old Columbia Ranch near Firebaugh. Mason knew the superintendent there, a man named Davis.

Both Mason and Cole told me all about this. Mason wrote a letter to Davis and asked him to give the boys work. I read this letter myself. In addition, Mason hitched his team to the buckboard and went around the country to his neighbors, borrowing riding rigs to outfit the boys to go to work. He borrowed a horse and outfit from one of his hired men for Grat to use until he made enough money to buy one of his own. From Frank Halter, a mule skinner on the neighboring Estrella Ranch, Mason borrowed a saddle and bridle. He got another saddle from his brother-in-law, Clark Bliven. Bob and Emmett rode away on two of Mason's plow horses, Foxie and Charlie. They had taken them instead of cash as wages for skinning mules for Mason. When they left, Mason gave them all the cash he could scrape together, almost fifty dollars.

Many reports have been circulated, stating that Mason helped plan the robbery, that he gathered up the equipment for Bob and Emmett, knowing that they were going to rob a train, and that he drove to the site of the robbery in order to get information for them. I don't believe it. Mason had more sense than to borrow equipment from his neighbors to be used in a train robbery. Up until the time the boys left, I am sure Mason expected them to go to work at the Old Columbia Ranch. After they left, however, Mason was uncertain and began to worry about their robbing a train. He told me this himself. He also told me that, while he had been gone, the boys had taken the ceiling from a closet in his house and made it into a sort of lid, or trap door, so they could get into the attic. It looked like they intended to hide when they came back.

CHAPTER FOUR

THE ALILA ROBBERY

The attempt to rob the Southern Pacific train at Alila, California, was made on the night of February 6, 1891. If Littleton Dalton had not decided to talk, the inside story of that robbery never could have been given to the public. He was the last living person who had heard from Bob and Emmett what had happened at the scene of the robbery, on the flight to Estrella, and from there to Indian Territory. The inside story of the robbery was not revealed for forty-seven years. Here is Littleton's story:

By now I hope I have established that Cole, Mason [Bill], and I did all we could to keep the boys from robbing a train. I know I did. And I took one more try at it before they went to Alila.

The boys left Mason's not half prepared for a train robbery. They had only a 44-calibre Colt six-shooter apiece and poor riding rigs. Two of their horses were common plow horses that they had been driving in an eight-animal team hitched to a Stockton gang plow, putting in a crop on Mason's ranch. I believe that Mason expected them to go to the Old Columbia Ranch and go to work, and I believe they started out to do it. What no one realized at the time, not even Bob, was that they were beyond work and would do nothing better than try to live by robbery and murder.

They stopped at Cholame and watered their horses and had drinks. They also bought a six-bit flask of whisky. A number of people there recognized all of their equipment, including the horses. I don't believe they would have stopped at Cholame if they were planning to rob a train.

The boys must have abandoned the Columbia Ranch idea when they were about where Tranquility is now. At least they told me they stayed on the Firebaugh road that far. Then they cut across east to Malaga, which was located on the Southern Pacific railroad, about four miles south of Fresno.

I was asleep in the bunk house at Clovis Cole's when I heard a single knock on the wall outside my bunk. The knock was repeated twice, about a half minute apart. This was a signal we brothers had used among us for many years. So I knew that one of the boys was outside and that he needed help. I got up and went outside without lighting a lantern.

It was Grat, and he had a fishy story. He and Bob and Emmett had started to go to Firebaugh to work, when his horse had gone lame. They had ridden to Malaga. The other boys were waiting in a barn on a ranch near Malaga. According to Grat's story, he had walked fifteen miles over to see me, and I was supposed to find him a horse. He wanted only a horse and bridle and would ride over to Malaga bareback. I afterward learned that Grat and Bob had ridden almost to Clovis Cole's and that then Bob had led Grat's horse back to Malaga. They did that so that Grat would be afoot, and I would be more apt to furnish him a horse.

We went into the bunk house and sat down in the dark to talk. In a few minutes I was positive that they were on a train robbing expedition, and I wouldn't ask Clovis Cole for a horse for such a purpose. Finally Grat had me light a lantern and let me read the letter Mason had written to Davis at the Old Columbia Ranch. Grat stated that at the Álamo Solo, near Dudley, a cattleman had told them there was no work at the Old Columbia Ranch. This didn't satisfy me, because I reasoned in that case that they would have gone back to Mason's. So I would do nothing about a horse. But Grat kept on talking.

About eleven o'clock I harnessed a horse to a buggy, left word for Clovis Cole, telling him I wouldn't be able to work next day, and drove Grat back to Malaga. I wanted to have one more heart-to-heart talk with Bob.

The boys were hid out in a barn on a ranch about a mile or more west of Malaga. There was no house on the place, which appeared to be a plow camp, not in use at that time. The situation didn't look good to me. I talked with them until daylight and finally agreed to help sell the grey horse Grat had been riding. They told me the horse had belonged to Mason, but that they had bought it off of him. The horse limped, so I thought I might have been wrong about the plans for train robbing. I had thought Grat simply wanted to get a horse that would be harder to identify.

To understand my willingness to believe Grat's story it is probably necessary to explain that when Bob and Emmett went to Mason's to skin mules about October first of '90, Mason had no money to pay them for their work. They needed saddle horses in order to get jobs punching cattle, so they said. They agreed to take Mason's horses, Foxie and Charlie, as pay. They had just about completed paying for the horses when they left in January of '91, to go on the train robbing expedition. They would have had the horses paid for some time before, except that they were gone too much of the time gambling in San Miguel, Paso, and San Luis. It was one of these horses that went lame. I learned all of this after they tried to rob the train.

Grat and I drove to a ranch near Fresno, leading the grey horse, and Grat sold it for sixty dollars, about half what it would have been worth if not lame. But Grat couldn't get another horse. We drove to at least six ranches and finally had to give it up. So I gave the boys a lecture and drove back to Owen's. This was the last I saw of any of them until after the Alila robbery.

It is interesting to remember that at Grat's trial the course of the boys from Huron to Traver was never learned. Between the two places they lost a day that was never accounted for. The officers never did pick up the trail around Malaga.

Well, Grat finally shipped the saddle and riding rig to Delano on the train. Then he took the train to Traver. There he met Bob and Emmett. They hung around the saloons, playing poker all night, and then went on down to Tulare, where they repeated the performance, Grat again riding the train. At Tulare Emmett bought a pair of spurs at a harness shop. Being of polished brass, with black leather straps, they were easy to identify and later made a good exhibit for the prosecution at Grat's trial. The boys then changed clothes with each other so as to mix up the testimony of witnesses. They were near enough of a size that they could wear each other's clothes, except that Bob couldn't put on the other boys' boots.

On this trip the boys were following the Southern Pacific pay car. On the first of each month the railroad company started a pay car from Oakland to pay off all the employees between there and Bakersfield. It reached Fresno about the second or third of the month and Bakersfield on about the fifth or sixth. This car was always followed by a swarm of gamblers, confidence men, and prostitutes, who took a good deal of the pay away from the railroad men. Grat and Bob had "followed the pay car" a number of times before. In fact, when he could, Father used to follow the pay car with his old spavined race horses.

When I left the boys at Malaga, Grat was wearing a good black Stetson hat. He always wore it without a crease or a dent in it. I never in my life saw him wear a slouch hat or one of any color except black. At this same time Bob was wearing new square-toed boots which we in those days called box-toed. He liked wide-toed boots, and, when he could get them, never wore anything else. The tracks of those box-toed boots were one of the best clues the officers found at the scene of the Alila robbery.

At Traver Grat had his moustache shaved off, together with about ten days' growth of beard. At Tulare they hung around saloons until dark. Grat played

Long-line plow team in use in the same area and at the same time that the Daltons robbed the train at Alila.
Photo in Bear State Library.

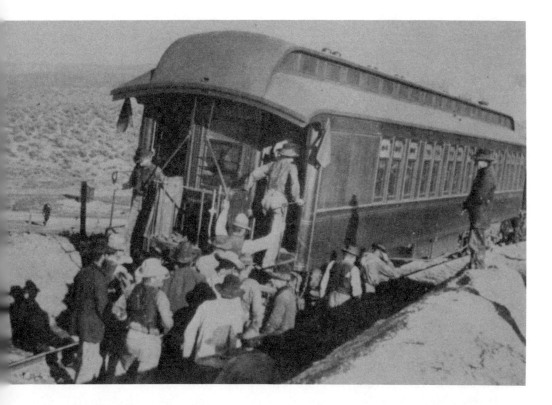

Southern Pacific Company pay car about 1895, when the company paid in cash. An armed guard stands at the extreme right, another on the ends of the ties at the left and looking at the camera. On bank at the left stands Paymaster Charles E. Robinson (right) and his assistant. Son of this paymaster, Paul D. Robinson, was for many years a locomotive engineer for the Southern Pacific Company. This photo was obtained through the courtesy of Paul D. Robinson, Jr., grandson of Paymaster Charles E. Robinson, and then Assistant Superintendent, El Paso Division, Southern Pacific Company.

Photo now in Bear State Library.

cribbage with Jim Ford, one of Sheriff Kay's deputies, for about four hours. Ford had known Grat for a number of years. At least a hundred other men in Tulare also knew both Grat and Bob from the days when the boys were following Father's race horses and were engaged in gambling and fighting in the bar rooms in Tulare. Grat tried to locate a horse, but didn't have enough money to buy anything he could use. He lost twenty dollars playing cribbage and poker, so he couldn't have had more than sixty dollars left, including what Mason had given him.

Bob and Emmett rode to Delano during the night, and Grat went down on the train, arriving before they did.

When going through Alila, now Earlimart, Bob and Emmett looked over the place where they had to jump the train and also the trestle where they later stopped the train.

At Delano the three boys hung around the saloons and livery stable. From evidence I heard at Grat's trial, and from what I later learned from Bob, Emmett, and Grat, they were all drinking heavily all the time.

Next morning they didn't have enough money left to buy a burro, let alone a horse; so Grat shipped the saddle back to Fresno, addressed to John Wilson, the name he had been using since he left Malaga. I don't know why he used an assumed name — too much whisky, I suppose. He met at least forty people in Traver, Tulare, and Delano who knew him and who called him by name. The use of an alias only helped to convict him. A dozen people identified him at the trial. Another smart thing he did was to stick around Delano until it was too late for him to get back to Fresno and establish a watertight alibi. He didn't leave Delano until after dark the evening of the robbery. He caught a through freight north and didn't get into Fresno until one o'clock the next morning.

The morning before the robbery, Bob and Emmett took their horses out of the livery stable. They bought some rolled barley for the horses. It was mixed with wheat and later proved an aid in convicting Grat. Then, while they got a lunch of about fifteen sandwiches from George Tilton, who ran a cigar store and chop house, they kept on drinking. It took them about two hours to leave Delano and during all of this time they were continually drinking. They had no less than a dozen drinks apiece and bought two quarts of whisky to take with them, leaving about ten o'clock.

In addition to the heavy drinking they had done in Delano, they kept it up from the bottles all day. They rode in broad daylight to a slough or sink about three miles west of Alila and stopped along the way to talk with ranchers and to inquire the way around Tulare Lake.

THE ALILA ROBBERY

No two real smart men could have stayed at the slough the same length of time as Bob and Emmett did and have left any more evidence of their stay. They ate a part of their lunch and threw the rest on the ground alongside the dated newspaper with the restaurant subscriber's name written on it. All the officers had to do was to scrape the remains of the lunch onto the paper and roll it up. The boys cut the tapaderos off the stirrups of the saddle that they had borrowed from Frank Halter. They threw the taps into the sage brush about thirty feet away from their camp.

In pulling off the taps they broke a piece of wood from the side of one of the stirrups. When the officers later found the taps, this piece of wood was hanging to some of the rawhide lacings and definitely placed the boys at the Alila location.

There was wool-covered sheepskin sewed around the bottoms of the stirrups. The boys decided they didn't need the sheepskin any longer, so they cut it off and threw it into the brush. Of course, the stirrups still had the marks of the rawhide lacings on them where the sheepskin and tapaderos had been fastened, and the hole where the piece of wood had been broken out. Frank Halter was later able to identify all three: the saddle, the sheepskin, and the taps.

The officers really wondered what kind of evidence planting had been done. Detective Hickey told me, "Lit, when I saw all that stuff I thought that special officer Bill Smith of the railroad company must have put the evidence there for us to find. But when I made the next find it was all explained. There was an empty quart whisky bottle about ten feet from the scraps of lunch." A dozen drinks of whisky apiece before ten o'clock and another pint apiece before dark explained everything.

By dark the boys probably felt equal to robbing the train without guns. At any rate, they got on their horses and rode straight to a telegraph pole beside a trestle a half mile south of Alila, leaving a perfectly plain string of horse tracks from the tapaderos, newspapers, lunch, and sheepskin. They tied their horses to the pole and walked up the railroad track to Alila.

While Bob and Emmett were waiting for the train to pull in, a tramp walked up and began talking to them. Bob asked the tramp where would be a good place to catch a ride on the blind baggage. The tramp showed them where the engine would stop. Bob and Emmett moved down there to wait. The tramp went with them. This made Bob uneasy. He didn't want to order him away, and he was afraid he might get wise to what was going to take place and notify the station agent.

The train pulled up at least two car lengths farther than the tramp had indicated and only came to a stop for about three seconds. The boys had to make a hard run, one on each side of the train, and almost missed the holdup. The train was under way when they scrambled aboard the engine.

Joe Thorne was the engineer, and George Radliff was the fireman on the train. Thorne saw what was coming and tried to keep Bob off; but Bob threw a gun on him and climbed aboard, anyway. Just as Bob climbed up behind the engineer, Emmett climbed up behind the fireman and covered him. Thorne was afraid they would hurt the fireman and ordered Bob to be careful and not hurt him, because he had a family. Bob came very near shooting the engineer before he would shut up.

Bob had on a mask made of a white handkerchief. In his anxiety over what the engineer might do, and to see better, he jerked the mask down around his neck. Emmett was in the front end of the coal tender with the fireman. Just as Bob pulled his mask down, the fireman opened the door to the firebox and, in the bright light, both the engineer and fireman got a good look at both of the boys. They knew one was sandy and the other dark. They could have identified both of them. Bob was mad about this and had about made up his mind to kill the engineer, but didn't want to kill the fireman too, because he had obeyed orders.

Emmett hit the fireman over the head with his gun and almost knocked him out. Emmett told him to shut the door, which he did. They finally got the train stopped with the front of the engine beyond the trestle not fifty yards from where the horses were tied. They all got off the engine on the east side of the train, opposite the horses, so that they wouldn't be scared at any shooting they might do, or be shot by any officers that might be on the train. Emmett marched Radliff ahead with his arms in the air. Bob made Thorne carry a coal pick back to the express car.

Emmett told Radliff to ask the expressman for a link, saying that they had broken one. In those days the cars were about one third the size they are now and were coupled together with a pin about an inch and a half in thickness and a heavy link about a foot long. They were forever breaking those links, and the expressman generally carried several extras. The boys expected the express car to be opened without trouble.

But the expressman had taken a look out the door when the train stopped and had seen the train crew being marched to the rear. He knew what was coming; so he put out his lights, closed and locked all the doors and windows, took off his shoes and wouldn't answer either the train crew or the boys. This expressman's name was Haswell. I heard him tell his story at Grat's trial. I also heard all of this from Grat, Bob, and Emmett.

Just at this time a brakeman walked up the side of the train with a lantern.

Thorne yelled at him to go back. Bob needed the light; so he told Thorne, "Say that again and I'll put *your* lights out." Bob put his revolver on the newcomer and made him put up his arms, with the lantern hanging on one arm. He told the brakeman to ask the expressman to open the express car door.

Up to this time there had been no shooting. It was too dark to see very much. Emmett crouched behind Radliff with one knee on the ground and Bob crouched behind Thorne and the brakeman.

There was a glass window in the express car door and, with the glow from the lantern, Emmett thought he could see a man looking through it. He told Bob, and Bob fired through the glass. Immediately the expressman began to empty his 44 calibre, double action Colt revolver through the broken glass window. He rested the muzzle on the window ledge and pulled the trigger until the gun was empty. At the same time Bob was emptying his revolver into the car door. One of Bob's bullets glanced off a steel bar across the little window and hit Haswell in the forehead, making a small, shallow wound.

During the shooting, Radliff turned as though he was going to run, and exposed Emmett. Emmett swore at him and told him to get back, taking a shot at him at close range, less than four feet. Radliff said, "I am shot." Emmett believed that, because he had just shot at him. He saw the man was badly wounded and would undoubtedly die. Until he met Grat, after Grat's trial and escape, Emmett thought he had killed that fireman. What he didn't know was that the expressman, Haswell, had hit Radliff with his first shot and that Radliff was shot before he turned around. There was positive evidence of this. Radliff was shot with old-style ammunition just like the expressman was shooting in his six-shooter. Bob and Emmett were also using 44-calibre Colts revolvers, but with up-to-date ammunition. Several of the boys' bullets were dug out of the express car and compared with the one taken from Radliff's body. They were not the same. Because of this, Haswell was indicted for the killing of Radliff. But Haswell was cleared at his hearing. We didn't know the actual results of the hearing. They were kept quiet until Grat's trial was almost over. Sheriff Kay first told me about it. I had thought until then that Emmett had killed Radliff.

As soon as Bob's gun was empty, Emmett began to shoot. This had been arranged before so that they would not be caught with both of their guns empty at the same time. When Thorne saw that Radliff got out of the line of fire by saying that he had been shot, he tried the same thing. He yelled that he was shot and tried to throw himself down under the car. Bob said, "Get out of that, you are not hurt."

After he emptied his gun, the expressman lay down on the floor between the safes. The wound in his forehead wasn't serious. He reloaded and lay quiet. He didn't move again until Bob and Emmett were gone. For about ten or fifteen minutes Bob and Emmett kept trying to get the expressman to open the door. They yelled at him, swore at him and threatened to blow up the car. They got no answer and finally decided that they had killed the expressman as well as the fireman. They had no tools with which to break in. They were less than half a mile from Alila, and help might arrive before they could get away. So Bob decided that they had better leave. They walked around to the west side of the train and went to their horses. While they were untying their horses, Bob fired several shots with his six shooter at a deputy sheriff who got off the train. I heard the deputy tell about this at Grat's trial. As soon as they were mounted, the boys ran their horses west as hard as they could go.

There were no returns from the Alila robbery. The express car was not entered and no money was taken. At Grat's trial, which I attended every day, the expressman stated that he carried that day eleven sacks of silver, totaling nine thousand and seven hundred dollars, consigned to New York, and that nothing was lost. . . . .

The killing of fireman George Radliff caused bitter feeling on the part of Southern Pacific trainmen toward Wells Fargo Expressman, C.C. Haswell. Although Bob and Emmett Dalton both thought Emmett had killed Radliff, both Radliff and Engineer Thorne knew he had been killed by Haswell. As Radliff was wounded in two places, it is possible that Emmett did hit him, but made only a minor wound, partially severing the little finger on Radliff's right hand.

Before any shooting was done, Thorne told the messenger that both he and Radliff were in front of the bandits and that if he shot he would get one of them. Disregarding this information the express messenger returned Bob's first shot by blindly emptying his revolver through the window and side of the car. His first bullet entered Radliff's body on the right side over the cartilage portion of the tenth rib, not even scarring the cartilage, and took a direct course downward and to the right. It pierced the small intestines in two places and finally lodged in the muscles supporting the lower abdominal cavity, having struck no bones in its entire course.

The mutilated condition of the bullet showed plainly that it had struck some hard substance before entering Radliff's body.

When told that he had but two hours to live, Radliff said, "I am not afraid to die." Asked if he knew who had held up the train he answered, "No, I don't know them. They are greenhorns." We know now that probably this was the first train robbery attempted by Bob and Emmett, and that undoubtedly Radliff's statement was correct. The last hour of Radliff's life was spent in conversation with his wife, who arrived several hours before his death.

Before he died, Radliff stated repeatedly that the messenger had shot him. His statement must be accepted as final authority. He knew from the position in which he was standing when shot that the bullet came from the express car. Both robbers were behind him. In addition, even before he was taken to Delano, he made the declaration that he had been shot by the messenger. This statement was repeatedly supported by Engineer Thorne.

George Radliff was a young man, only twenty-six years of age. He had fired for Joseph Thorne for some time and was exceedingly popular among his railroad associates. His death brought a flood of condemnation on Haswell. Old trainmen of that day remembered that threats of violence came from the San Joaquin valley trainmen and that for some time Haswell's life was in danger. But this feeling was kept very quiet so that it would not prevent the conviction of Grat Dalton, who then was being held for the attempted robbery.

Engineer Thorne claimed to have felt a sawed-off gun under Bob Dalton's coat and Express Messenger Haswell claimed that Bob had a shotgun in his hands and that a charge of buckshot from it was fired through the window, one of the shot striking him on the forehead. No other witness claimed to have seen a shotgun. In fact, several denied that the robbers had anything but revolvers.

During many years of investigation I have found one explanation of the wound received by Haswell. It stated that the revolver bullet fired by Bob struck a bar across the glass in the window, split, and a fragment wounded Haswell slightly. A similar explanation has been offered concerning Radliff's fatal wound, caused by a badly deformed bullet which had passed through nothing but flesh in penetrating his body. According to a statement made by Sheriff E.W. Kay, the first bullet fired by Haswell is said to have struck a bar over the window and to have been deflected downward. All newspaper accounts and all records are silent on this subject.

Among those interviewed, Littleton Dalton is the only person who actually investigated the bullet marks on the express car. Here is what he had to say about the guns, as well as what followed when Grat returned to Fresno:

At Grat's trial one of the amusing things was the descriptions given of the guns used by Bob and Emmett. Several of the witnesses claimed to have seen them holding shotguns. In spite of all those stories, neither Bob nor Emmett had anything but 44-calibre Colt revolvers. They just *looked* as big as shotguns to those witnesses. Besides, there was not a shotgun pellet in the express car anywhere, only a dozen or so holes made by revolver bullets. After the robbery the car was brought to the Fresno railroad yards. I went to the yards to examine the express car and saw this for myself.

During the robbery attempt, Grat was on his way back to Fresno on a through freight. The freight met the passenger at Alila — was leaving the siding there when the boys jumped the passenger. This north bound freight pulled out as soon as the passenger train cleared the north end of the switch. This left absolutely no chance for Grat to have taken part in the robbery. There was no way for him to get to Fresno after the robbery, except on the freight. The freight was ten miles on its way north of Alila when Bob and Emmett left the express car.

When Grat got into Fresno from Delano, I was in Fresno. We had heard about the attempted robbery about ten o'clock. In the Reception Saloon was a blackboard on which was posted important news, results of horseraces and baseball games being most common. While I was talking to someone in the bar room, news came about the train robbery and it was written on the blackboard. I was ready to go back to Owen's and to bed, because I was to drive a plow team in the morning and had to get up at four-thirty. But when I saw that notice I lost all interest in plowing. I knew the boys had done just what I had hoped they wouldn't.

At that time Radliff was not dead, but he and Haswell, the expressman, were both reported to be fatally wounded. I was sick. While I had decided at Malaga to cut loose from the boys, I knew then that I would have to do all I could to keep them from stretching rope. Of course I thought Grat was in on the robbery. About a dozen of us sat around the bar room and talked. Finally I walked over to the Grand Central Hotel bar room.

While I was listening to some men talk about the robbery, who should walk in but Grat. I almost fell over backward. My first impulse was to knock him over the head with my chair. Then I thought that maybe the boys had not robbed the train, after all. But it didn't seem possible that someone else had robbed the train in that locality when they were there. I didn't know what to think.

Well, Grat walked up to me and said, "Hello," as though nothing had happened. At the time he hadn't heard a word about the robbery. I started into the lavatory, and he followed me. There was no one else in there; so in about a half a minute Grat told me how he had left Delano and I told him that I had heard about the robbery. I immediately took him out into the hotel lobby and had him register. This was about one-thirty in the morning. I had him talk to three or four persons right away so that he could establish an alibi as early as possible. Then we went up to his room, and talked for a half hour. He told me all he knew and I told him what I knew about the robbery.

I slept with Grat that night and stayed around Fresno next day, read the news of the robbery as it was posted on the blackboard in the Reception and listened to the stories the trainmen brought back from the railroad depot. Then I went back to Owen's and took my plow team out again.

While I was plowing, I kept thinking about some of the things Grat had told me. During the trip down to Delano, Grat had done all of the scouting for information and had pretended that Bob and Emmett were strangers to him. He had gone in each place alone and had pretended he didn't see Bob or Emmett. He didn't eat with them or room at the same places they did. This was because Grat was well known all along the line, and he was continually meeting people he knew. But Bob was also well known in Tulare and Traver, and I knew that the moustache and beard he had grown couldn't prevent many persons from recognizing him. I became thoroughly convinced that the jig was up for all three of the boys. I said to myself, "Lit, from now on you're going to 'tend your own business!"

Grat hung around Fresno for about a week, expecting to be arrested at any time, because so many people had recognized him between Malaga and Delano. Detectives Smith and Hickey questioned him a half dozen times. Finally, one day Grat was talking to Hickey on the street, when one of Grat's acquaintances came up and began talking to him. Hickey ordered the fellow away. Grat told Hickey he couldn't do that. Hickey said, "The hell I can't, mister. You are under arrest."

Grat went with Hickey and was slapped in the Tulare County Jail at Visalia. He was questioned for several days and then was turned loose. Sheriff Kay was convinced from what Grat said and from what he knew from the chase following the robbery that Grat was not at the scene of the robbery at all. Kay told Grat this, and he also told it to Smith and Hickey. But he told Smith that if they turned Grat loose and set someone to follow him, he would probably lead them to the two brothers who did stop the train.

Well, Grat was released all right and went down town. There he met a fellow he had known for several years, a man named John Harris. Harris had been planted to trap Grat. It wasn't hard for him to get Grat's confidence. Grat was broke and wanted to borrow money. Harris loaned him fifteen dollars and also drove him to Hanford, where Grat thought he could get work. While Grat was looking for work, Harris found Frank Griffith, who was a Tulare County deputy sheriff, and who lived near Hanford. Harris arranged for Griffith to trail them and to follow Grat when they separated.

Grat could find no work. It was then late at night and the last train had gone from Hanford to Goshen. So Grat asked Harris to drive him to Goshen so that he could catch the midnight train north. Harris found time to tip Griffith off to Grat's plans, and made arrangements for him to follow Grat and split any reward he might collect. There was at that time a reward of three thousand dollars offered for Bob and Emmett. Griffith drove to Goshen ahead of Grat and Harris and had already purchased a ticket to Fresno when they arrived. Grat went through Lathrop and on to San Jose. . . . .

In 1925 Frank Griffith was living a mile or so east of Hanford. He furnished an important statement concerning the second arrest of Grat Dalton, taking up where Littleton Dalton left off. His story is of interest:

As soon as Grat landed in San Jose he got into a poker game. I was afraid to shadow him very closely because he had seen me get on the train at Goshen, and I was afraid he would become suspicious if he saw me again. So I hired a night watchman to keep Grat in sight. He was a California Spaniard I had known for thirty years; so I felt I could trust him.

I was completely exhausted for want of sleep. I rented a room in the back of a nearby saloon and went to sleep, lying on top of the bed with my clothes on. My paisano friend had orders to awaken me the minute Grat prepared to move from the saloon where he was playing poker.

About midnight the poker game broke up. My paisano guard challenged Grat to play coon-can for a dollar a game and drinks on the side. Grat cleaned him out of about twenty-five dollars in two hours. The fellow was both drunk and mad. He called in a night policeman and told him who Grat was. The result was that they arrested Grat and threw him in jail.

The night watchman forgot all about me. When I awakened it was broad daylight, he was broke, asleep, and dead drunk. There was nothing to do but return Grat to Visalia.

For an account of the flight of Bob and Emmett from the scene of the Alila robbery attempt we return to the account furnished by Littleton Dalton:

In a few days Sheriff O'Neal of San Luis Obispo County and Bill Smith, the railroad detective, came to Mason's and had long talks with both Cole and Mason. The result was that they were both arrested, taken to Visalia and jailed. Cole Dalton was released as soon as he was questioned. Mason [Bill] soon obtained bondsmen and was released, but Grat stayed in jail for several months, awaiting trial on a charge of robbing the train at Alila.

Well, when Bob and Emmett left the scene of the attempted train robbery, they almost immediately began to have trouble. The ground was crusted with alkali and was soft from recent rains. The plow horses they were riding soon winded and almost gave out. The boys were arguing and quarreling over their failure. Bob kept telling Emmett, "You damned fool, you shouldn't have shot that fireman. You should have hit him over the head with your gun like you did in the tender!"

It was a pitch dark night and foggy to boot; so they couldn't see the stars. Soon they lost their way and rode around out there on the plains south of Tulare Lake. The horses had never been over the route before; so they couldn't be given rein. Bob told afterward that they must have ridden over every section of land between Tulare Lake and The Bubbles [Now called the Lost Hills F.F.L.].

Finally, after daylight, the fog lifted. When they got their bearings, they were only about two miles from the Álamo Mocho Ranch and saw a boy riding to meet them. It was too late to avoid him; so they rode toward him. It turned out to be a boy Bob knew. His name was Din Light and his parents lived at the Álamo Mocho Springs in the Kettleman Hills. Din was looking for strayed stock. Bob asked him if they would be able to get something to eat at the Álamo Mocho and Din said, "Sure, go right to the house. Mother will have hot biscuits and coffee."

After breakfast at the Álamo Mocho, the boys rode on by the Álamo Solo and left Dudley to one side, hitting for a spring in the Cottonwood Pass where they could water their horses and conceal themselves during the day. After leaving the spring they began meeting people and were driven from the road in order to avoid them. Once they had to wait more than an hour to avoid a traveler.

Too many people knew them around Cholame for them to travel the main Paso Robles road; so they left that road and cut through the hills for about twenty-five miles, directly toward Mason's ranch. Even then they happened onto several cow-punchers they had known at the Estrella and at neighboring ranches and who recognized them.

When Bob and Emmett got within sight of Mason's place they saw a strange rig beside the corral. Mason's buckboard was gone. They were afraid to go to the place. They then rode to Clark Bliven's ranch. Mason was out looking for the boys.

Before the boys arrived at Mason's, Sheriff Kay of Tulare county and one of his deputies came to Mason's and put up for the night. They had tracked the boys from Alila to a point west of Cholame, where they had lost the tracks. They did not know who had attempted the robbery; so had no suspicion of Mason or the other boys.

After dark Mason arrived at Bliven's. He took the boys to his place. They saw Sheriff Kay's buggy beside the corral, but had no idea who it belonged to. Mason told the boys to sleep in a straw stack, and he went into the house alone. Mason did not know either Kay or his deputy and did not suspect that they might be officers.

In the morning when Mason and his wife got out of bed, Kay and his man were gone. No one was surprised at this, as Kay had told Mason's wife that she did not need to cook breakfast for them, that they would leave as soon as they awakened. In fact, nothing was suspected until supper time, when another rig drove up beside the house.

Mason recognized the newcomers as Sheriff O'Neal and a railroad special officer known as Bill Smith. No one tipped Mason off that O'Neal was coming, as has often been stated. Otherwise, Bob and Emmett would have left the house before the officers got there.

Bob had cut a trap door entrance to the attic in the ceiling of a closet and he and Emmett climbed aloft while Mason went outside to meet O'Neal. The boys had a bed in the attic and, knowing they had to keep absolutely quiet if O'Neal came into the house, they lay down on the bed with their six-shooters in their hands and their feet toward the trap door. Bob told me afterward that if Bill Smith had put his head through that trap door he would stopped two 44-calibre bullets before he could have batted an eye.

Well, O'Neal talked a few minutes and then asked if they could put up for the night. Of course Mason couldn't refuse him. Bill Smith came into the house immediately, while Mason and O'Neal put the team in the barn.

Smith began to question Mason's wife and even Charlie, the little boy, about Bob and Emmett. They told him the boys had gone to Seattle. As soon as Mason came in, Smith began on him. He disputed everything Mason told him and bragged about what he was going to do to Bob and Emmett when he caught them.

Bill Smith was the most objectionable man I ever knew. He made me mad every time I looked at him. Mason was one of the best natured men in the world, but he was soon so mad he could have killed Smith without hesitation. He argued with Smith as loudly as he could, in order to cover any noise the boys might make in the attic.

Finally O'Neal became disgusted with Smith. He saw a guitar and asked Mason if he could play. This fitted into Mason's program perfectly, so he sang and played until after midnight. All this time Bob and Emmett lay aloft, afraid to move. There was no way out until O'Neal and Smith were gone. Not only were they tired from their two-day ride, but they had developed a deadly hatred for Smith.

About one o'clock in the morning, Mason showed Smith and O'Neal to their room. As soon as Smith got to sleep, he began to snore. He not only kept O'Neal awake, but also Bob and Emmett. By daylight Bob was so furiously angry at Smith he could hardly keep from going below and killing him.

Smith and O'Neal had breakfast and hung around the place until about ten o'clock, talking to Mason. Then they left.

Bob and Emmett came down from the attic and prepared to leave. They then found that a saddle they had hidden was gone. They had hidden it in the manure pile the night they came in from Alila and had not missed it before. They didn't know whether it had been found and removed by Kay and his man, or by O'Neal and Smith. In either case they knew it was dynamite as evidence. So Mason arranged to get them out of the state as soon as he possibly could. . . . .

> In talking with pioneers of the Estrella, Cholame, and San Miguel country, I found them positive that Emmett Dalton was here in California with Bob at the time of the Alila robbery. The newspaper accounts also freely mentioned Emmett. When I talked with Lit he was just as positive. He had talked with Emmett here at that time on three different occasions. In conversation, Emmett had also admitted to me that he had been here. But I wanted documentary evidence.
>
> Lit and I were sitting in the study. At my elbow was a copy of Emmett Dalton's book, *Beyond the Law*, also a copy of his later book, *When the Daltons Rode*. I took up the first book and read to Lit from page thirty-nine the statement describing how Bob Dalton and McElhanie had ridden on the train together from Kingfisher to California and how McElhanie had assumed Emmett's name while he was here. The book states that the writer, Emmett Dalton, had never been able to

understand why McElhanie had used the name of Emmett Dalton, unless it was because McElhanie was wanted and he was not.

When I finished reading, Lit gave a snort of disgust.

"That McElhanie that Emmett has mentioned there was no one in the world but Emmett Dalton himself."

I was positive Lit was right, but I was wishing for proof other than the memories of pioneers such as I had been receiving. Thumbing through the pages in the book, a sentence on page thirty-four took my eye. The topic was an encounter with a posse in New Mexico after Bob and Emmett had robbed a gambling game in a saloon.

I said to Lit, "Listen to this." Then I read to him the account of McElhanie's being shot in the arm and of Bob's shooting the horse from under the rider, who hit the ground, running; also of the bathing of McElhanie's arm in the stream and the bandaging of a large cud of tobacco over the wound.

Remarking to Lit that I believed I had seen something of the same encounter mentioned in the other book, *When the Daltons Rode,* I took that volume down and carefully began to go through it. Almost as soon as I opened the book my eye fell on a statement on page one hundred twenty. I said to Lit: "Here is something," and read the statement that the railroad and express companies of California declared that McElhanie was none other than Emmett Dalton, and that he, along with Bob, was charged with the Alila robbery.

"You're darned right there was a charge against him for the Alila job," spoke up Lit. "You have noticed that he never hung around the Estrella and San Miguel when he was gathering material for his book. Too many people there knew him."

Running through the book I found on page six a description of the same encounter with the New Mexico posse described in *Beyond the Law.* Again I read to Lit how Bob had shot the horse, and how the rider had hit the ground running. But from there on was a very distinct variation from the account given in the earlier book. It stated that *Emmett Dalton* was the *only* one wounded and that he (Emmett) bathed *his* wounded arm at a small stream and tied it up with a cud of tobacco.

"There you are," broke in Lit, "You have Emmett's own printed word that he was McElhanie."

And Lit was right. There, discovered almost by accident, was the record I had wanted.

THE ALILA ROBBERY

The first train wreck on the present San Joaquin Valley Division of the Southern Pacific Railroad. It occurred at Tulare when a switch engine pulled onto the main line in front of a freight train. When this wreck occurred, there was no railroad service to Porterville. Billy Brown was driving an Overland Stage Coach from Tailholt, later known as White River, through Porterville, to Tulare. He arrived as the railroad photographer was making this picture and ordered several copies from him. This one he gave to the author.
   Photo in Bear State Library.

"Tall man, straight as an arrow, big black sheriff's-style Stetson hat, eyes sharp as an eagle's — ." Eugene W. Kay as he appeared one rainy day when the author found him in San Francisco, forty years after the Alila robbery.
Photo now in Bear State Library.

CHAPTER FIVE

THE ANDY NEFF SPECIAL

In approaching the Dalton Gang's San Joaquin Valley activities, the key man was Eugene W. Kay. He had entered office as Sheriff of Tulare County an heir to two train robberies and just in time to be deluged with a continued series of such robberies which lasted through his two terms of office and continued for several years after he retired. Kay was recognized by all authorities as one of the most active men ever to hold the office of sheriff in any California county. He had few equals anywhere.

The difficulty was that "Gene" Kay had dropped completely from sight as soon as he left office. Perhaps half a hundred persons had told me that Kay had been dead for many years. For about ten years I took these statements at full value. Finally Harry Charters, Tulare newspaper editor of Dalton days, told me, "Gene is not dead. At least he was not a year ago. I met him on Fremont Street in San Francisco, where he had a small office. We talked for a few minutes, but he wouldn't discuss the Daltons; said they and the other train robbers had broken him financially and that he had never spoken a dozen words about any of the train bandits since he left office. If you will talk to him I think he will loosen up."

It was not difficult to locate or to approach Gene Kay. Following Charters' instructions, I stood on the curb on Fremont Street and watched for a "tall man, straight as an arrow, big black sheriff's-style Stetson hat, eyes as sharp as an eagle's and actions just as sharp."

The first man I stopped was Kay. He was as straight as ever, but had failed considerably since Charters had seen him, and was carrying a cane. We went into his office and talked for three hours. He inquired about almost all of the remaining Tulare pioneers, but his mind was set against discussing any train robberies. But I was invited to visit him that night at his home on Scott Street. We talked for two hours more before Kay decided to discuss the robberies. My break came when I told him that Harry Charters had informed me where to locate him.

Dan Overall, once Sheriff of Tulare County, father of Orville Overall, Big League ball player.
Photo courtesy of Bob Hill and now in the Bear State Library.

"Harry Charters. Harry was one of the best friends I ever had. Harry helped me electioneer when I first ran for sheriff.

"Funny thing happened when I was electioneering at Alila, two funny things, in fact. The first happened when I was with Maurice Power and the other with Charters."

Knowing that the gates of Kay's memory were about to be unlocked, I was afraid to say a word. He studied a moment, ran his hand over his head, laughed, and broke out into the sort of story that only old-time southerners can tell. It furnished a picture of Alila in the late '80s that could be equaled by nothing else.

I was electioneering for sheriff, and Maurice E. Power, the silver tongued orator from Visalia, was electioneering for district attorney. There were sixteen votes in the Alila precinct, all democratic. We decided to pool our traveling facilities and make the trip together. Power rode to Tulare from Visalia on the little dinkey train and we drove from Tulare to Alila in my buggy.

Public meetings were held in the little school house a short distance east of the present town of Earlimart. The surrounding country was settled by "timber culturalists". They took up a timber culture of a hundred and sixty acres and held their claim by building a cabin and digging a well and scratching in about forty acres of wheat or barley every fall. They tried to scratch out a living by collecting the bounty on squirrel and coyote scalps. The squirrels scratched a living out of the wheat and barley and the coyotes scratched out a living catching squirrels.

Each settler had a saddle horse and from two to ten greyhounds to run squirrels and coyotes. The greyhounds scratched out a living catching jack rabbits. Those greyhounds were just as important to us politicians as their owners, for it was surely a case of love us, love our dogs.

The inside of that little school house was crowded. The sixteen voters crowded into those little desks and at least forty greyhounds crowded into the rear of the room. They were led by a big spotted hound that seated himself a few feet in front of the rest.

I talked first and had a fairly easy time, as I was a Democrat and needed only to present myself to get every vote there. I had only one difficulty. Every time I looked at those darned greyhounds I had to grab my handkerchief and cover up my laugh by blowing my nose.

Those hounds sat there on their haunches as quiet and erect as Egyptian images. Their noses were pointed as straight at my face as so many double

"The little dinkey train" and the section crew which kept up the line on the Visalia and Tulare Line. Eleven miles in length, this was, during the Dalton Gang Days, Tulare's most rapid means of communication with the county seat at Visalia.

Many well known Tulare county citizens appear in this photo. Left to right: Charles Roby, Ed Whiteside, Mank Morre, F.M. Busby, Lon Busby, Charles Busby, Charles Rose, Clarence Rush, and James Galian.

Photo courtesy of Mrs. George Beckwith, now in the Bear State Library.

barreled shotguns. They never so much as flicked an ear. The voters chewed tobacco and spat and talked between themselves and didn't look half as attentive as the greyhounds.

I'd talk as long as I could, would grab my handkerchief and blow and say something about a cold. I blew until my darned old nose was as red as a beet. When I sat down, Power said to me, "Gene, what in the world is wrong with you? You haven't any cold." He didn't know that the dogs were in the back of the room. They had entered after we were seated. While the chairman was introducing Power I whispered to him, "Maurice, we'd both carry the county if we could count the votes in the back of this room."

When Maurice faced that room I thought he would have a stroke of apoplexy. He would say a few words and then blow. In spite of his great ability as an orator, he never did make three connected statements while he was on his feet.

By this time the voters were as restless as could be. The chairman said to me, "You fellows must have taken a hell of a cold riding down here in that buggy."

Power was a Republican and he didn't get anywhere with those Democrats. They talked back and forth among themselves and contradicted everything he said.

Outside, the horses also were restless. One snorted. Several of the greyhounds glanced sidewise at the leader, but he didn't move, so they quieted down again. Another horse rattled a halter chain and a dozen of the hounds looked anxiously at the leader. Still he sat tight.

Finally our horses cramped the buggy and scraped a wheel against the body. At this the hounds all looked at the leader, who probably decided that, in spite of the interesting program, this new, strange noise needed investigating. He turned and made a long, rubbery jump out of a window and was followed by the other thirty-nine as noiselessly as the strokes of a steam piston. Not a toenail scraped the floor.

Power turned his back and blew his nose until I thought he was going to blow off the top of his head. Then he turned around, pulled out his watch, snapped open the cover, looked at the time, rubbed his thumb over the crystal, and said, "Well, as the hour is growing late, and most of the audience has already departed, I think we had better go back to Tulare."

We laughed and talked about that audience all the way home. . . . .

Seeing that at last the ice was broken, I hoped to steer Kay into a discussion of the Alila robbery, but he was not ready for train robberies. He laughed, was silent for awhile, ignored my questions and then again began another of his recollections of the days when he was electioneering.

I had one other electioneering experience north of Alila where there was a settlement of Prohibitionists. Their vote was completely controlled by a woman political leader, who, in those days, of course had no vote of her own. I was new at electioneering, so Harry Charters went with me to try and corral the Prohibition vote. He said there was no use talking to anyone else in that locality, so we drove directly to the home of our political boss.

We met the lady at the gate. She looked us over with an eye as cold and glassy as a frozen nest egg. I began to talk, and I surely had uphill business. I got as nervous as though I was facing drawn guns in the hands of the whole Dalton Gang. Each time I would say anything I would paw nervously with one foot, then the other. The soil was sandy and each time I pawed I dug a little deeper into the sand. The harder I talked, the worse I pawed and the deeper I got. Afterward Harry said, "Gene, if you had talked three more minutes you would have been in a hole so deep the sand would have been running into your hip pockets."

Finally the lady spoke. "I can't support you, Mr. Kay. I understand that you are a drinking man." That sure hit me square between the eyes, for I had never taken a drop of any kind of fermented liquor in my life. I couldn't find a word to say. While I climbed out of the hole I had pawed, Harry began talking.

Harry was as mad as could be. He offered to bring that lady a hundred men who would swear that she couldn't prove that I had ever taken a drink of anything. "Why," said Harry, "Mr. Kay is a teetotaler," and he named a dozen prominent men in and around Tulare and Visalia who would prove it.

The lady never said another word, so we decided that the Prohibition vote was lost, told her goodday and drove back to Tulare. When it came election time I got every single Prohibition vote in Tulare County. That woman had investigated me and electioneered for me among all the Prohibitionists. . . . .

Thinking to lead Kay into more of the pleasant things he could remember of Dalton Gang Days, I remarked that there were many worthwhile recollections about the train robberies that he could tell.

His first statement was, "I have tried to forget all about those days and I am afraid I can't remember what you want to know."

"Gene" Kay as he appeared in January of 1891 when he was sworn in as sheriff of Tulare County.
Photo now in Bear State Library.

Kay may have tried to forget, but he only had built a wall around his memories. I hope mine are as complete when (and if) I approach the age of ninety. The interviews with Kay continued over a period of several years and ended only at the time of his death.

From the moment when I got the telegram reporting the Alila robbery, things started off with a bang and they kept banging until I left office. I had just returned from a trip into the Kaweah River swamps to serve some papers. Two brothers didn't count hogs the same. By the time I had returned to Visalia it was about nine o'clock. I had stopped at the office to see what was new before going home and to bed. While I was talking to Williams, the night jailor, the telegram was handed to me. An attempt had been made to rob a Southern Train at Alila and the fireman had been mortally wounded.

I believe I made the best time that had ever been made from the Sheriff's Office in Visalia to Alila. I told Williams to telegraph the roundhouse at Tulare to have an engine and express car ready to take me and my driving team to Alila, also to have Perry Byrd check on some of our Visalia citizens whom I knew had been implicated in the Goshen robbery, and to telegraph me at Alila what he learned. I jumped in the buggy alone and was at the depot in Tulare, eleven miles away, in exactly thirty minutes. I drove right onto the station platform beside the express car. Two of my deputies, George Witty and Bob Hockett, were there to meet me.

Jim Ford had been working for me on my ranch at the Buzzard's Roost, now called Waukena. Jim just happened to be in Tulare and was standing in the crowd at the depot. He helped me unhitch. He led the harnessed horses into the car and held them while I had some trainmen push some planks and the buggy into the car. I telegraphed the Alila constable to keep people away from any tracks at the scene of the robbery. As Jim was used to managing stock, I yelled at him to hold the horses and I jumped on the engine. That's how Jim came to be a detective.

Andy Neff was my engineer. I have forgotten the name of the fireman. Andy had pulled the first train into Tulare when the railroad was being built, nineteen years before, and was later engineer on the train stopped by Evans and Sontag at Ceres.

Andy pulled the throttle open and away we went. Now, I suppose you are imagining a thundering passenger locomotive, pounding the rails at about seventy miles an hour and a shrieking whistle that sliced across the country as far as Tulare Lake. That makes me laugh.

It was one of those little old, red and gold, whistling-teakettle locomotives

The Southern Pacific roundhouse in Tulare in 1889 when the first train robbery occurred on that line, showing some of the four-driver, pot-bellied smokestack locomotives such as were described by Ex-Sheriff Eugene W. Kay.
Photo courtesy M.C. Zumwalt and now in Bear State Library.

— "Kerosene headlight that would light up a white cow at sixty yards, pot-bellied smokestack, and a whistle that went peep, peep" — Cow's-eye-view of a locomotive such as was described by Gene Kay.

"Yes, I'm funny now, but in my day I hypnotized half the kids of the nation into wanting to become locomotive engineers."

Photo courtesy Southern Pacific Company and now in Bear State Library.

with polished brass all over it, a pot bellied smoke stack, four drive wheels little higher than your waist, and a whistle that went peep, peep. I suppose the Southern Pacific had larger locomotives at the time, but they didn't furnish us with one, and I'm glad they didn't. Of all the locomotives I ever saw it is the only one I can remember.

The kerosene headlight would light up a white cow at least sixty yards ahead, but you would run over anything else before you saw it. The cars were about the size of those the Forty and Eight pulls around at the Legion conventions and were hooked together with links and pins. You could actually put your shoulder against an express car and move it to couple·up. That's the kind of train the Dalton boys stopped, did it with six-shooters.

Andy was a humorous sort of fellow. As the little old firepot clattered over the little rails, uh-chuck uh-chuck; uh-chuck uh-chuck; uh-chuck uh-chuck; he told me what he knew about the Alila job. It wasn't much.

We didn't stop at Alila. The station agent handed Andy some orders as we pulled through. With them was a telegram for me from Perry Byrd at Visalia. It read, "Chris and John in bed." So I knew I had a fresh job to work on. The robbery attempt might have been the work of anyone.

Jim Ford got out the planks and some of the audience helped him unload the team and buggy and hitch them while I measured the boot and horse tracks.

Tom Orr, Delano Constable, had guarded the tracks he had found at the place where the express car had been stopped and at the telegraph pole, where the horses had been tied. I picked up some pieces of glass from the ground. They had come from the express car window. I talked with Engineer Thorne and a brakeman who had been held up by the bandits. George Radliff and the express agent had been taken to a hospital in Delano.

The boot tracks could have been identified anywhere. One pair had been halfsoled and left a distinct pattern. The other pair had a pronounced square toe. The soil was moist and had received perfect imprints in a dozen or more places, both at the telegraph pole, where the horses had been tied, and beside the trestle, where the holdup had been attempted. The horse tracks were also easy to identify. One horse was unshod. The other was shod in front. One set of tracks was much smaller than the other and was narrow, or pinched, at the back, like the tracks of a mule. One hoof of the other set had two large places chipped when a shoe had been thrown. I measured all the tracks and made drawings of them. I did this while seated on the ground beside a lantern. I also cut some sticks to size to measure the tracks while on the road.

The robbery had been attempted just north of the Kern County line, so the

Kern County Sheriff, Borgwart, and some of his deputies came north from Bakersfield on a special train, arriving about two hours after Jim Ford and I with our Andy Neff Special.

We talked over the evidence while we waited for daylight. From the first there was a conviction on the part of the Kern County force that the holdup was a local job and that the robbers had gone east, toward the Sierra. The reason for this was that the Pixley job, done about ten miles north of Alila two years before, had been done from the east.

Of course I really had no idea in the world who had attempted to rob the train, but I always tried to approach every job with an open mind. None of us had seen which way the tracks led. I took the attitude that anyone within operating distance could have done it.

After I found the way the Kern County force felt, I suggested that we wait until daylight and could see the tracks of the horses. By this time railroad detectives Hume and Thacker arrived and immediately sided with the Kern County people. Dan Overall, ex-sheriff, whom I beat at the previous election, had arrived also and sided with them. It seems stranger today than it did then that I was absolutely alone in not jumping at the conclusion that the tracks were going to lead to the east. Perhaps it was because of the telegram I had received from Perry Byrd.

As soon as it was light enough to see, Jim Ford and I got in my buggy and made a circle around the place, about a half mile in diameter. There was no use in starting any closer. By daylight at least a hundred people had visited the scene of the holdup. About half of them came across country on horseback, and the scene of the robbery was a mass of horse tracks. If the tracks around the telegraph pole and that little trestle had been obliterated, I don't know how we ever would have known what tracks to follow.

Both Jim and I looked for tracks as closely as we could. We measured at least twenty sets of horse tracks and made at least three fourths of a circle before we struck what we were looking for, the tracks of two unshod horses that tallied with our measurements. One set was larger than the other and had the chipped hoof. The tracks led directly west and had been made by horses running at full speed. We followed these tracks some distance, until we struck a thick bank of fog. By then I was certain our train robbers had struck for the Coast Range.

The closest place of any size to the west was Coalinga and it lay about thirty miles north of the direction in which the tracks led. Directly west, San Miguel and Paso Robles were the closest towns. There were ranches and wayside stations closer, but no place where train robbers could find cover.

THE ANDY NEFF SPECIAL

By this time I found that Jim Ford was one of the best trackers and detectives I had ever worked with. He could read those horse tracks as fast as my team could travel. Finally he suggested that we go back to the train, load up again, and go to Huron on the train.

Said Jim, "That way we will gain on them, whichever way they have gone. If they are on the way to Coalinga or the Coalinga back country we will meet them. If they keep on west we will either head them off or cut their trail."

At that time Huron was the end of the railroad which ran from Goshen through Hanford, Lemoore, and Armona. Huron was on the barren, unsettled plains north of the Kettleman Hills. I immediately saw that Jim's plan was good. So we turned around and drove back to the train as fast as the team could go. While Jim put the team and rig aboard, I talked with the rest of the officers. They wouldn't listen to me. Hume was as angry as could be with me. He said, "Kay, if we start for the Sierra right away we can cut them off. You are going to make us miss our men." I told Hume that I had found the tracks of the running horses still leading to the west, at least three miles away; that they had gone too far to double back. I said, "Hume, those fellows are headed for home. We are going to find them in the Coast Range."

I told Hume what I proposed to do and invited any of them to go along. Dan Overall had changed his mind and said, "Gene I believe you are right. What do you want me to do?"

I told George Witty and Bob Hockett, "I want you boys to go with Dan." Then I thanked Dan and told him I wanted him to take a few men with him and follow the tracks west to connect with Ford and me west of the Kettleman Plains. As soon as we left, Dan did start on the tracks. He had with him Jim Wagy, Tom Orr, George Witty, Bob Hockett, Pat Murry, and Milt Wagy.

Andy Neff had run up the line to Poso, now called Famosa, where there was a turntable, had turned the engine around, loaded up with coal and water and even had some hay thrown into the express car. Jim had everything loaded long before I finished arguing with Hume, and Andy was jerking the whistle cord lightly and making that old tin whistle do an impatient peep-peep, peep-peep, peep-peep. I ran for the engine and we started to Alila.

At Alila I sent telegrams telling the Visalia deputies of my plans. I also asked the station agent to clear the track for us to Huron. Then, away we went again, uh-chuck uh-chuck; uh-chuck uh-chuck; with that darned old whistle going peeeep-peeeep, peep-peep; peeeeep-peeeeep, peep-peep; peeeep-peeeeep, peep-peep; continually. Andy made a great skylark of the run. It was the first time he had ever been turned loose on a railroad and he

James B. Hume, Wells Fargo & Company detective, who was active during the careers of the Daltons and of the other train bandits, Evans and Sontag. He disagreed with Sheriff Kay about the route taken by the Daltons after the Alila robbery attempt.

Photo courtesy Wells Fargo Bank and Union Trust Company and now in Bear State Library.

"Andy" Neff as he appeared when he made the famous run from Alila to Huron after the Daltons.

Photo courtesy Mrs. W.J. Higdon (sister-in-law of Andy Neff) and now in Bear State Library.

made the best of it. The fireman shoveled coal all the way and was all in when we got to Huron.

When we went through Tulare it was about eight o'clock in the morning and Andy had that old teakettle open, the whistle cord tied back, and was out in front of the cab, whipping the sides of the old boiler with a tie rope he had taken from some Alila rancher. The crowd at the depot yelled as loud as they could, but we could only see their mouths move. The heat waves from the sides of that boiler made it go in and out like the sides of a winded horse.

Everything was clear at Goshen, so Andy clattered over the switches and around the curve onto the Huron branch with the front end of the old firepot jerking right and left like it didn't know which way it wanted to go.

In Dalton Gang days, Goshen Junction was a busy place. [It was in this sentence that Kay supplied the name for this volume.] An average of a train an hour was dispatched out of the place. But it was impossible to go through on a train without laying over. Coming from Fresno to Tulare, less that fifty miles, you generally had to lay over from two to four hours.

Waiting at Goshen Junction was a standing topic of conversation from one end of the state to the other. Only recently a traveling salesman told me he had been on the road for thirty years, ten years of which had been spent in Goshen, waiting for trains. Another traveling salesman bought a home in Goshen so he could spend his lay-over time with his family.

Well, when Andy saw the switch signal set open at Goshen Junction he let out a whoop you could hear above the shriek of the whistle. "Oh Boy!" he yelled, "here is the first time I ever got through Goshen without a layover." I yelled back to Andy that the same thing went for me.

We made a non-stop, wide-open run from Alila to Huron, the only time it was ever done and in just about as good time as that old engine was capable of doing.

At Huron Jim and Andy unloaded the team and hitched them to the buggy while I got some lunch from Mrs. Martin, who ran a little restaurant there. Inside of thirty minutes Jim and I were on our way again. But what a come-down.

Jim was driving. He kept saying to me, "Gene, what the hell is wrong with this damn team. Looks to me like they're backing up, instead of going ahead." We almost ran that poor team to death before we found they couldn't keep up a locomotive pace. By the time we were out on the Kettleman Plains about twenty miles, we were back to normal and settled down to a steady, ten-mile-an-hour clip.

We drove from Huron to the head of Sunflower Valley, west of Dudley and the Álamo Solo, without seeing another human being. Then we met a man who rode to meet us. There was where we lost out by being afraid to talk enough. We were afraid to ask all the questions we wanted to. We thought the bandits would avoid ranches and watering places like Álamo Mocho, Álamo Solo, and Dudley. So we asked our traveler if there was any place around there in the hills where a traveler could water his horses. We had figured that was a safe question. He would think we wanted to water *our* horses. He directed us to a spring surrounded by willows in the hills near Cottonwood Pass.

We learned afterward that this man was Louis Merrill, whose home was at Avenal Ranch, about six miles north of where we met him. He had been at work for Bill Dalton and had actually loaned to Bill the horse that Grat had ridden away from the Cotton Ranch when they started out on their train robbing expedition. Merrill had ridden directly from Bill's place, where he had been blacksmithing, and could have given us plenty of information if we had asked him more questions.

Well, Merrill rode home and Jim and I drove into the hills and found the spring. We were no sooner out of the buggy than we saw both sets of horse tracks we had been looking for. In addition to the horse tracks we found both of the boot tracks we had found south of Alila.

We measured the tracks and compared them with the drawings I had made. There was no question about it. The tracks were made by the same horses that had been tied to the telegraph pole south of Alila. We were as happy as kids. The tracks were fresh — had been made that day, so couldn't be more than three or four hours old.

Just as we were congratulating ourselves, I saw a small piece of thin, fresh, brightly polished hardwood lying beside one of the boot tracks. I picked it up and we looked it over for several minutes. We agreed that it was broken from the side of an old, thin-worn saddle stirrup and had been lost by the men we were chasing. Although we didn't fully realize the value of it at first, this piece of stirrup turned out to be the one additional clue we needed in order to trace the bandits to their very lair.

I had probably better clear up an old misunderstanding about this piece of stirrup. A man named Talmage, of Delano, found a similar piece of the same stirrup attached to one of the tapaderos which had been cut from the saddle at the camp of the robbers three miles west of Alila. This was not the piece of stirrup we had. Talmage didn't discover his piece until about the same time Jim Ford and I discovered ours, fifty miles away. We first saw the Talmage find at Visalia, when we returned from our chase to San Luis Obispo county.

When we finished looking at the stirrup fragment it was late in the afternoon and the horses had been on the road most of the time for about twenty hours. We figured they had traveled thirty-five miles since we left Huron. They were worn out. So we unhitched them, watered and fed them and let them rest for an hour. Then we started on, following the tracks to the main Paso Robles road. There a third set of tracks was with the others, but never crossed the others so we could tell which was the oldest. Finally Jim said to me, "Gene, that lone rider is ahead. Those other fellows are avoiding his tracks so no one can tell which is ahead." Jim was already showing his ability as a detective.

Before sundown the team was exhausted, so we pulled off the road and made a dry camp. This camp was about five miles northeast of Cholame. We afterward found that our parties had stopped for the night not three miles ahead of us. In the morning we followed the tracks, but lost a lot of time, because twice the tracks left the road for a mile or so at a time. We soon learned why.

About nine o'clock we met an elderly man and lady in a buckboard. We asked them about traveling horsemen. They had seen two, traveling together, but these riders had left the road and avoided them. But from the lady we did get a fair description of both men and horses.

Soon after we started again the tracks were out of the road most of the time. Jim had to follow them afoot a lot of the time, when they led over hilly ground where the buggy couldn't be driven. Finally we missed the two tracks altogether. The road was hard and the tracks difficult to follow. We couldn't locate them again. We followed the third set for several miles, expecting the others to reappear, but they didn't. We caught up with our third traveler about six miles east of Paso Robles. We took him into Paso and found that he was a well known Paso paisano who could tell us nothing about the other parties. He had not noticed any tracks and hadn't seen the travelers.

We put up our team in Paso for the night, got a good room and all we could eat and slept like logs all night.

Before sunup next morning we were on the road with lunches, hay, and some extra water for the horses. We drove about twenty-five miles back to where we had lost the horse tracks the day before. They led from the road through a gate and across a large field. After we had spent about three hours following the tracks they took southwest to hilly country where we couldn't follow the buggy. On a fast trot Jim followed afoot for at least three miles. Finally he climbed a hill and looked the country over. He decided that the men had hit directly for San Miguel. He came back and we decided to return to the main road and go to San Miguel, watching for those tracks to appear in the road again.

My two days on the road with Jim Ford had shown me that he was an excellent tracker and also a good detective. He told me he had never done anything before but common ranch labor, but he turned out to be the best deputy I ever had and we later chased Bob and Emmett Dalton through seven states and Old Mexico; but that's another story and I will have to tell about it later.

When we were about eighteen miles from San Miguel, the team began to give out again. We had found no more tracks after we left the hills. We had branched off the main Paso Robles road and were traveling toward San Miguel and decided to stop at the next farmhouse. We reached it just at sundown.

Jim sat in the buggy while I went to the door. I was met by a very pleasant woman who told me that her husband wouldn't be in until late, but that we would be welcome to spend the night if we would put up with some inconveniences. She had two little children at her side. I remember that one was a chubby little boy who couldn't talk very plain, but was anxious to get lots of practice.

Jim and I put our team in the barn and sat down to a fine supper. While we were eating, the husband returned. We talked for an hour or so about the country and then went to bed. Jim and I had a spare bedroom, the only one in the house besides the one occupied by our hosts and the two children.

There have been a lot of stories circulated about our stay at Bill Dalton's place, for that is actually where we stopped. Half the people in California believed that Bob and Emmett Dalton stayed in the same house with us that night. The story was also told that I suspected the Daltons before I left Alila. Ford and I were criticized because we didn't arrest Bill Dalton and search the house.

Well, it is very easy to look back and tell what should have been done. But here are the actual facts. There was not an officer in California, myself included, who suspected any certain persons until next morning. None of the other officers suspected any of the Daltons until we had made our investigations in Paso Robles next day. I had met and talked with Grat Dalton on the street in Visalia after the Goshen robbery, but he had cleared himself of any suspicion.

About Bob and Emmett having spent the night in the same house with us at Bill's, I can only say that neither Jim nor I saw them, or any sign of them. Emmett later told a story that they were trapped in a blind bedroom and couldn't get out all night. There was no "blind" bedroom for them to get trapped in. Both bedrooms had outside windows. There may have been a trap door in the ceiling of a closet, leading to a blind attic. At Grat's trial I heard talk to that effect, and Bill Dalton later told me the same thing. But both Grat and Bill afterward told me that neither Bob nor Emmett were in the attic when we were there. To the contrary, they told me that it was San Luis Obispo County Sheriff O'Neal and S.P. detective, Bill Smith, who spent the night at Bill Dalton's when Bob and Emmett were trapped in the attic. This was after we had been there. That was the night Bill sang and played the guitar. He wanted to drown out any noise the boys might make upstairs.

Bill didn't come in until after we were in the house. I am now positive that he brought Bob and Emmett home with him and hid them outside. I believe this to be true from what Bill afterward told me and from what I learned next morning.

Everything was quiet that night. After supper we sat and talked quietly for about a half hour and then all went to bed. Upstairs a man couldn't have moved in his seat or turned over in bed without our hearing it. The house was one of those pioneer affairs with a muslin ceiling. The kitchen may have had a wooden ceiling and there may have been a bed above it, but there was certainly no one in such a bed the night we were there.

Anyone can see that it would have been foolishness to search every house where we stopped. We would have been thrown in jail, or filled with lead, before we got to Paso Robles. For Jim and me to have searched Bill's house with Bob and Emmett trapped there would have been the most sudden and sure kind of suicide possible. Subsequent events make this certain.

Well, nobody suspected anything until about four-thirty next morning. So far as I know, Bill Dalton didn't even suspect that Ford and I were officers. Jim and I awakened early and lay there talking for some time. He did most of the chasing afoot the day before, so I told him we wouldn't leave until we ate and for him to stay in bed until breakfast was ready and I would feed and water the horses. I dressed and went to the barn.

I led the horses out to water, fed them, curried them and then harnessed them. I thought it would be the right thing if I cleaned out the barn. So I began forking the manure out the small window behind the horses. The first forkful knocked the top off the pile of manure outside. When I started to throw the second forkful, something in the manure pile attracted my attention. It was a clean piece of tan leather. I reached out and took hold of the leather, pulling a saddle from the manure. A stirrup popped up in front of me. The side of it was worn thin and had a piece of wood broken from it.

Reaching in my pocket, I brought out the piece of broken hardwood I had picked up at the spring in the Cottonwood Pass. It fitted into the stirrup perfectly.

Then I began to think fast. That was the end of the trail of those horses. It was clear what had happened. My host had brought the train robbers home with him. Perhaps he was one of them. When he found he had company he had sent them away. What I didn't know then, was that Bob and Emmett Dalton slept in a straw stack near the barn and were at that time still in bed.

The moisture from the manure hadn't penetrated the leather. I cut into it to determine this. The saddle had been covered up in the manure pile that night.

As soon as I was certain of my find I led the team from the barn and put the saddle in the buggy, which was outside the corral, near the house. I covered it up with our lap robe. Then I went to the window of Jim's bedroom and told him to hurry out. Jim pulled on his clothes without buttoning anything and was out through the window in less than a half minute. We hitched the team and left before Bill Dalton was up.

Driving to Paso Robles I found that Overall and Witty and their posse were put up at a hotel there. Overall told me they had followed the tracks through to a point just east of Dudley.

We got together in Overall's hotel room and checked our stories. We had a connected chain of evidence. The tracks led from Alila directly to a point less than six miles from where we had found the piece of stirrup. At this place we had found both the horse tracks and boot tracks, also the piece of stirrup. From the spring we had tracked the horses to within twelve miles of Bill Dalton's place. By finding the saddle, we had actually traced the riders to their lair.

We planned to spend the day around Paso checking on the Daltons. Before noon railroad detective, Bill Smith, showed up. He had followed Overall's posse across country. We told him what we had learned. Then we went on with our investigations.

We learned plenty in Paso about the Daltons: that there were five brothers of them, that three of them were heavy drinkers and gamblers, and that they were well known in the saloons in Paso, San Luis, and San Miguel. Bill seemed to have a good reputation.

By this time telegrams began to fly back and forth between Paso Robles, Visalia, Alila, Traver, Tulare, and Delano. A trio of men had gambled from Traver to Delano for three days before the robbery, following the Southern Pacific pay car as it made its monthly journey. This was not an unusual occurrence. One of the gamblers was positively identified at both Traver and Tulare as Grat Dalton. The descriptions sent me tallied exactly with those we got of the Paso Daltons.

"Hell," said Jim Ford to me, "I know both Bob and Grat Dalton. I played poker with all three of those fellows when they were in Tulare on their way to rob that train."

There was no question about it. The Daltons had attempted the Alila job.

It is still painful for me to express my feeling with regard to Bill Smith, the railroad detective. I can only second what has been so often said and written about him. He was absolutely unreliable. He was an active detective, and under certain circumstances, I believe he could be brave. But he did try to undermine my work as soon as I went into office, and he jumped the gun after the Collis job. At Paso he did the same thing. Unknown to the rest of us, he got Sheriff O'Neal to go with him to Bill Dalton's, expecting to surprise and arrest Bill, Bob, and Emmett Dalton. Instead of surprising *them* he just missed getting the last surprise of his life. If he had run onto Bob and Emmett they would have killed him, and would probably have killed O'Neal, too.

About five o'clock in the afternoon we began to assemble a posse of about ten men to go out and surround Bill Dalton's house and search the place. It didn't seem likely that we would find our men there, but we might find evidence. In making our preparations we talked to one of O'Neal's deputies. "Hell", he said, "Bill Smith took O'Neal out there to arrest them three hours ago."

There was no use in taking a posse to Dalton's. We sat down to wait for Smith and O'Neal to bring Bob and Emmett in. I am still waiting.

Smith and O'Neal came back into Paso the next day about noon, empty handed. I believe it is an actual fact that they spent the night in the same house with Bob and Emmett, for this was the night that the singing and playing went on.

There isn't much of interest about the rest of it. We did a lot more work around Paso Robles, San Miguel, Santa Margarita, and San Luis Obispo, but learned little more than we had the first day in Paso. Jim Ford hurried to Tulare and gathered most of the evidence I got about the trip of Grat, Bob, and Emmett Dalton through Traver, Tulare, and Delano. I went to San Francisco on the train to confer with Southern Pacific officials and then returned to Visalia.

Grat was arrested twice and finally lodged with Bill in the Tulare County Jail at Visalia. Bill soon got bonds, but Grat did not.

Then, on March 17, the Tulare County Grand Jury indicted four of the

Dalton brothers for the Alila robbery attempt: Bob, Emmett, Grat, and Bill. The indictments were for attempted robbery and assault with intent to commit murder.

A few days after Grat and Bill Dalton were placed in the Tulare County Jail for the Alila robbery, a man came to the office of the jail and asked for me. Williams sent him across the corridor to my office. I looked up to see in the doorway a typical San Joaquin Valley mule skinner. He was dressed in boots, with overalls and a jumper that buckled around the waist. In his hand he held a narrow-brimmed Stetson hat.

When I first looked at the man I thought I should know him, but I couldn't place him. He was not heavy, but was well built, with dark hair and eyes and a rugged countenance. He waited for me to speak.

I said, "What can I do for you, my man?"

"My name is Ben Dalton, and I understand that you have two of my brothers here in jail. I would like to see if they are really my brothers."

I told him he would have no trouble in seeing them, expecting him to go to the jailor and be escorted to their cells. But he didn't move. Finally I said, "Well, go on in and see them." He came back at me, "Aren't you going along?" I told him I wasn't, and he left.

After about an hour Ben again appeared in the door. What he had to say has since amused me many times.

"Well, Grat Dalton could hold up a train. I don't know whether he did or not. He says he didn't. But you are just wasting the taxpayers' money keeping Bill in jail. He would like to have you think he had held up a train. He couldn't hold up anything. He couldn't hold up an old setting hen while you took the eggs from under her."

But subsequent events showed that Ben was wrong about Bill's courage.

It was only after Ben left my office that I realized that I knew him and had also known two of his brothers, Littleton and Frank. In 1878 I hired two of George Crossmore's mule teams and plowed with them on my ranch at the Buzzard's Roost, now called Waukena. When I was through with the teams, Crossmore hired them to Ed Benedict, who had homesteaded just at the eastern edge of Hanford.

Benedict had hired two extra mule skinners and he wanted the Crossmore stock for them to drive. He sent three men over to get the mules. These three mule skinners were Ben, Frank, and Littleton Dalton. I went to the field horseback, ran the mules into the corral, helped harness them and got the boys started toward Benedict's place.

For a few years I saw the three boys from time to time and then they dropped completely out of sight. I had never associated them with the Estrella Daltons and the train robbers we were after. This was natural, as all three were good, square men. I never saw Ben Dalton after the day he visited Grat and Bill in the jail at Visalia. I got acquainted with Lit again at the time of Grat's trial and verified all of this when I reminded him of it. . . . .

Southern Pacific Pay Car at Kern City, now East Bakersfield, about 1888.
   The Daltons regularly followed the pay car in order to gamble with the employees.
   Photo courtesy Paul Robinson and now in Bear State Library.

CHAPTER SIX

Six Thousand Mile Manhunt

There had been so many stories told and published about the happenings after Sheriffs Kay and O'Neal visited Bill Dalton's ranch that I had given up hope of ever getting them straightened out. Kay's story helped some, and so did some of the newspaper stories, but still there was a large gap to be filled and most of the printed material did not check with what I was told by Kay.

Billy Russell of Traver, John Hazen of Visalia, and Harry Charters of Tulare, helped in many ways, but they really knew little that Kay had not already told me. Russell and Hazen had worked under Sheriff Kay at the time of Grat's trial. Charters had been a Tulare newspaperman at the same time.

For one thing, there was a considerable amount of mystery as to how Bill Dalton had avoided the officers when he started to take Emmett and Bob to Indian Territory. While discussing this with former U.S. Deputy Marshal, Chris Madsen, at his home in Guthrie, Oklahoma, in 1938, he repeated to me one of Bill Dalton's typical wild stories. It had to do with Bill's departure from the Estrella when he took Emmett and Bob to Ludlow. Said Madsen, "I had a long talk with Bill at Kingfisher. I asked him about his get-away from California. He told me, 'That was the easiest trick I ever played on anybody. I simply got me a loud, striped suit and took my wife out riding just after dark. I kept that up for some nights until the deputies, or detectives, got so they just watched for that loud suit and did not know that I was not in it. The night when I was ready to leave I had another man dressed up to represent me. He took my wife out and remained out long enough for me to get out of sight. That man and my wife kept up the play for several nights, until I was well on my way.'

"That was Bill's own story. How much of it is true I do not know, but he got away, anyway."

It remained for Littleton Dalton to furnish what was needed to complete the story and to straighten out the mix-up in printed material.

Littleton's story was told at least ten years after the task had been given up as hopeless:

It was some time before Bob and Emmett could make a getaway from the Cotton Ranch. They hid out in the mountains near Mason's (Bill's) for at least two weeks. Mason was afraid to go near them. He put supplies out for them and several times they came to his house in the night.

Mason went to Paso Robles and bought a saddle, but he was then entirely broke and had no money for any more saddles or horses. It took real money in those days to buy a good saddle horse and riding rig. The officers had taken the saddle borrowed from Clark Bliven. The one borrowed from Frank Halter was in the express office in Fresno. Try as he could, Mason couldn't get any more saddles or any horses fit for a hard ride.

Finally Mason got the loan of some horses that were on pasture at Frank McAdams' place in Bitterwater Valley, almost on the line between San Luis Obispo and Kern counties. He hitched his driving mare to the buggy and took Bob with him, starting shortly after dark. Emmett rode the new saddle on a mule. They cut through the hills over a back road and reached McAdams' place before morning, bedding themselves down in the barn.

Mason and Bob told the man in charge of the stock that they were going to the Carrizo Plains to look for farming land and wanted to borrow three horses and two saddles. Their story satisfied the man, so he let them have the stock, also one saddle which belonged to Frank McAdams.

Well, the boys were all fixed, except for a third saddle. They told the man at McAdam's ranch that they would borrow a saddle from a neighbor and left, Emmett riding one of the horses with a blanket and surcingle. They headed for the swamp country west of Delano, where Mason had a friend working on Tom Fowler's Lake-House Ranch about ten miles south of Tulare Lake.

But the boys could get no saddle, and the horses Emmett and Mason were riding were not in condition to make a hard run. They wore them out getting in from Bitterwater. They all talked until dark about what to do.

Finally they decided to come to me at Clovis Cole's, southwest of Fresno. Mason stayed at the Fowler place and Bob and Emmett rode all night and landed at Joe Middleton's place near Hanford after daylight next morning. They stayed there until late in the afternoon and rode on to Clovis Cole's during the night. I was plowing at a plow camp at that time and not at Clovis' home place.

I heard the three knocks on the side of the bunk house outside my bed. I went out and found Bob and Emmett there. As soon as I saw them, I knew I had to help them, in spite of all the promises to the contrary I had made to myself. Bob told me that Emmett had killed the fireman at Alila. I asked Emmett about it. He said, "I did, all right. I shot him through the middle. He wasn't four feet from me."

Bob said, "Lit, we have got to have . . . ."

I broke in on him, "Yes, I know: a horse, a riding rig, a winchester rifle, ammunition, and money."

Bob said, "Yes, Lit, that's it. We're going back to Indian Territory and hide out until this thing blows over."

I studied quite a while. I knew they could never hide out anywhere until that Alila affair blew over. Besides, they had just run away from Indian Territory to hide in California. I didn't feel that I could go to Clovis Cole for help. Finally I said, "All right, I'll help you fellows just this once. Don't either of you ever come to me for help again. You've kept me broke for years and you're now traveling too fast for me. I'll never help you again."

I found I had just twenty dollars in my pocket. I had no horse or riding rig. I took Bob's horse and rode across the field to Charlie Owen's. I awakened Charlie and told him I had to have a hundred dollars. Charlie never said a word, but picked up his pants, took out his purse and gave me five twenty dollar gold pieces. At thirty-five dollars a month it took me more than three months to earn that money back.

I went into Charlie's barn, fitted one of Charlie's race horses with a saddle and bridle, led it back to Clovis Cole's, and gave Bob the horse and the hundred and twenty dollars. When they left they told me they were headed straight for Tehachapi Pass.

Next morning I went over to see Charlie Owen and told him I had taken a riding rig and one of his horses. Again he never said a word. Nor would he let me pay for the horse, saddle, or bridle. He said, "Lit, I think I'll be better off *without* that horse. He's lost me lots of races." If Charlie had accepted pay for that horse and riding rig it would have taken me eight months more of hard work to pay it out.

The boys joined Mason at the Fowler place and they skirted along the fringe of tules on the west side as far as the Miller & Lux Buttonwillow Ranch, where the town of Buttonwillow is now located. On the way they turned loose the lame horse that Emmett had been riding and started it back toward Bitterwater. Then the horse I got from Charlie Owen went so lame they all knew it could never cross the valley, let alone make the run over the Tehachapi Mountains. So, at the Buttonwillow Ranch, they roped and sad-

The Tom Fowler Lake House, from a photo made in June of 1938. This house was built on a mud flat in the middle of Tulare Lake in 1873 when the lake was at low ebb. Lumber was carried to the site by a steamboat. The builders expected that the lake waters would return, which they did on four occasions, one as late as 1938, when this photo was taken. It was to such remote, isolated places as this that the Daltons turned their horses when they wanted help in a getaway.

Photo by Frank F. Latta and now in Bear State Library.

dled one of Henry Miller's horses and turned Charlie's horse loose. I don't know what they did to kill that horse off. It was a good horse and I never knew it to go lame before. They must have simply ridden the life out of their stock. I afterward tried to recover Charlie's horse, but was never successful.

They made a hard ride from the Buttonwillow Ranch across the valley to the railroad below Bealville, where Mason decided to take the train and locate a hideout, guns, ammunition, and horses, and make all the rest of the usual preparations for Bob and Emmett when they arrived. There were special rates on at that time and a railroad ticket from California to Indian Territory could be purchased for about twenty dollars.

Bob and Emmett rode on alone, passing through Tehachapi several miles and staying in the canyon all day with an old fellow named Monroe. They had ridden their horses almost to death and had to lay over until next evening. Then they dropped in north of Mojave and struck out across the desert as though they were going to find water every place they wanted it. It almost cost them their lives. Bob told me that they had water for their horses only once between Mojave and Barstow. It must have been a ride of almost seventy-five miles by the route they took, and over the worst kind of desert, too. After that they kept close to the railroad, so as to get water at the section houses, but by doing it took the chances of being picked up.

Mason told me that when the train left Barstow and started across the desert toward Needles, he decided that the boys could never make the trip across the desert horseback. So he decided to get off and stop them. He did this at Ludlow and had to wait three days for them. Mason claimed to be a cattleman waiting for some cow punchers to join him. I don't know what those people in Ludlow thought of cattlemen loose in that country, but Mason could talk almost anyone into believing anything.

When Bob and Emmett came in, the three of them had another long talk. They decided it would be as safe to take the train and ride into Indian Territory as it would be to go horseback. They couldn't sell the horses and riding rigs and there wasn't enough money for all three to go to Oklahoma on the train, so Mason started back to Paso Robles on the train and Bob and Emmett started for Kingfisher. They left the horses at Ludlow, explaining that more of the cow punchers would be along after them in a few days. The railroad detectives found the horses in a few weeks, and they were returned to Visalia in time to be used as evidence at Grat's and Mason's trials.

Mason arrived in Paso Robles on the train and was arrested by Sheriff Eugene Kay, of Tulare County, within fifteen minutes after he stepped off the cars. He was taken to Visalia. After a hearing he was held for trial for robbing the train at Alila. He soon secured bondsmen and was released. He had as bondsmen a half dozen of the most respected men around Merced, Livingston, and Paso Robles. . . . .

It was several years after I met Eugene W. Kay, before I realized why I had been puzzled by the published news and historical accounts of the Dalton Gang. It had been due to Kay's natural hatred of publicity. None of the stories came from Kay. He never had talked. All stories printed or related orally had come from some of his deputies or from someone else who enjoyed being in the limelight. At Mojave I talked for many hours with Jo P. Carroll. Jo P. had been a news reporter at Viaslia during the Dalton and Evans-Sontag days. Said Jo P., "I soon found how to get news out of Kay. As soon as he knew I wouldn't mention him, or write anything that would hinder his work, he became the best source of news I ever had. Why, he even let me go with him on three of the most important expeditions. Wonderful fellow, Kay. Finest man I ever knew. I would give the rest of my expected days just to sit beside the Kaweah River under one of those old Visalia oaks and spend an afternoon visiting with him."

There is not room in this volume to print all the similar statements I have heard made about Gene Kay.

The most remarkable exploit of Kay's whole career as sheriff was the pursuit of Bob and Emmett Dalton, begun just after their horses were discovered at Ludlow on the Mojave Desert east of Barstow. It might also be stated with little fear of dispute that it was one of the most remarkable pursuits of criminals ever waged by a determined officer of the law. It began at Visalia, extended through seven western states and a portion of Old Mexico, blazed a trail six thousand miles in length by every existing means of transportation, and lasted more than three months.

In the forty-five years that had elapsed since Kay made the journey, most of the details had passed from his memory, so he could give only a brief description of the route and relate a few of the incidents that occurred along the way. Emmett Dalton was alive at the time Kay told me his story and wanted me to write for him, splitting the proceeds fifty-fifty. I sent Emmett a type-script of Kay's story, knowing that his account would make a tremenduously interesting addition when dove-tailed to that given by Kay. Emmett was interested and was willing to tell a story, provided it would not conflict with any of the statements in

Emmett Dalton when he was released from prison in 1907. Photo now in Bear State Library.

his book, *When the Daltons Rode* and providing Kay would be portrayed as a relentless, bull-dog nemesis, driving Grat and Bob and him into banditry. The reader knows the result. I didn't get Emmett's story, and it would have been entirely valueless if I had. But here is Kay's:

> Author of
> "When The Daltons Rode"
>
> EMMETT DALTON
> HOLLYWOOD, CALIF.
>
> MAY 25, 1934
>
> MR F.F.LATTA
> TULARE, CALIF
>
> DEAR MR LATTA:
> THANK YOU FOR YOUR LETTER OF APRIL NINETH.
> I HAVE JUST BEEN THINKING THAT IF YOU WANTED TO TACKLE
> WRITING TWO OR THREE REALL WESTERN STORIES REGARDING
> FAMOUS WESTERN CHARACTERS, I AM SURE I COULD SELL THEM,
> AND WE WOULD SPLIT FIFTY-FIFTY.
>
> THINK THIS OVER AND LET ME KNOW IN TIME
> SO I WILL NOT BE TIED UP ON SOME OTHER PROPOSITION.
>
> WITH KINDEST REGARDS I REMAIN
>
> YOURS TRULY
>
> *Emmett Dalton*
>
> 4350 PRICE ST
> HOLLYWOOD, CALIF

When the horses were discovered at Ludlow, and the descriptions of the two men checked with those we had of Bob and Emmett, I decided to capture them, if it was humanly possible. It was not advisable to travel alone on such a journey, so I planned to take with me the best man I could find. This proved to be Jim Ford. From the time of the chase to Paso Robles and to Bill Dalton's ranch after Bob and Emmett, I had worked with no one in any way the equal of Jim.

We arranged a code with George Witty whereby we could send telegrams without their contents being known, provided ourselves with credentials carrying our photographs, my sheriff's badge and some money, and started out with nothing in the way of weapons except our revolvers.

Our first investigation was made at Chico. There we expected to pick up the trail of Cole Dalton, who was to meet Bob and Emmett at Salt Lake. I knew that they were not headed for the Indian Territory. Information had been given me by one of Bill Dalton's neighbors and his brother-in-law, Clark Bliven, that they would meet Cole in Salt Lake. We expected Cole to lead us directly to them.

At Chico we found Cole had preceeded us by a few hours to Marysville. There we found he had gone into Nevada. We took a stage and finally landed in Winnemucca about two hours after he had taken the road for Salt Lake. We had to lay over almost twenty-four hours in Winnemucca in order to get transportation and got farther behind than we had been since leaving Chico.

It took us two days in Salt Lake to learn what we needed to know; where the three had lodged and where they had gone. Upon arrival we found that no one answering the description of Bob or Emmett had secured passage on the railroad. They didn't know that they were being followed, and we expected them to travel the trains openly. At the end of two days we found a rooming house where they had stayed overnight. They had burned a light in their room all night and had carried on a low conversation, accompanied by hammering and sawing noises during all of that time. This we learned from the proprietor. Then they had slept all the following forenoon. They had checked out with their baggage just after noon.

Checking again at the depot we found that Bob and Emmett had bought tickets for Ogden. They left with a large telescope bag apiece. As we had expected, Cole Dalton had furnished them with money, guns, and ammunition. We found the place where the guns and ammunition had been purchased. All three had undoubtedly spent the night at the rooming house, shortening the barrels and magazines of their winchester rifles so they would go in their telescope bags. It looked to us like they were going to follow out the plan outlined to me by their neighbor and rob a train.

We took the train to Ogden, contacted the police upon our arrival, and explained who we were after and what we expected. We no sooner left police headquarters than we ran onto Emmett. While I was walking down one side of the street and Jim down the other, Jim saw Emmett come out of a store directly in front of him. But just at the moment Jim saw Emmett, Emmett saw me. He ducked back into the store.

Jim hailed me. He pointed to the door and motioned for me to watch it. Then he ran through another store to the alley to head Emmett off. In a few seconds I saw Jim come in the rear of the store.

In the store I found that men answering the descriptions of both Bob and Emmett had been in, but had left hurriedly by the back door and ducked into the rear of a saloon across the alley. Cole Dalton wasn't with them, nor did we again get any trace of him on our entire trip. I later learned that he had returned directly to Chico. I sent Jim Ford after Bob and Emmett and got hold of the Chief of Police and started a search of Ogden, which in 1891 was really not much of a city.

I hope it is understood that Jim Ford was taking his life in his hands when he planned to arrest Bob and Emmett with a revolver, particularly after they had been alarmed. Eight months after this occurred I arrested Riley Dean, a companion of Grat Dalton. Riding from Kings River back to Visalia in a buggy with Dean I told him of the experience Ford and I had in Ogden.

Dean laughed and said, "Hell, you fellows never got near Bob and Emmett. If you had, they would have shot you dead before you could have batted an eye."

Well, I suppose they would have killed *me*, because I would have tried to arrest them without killing *them*, but in killing Jim, one of them would certainly have met instant death. Jim had absolutely no fear. He was never a particle unnerved or excited in his life and he was as quick as chain lightning.

On the plains when we were riding along horseback, Jim showed me the quickest and most accurate shooting I have ever seen or ever expect to see. He did it with a 38-calibre Smith and Wesson revolver on a 44 frame.

There were lots of prairie dogs along the road. They would stand up within fifty feet of us and bark and flip their tails as we passed. I tried Jim out on them. I would point at one quickly, stiffening my arm like I was shooting as I straightened it, and then jerk it down as quickly as I could.

Jim would start jerking his gun as soon as I moved a muscle, locate the prairie dog and shoot at it as soon as I could get my arm down. This was much harder than beating me to the draw. At a distance of fifty feet, from the back of a walking horse, Jim would hit three out of five prairie dogs and would never miss one three inches. At a gallop he could do almost as well.

Jim had told me that until I put him in the express car with my horses at Tulare to go to the scene of the Alila robbery, he had never fired a revolver since, as a boy, he had shot his father's old cap and ball "leg o' mutton." [Note: This statement, made by Jim Ford, probably was not true. Porterville friends of Jim have stated that he was a first cousin, or a brother of Bob Ford, who killed Jesse James, and was an experienced detective and gunman before he came to California F.F.L.]. In addition to being quick and accurate, Jim's wits were set on a hair trigger. He was a natural gunman.

That day in Ogden, when Jim went into that alley, he had already drawn his revolver and would have instantly shot anyone he saw with a gun in his hand. I never had any fear of anyone killing Jim Ford. Considering the way we were working it was wonderful support to have such confidence in him.

Well, as Dean and I were riding along the road north of where Cutler is now, I decided to have Jim Ford show Dean some real shooting. I had Jim near us as a guard all the way to Visalia. He had a fine horse which loped slowly near my buggy team. The rest of the posse came behind on horseback.

I felt it was necessary to keep Jim close by. My revolver was strapped under my overcoat and I had only a British Bull Dog revolver in my right overcoat pocket. Dean was a tremendous, powerful man and otherwise could have taken me unawares, overpowered me, and escaped.

I motioned to Jim to come closer to us on the right side of the buggy. Then, without explaining anything to him, I suddenly pointed at a granite boulder about fifty feet from the road. It was about the size of the crown of my hat. Instinctively Jim jerked out his revolver and hit that boulder before Dean saw what he was doing. Before we had gone a half mile Ford had shot two squirrels, both sixty or more feet away and had hit a dozen fence posts and rocks, all as soon as I could point at them.

When Ford shot the second squirrel Dean said, "I don't believe it. There ain't *nobody* can shoot like that."

Neither Bob nor Emmett had left Ogden on the "cushions". We checked all stages and trains. We telegraphed ahead of all trains and found that they hadn't paid fares after boarding the trains, nor were they on the rods or blind baggage. We also telegraphed ahead to check all freight trains. These were the only means they had of leaving a place like Ogden, as they were surprised before they were able to locate horses.

Late that night we received a telegram telling us that two men of the description of Bob and Emmett had been seen on a south-bound freight many miles south of Salt Lake. A few hours later, just as we were ready to follow, another telegram placed them in the southeast part of the state. I have forgotten the name of the town. Apparently the boys figured we would think they were headed east and expected to throw us off the track by heading south. The unfortunate thing was that it was impossible to get officers to attempt to arrest them. We had several descriptions from train crews who had seen the boys, and wired ahead all day to officers, but with no results.

We followed on a passenger train and spent the greater part of a week tracing clues across eastern Arizona and western New Mexico, traveling by stage, and horseback. During this time the boys knew that we were on their trail and once, when they were traveling horseback, they doubled back and learned all they could about us at a ranch-house where we had stayed a day or two before. We later learned that during that time they were using stolen horses and riding rigs.

Generally Bob and Emmett rode with different train crews than we did. In order to get information, we questioned the train crew we were traveling with and learned where the crew ahead stayed when they laid over. Then Jim or I ran down the train crew and questioned them.

Sometimes, when Bob and Emmett were more than a day ahead of us, we might be traveling with the crew that had carried them. Then we could get our information without delay, but this was not often.

It is impossible to give any idea of how tired we got on such forced rides. One of us had to keep awake almost all of the time, and neither of us averaged as much as four hours of unbroken sleep a night on the entire expedition. The interest of the chase kept us awake, but we became skin and bones and, if we relaxed for a minute, we simply lost consciousness.

At last we learned that Bob and Emmett had taken a train for Needles. Jim and I jumped the first train we could get and learned at Needles that our men had left the train at Kingman. We doubled back to Kingman in time to miss them again. They had played poker at Kingman all night and had won about a hundred dollars. The poker playing natives of Kingman were still up in arms. Bob had played, while Emmett, who pretended not to know him, tipped off the hands of the others. As we left, Jim Ford said to the poker players, "That's all right, boys. Those were two of the Dalton boys. We were going to arrest them and will bring them back and let you finish your game with them."

I cannot trace accurately all the stops we made and tell all the things that happened. Beginning with the trip to Bill Dalton's and Paso Robles, we were out almost three months together and traveled more than six thousand miles by train, stage, horse and buggy, wagon, horseback, and afoot, crossing and recrossing several states and entering for a few days into Old Mexico. Jim Ford was out a month longer than I was. One of us slept while the other watched, so neither of us saw everything. After it was over, it took us another three months to get rested.

From Kingman we went to Ashfork and then to Prescott, Gila Bend, Tucson, and to Nogales, in the state of Sonora, Old Mexico.

Until we reached Tucson we traveled by stage, train, and horseback. We rented horses when we needed them. But at Tucson we found Bob and Emmett had bought two saddle horses and riding rigs, probably using the money they won at Kingman. This meant that we again had to follow them horseback for some distance. We bought horses and riding rigs, a winchester rifle apiece, and a good supply of ammunition, for we had decided the boys were headed for Old Mexico.

Bob and Emmett entered Mexico at Nogales two days ahead of us. To the immigration authorities they gave Guaymas as their destination. They entered under assumed names, but the descriptions we received checked in detail with the information we obtained at Tucson.

We presented our credentials and were given what they called *la carta blanca*, the white card. This was simply a white card on which was a note from the head Mexican official ordering all Mexican officials and citizens to furnish us all aid within their power and to exempt all of our possessions from seizure. We were also offered a military escort and everything at the disposal of the Federal Department at Nogales.

Neither Ford nor or I had ever been out of the United States before, but Jim could talk quite a lot of Spanish and I could understand some of it. We changed two hundred dollars into Mexican pesos and felt rich. We got back three times as much money as we handed over.

When we left Nogales we began questioning everyone we saw, and soon picked up the trail. Before we reached the first village below Nogales we could get no further trace of our men. We had to backtrack, and found that they had cut through the mountains east on an old road toward Cananea. From this we decided that the trail would soon lead back into the States.

If we had not been under such a strain, both Jim and I would have enjoyed our trip through the state of Sonora. Everything we saw was interesting: burros loaded with firewood, everyone drawing water from dug wells and carrying it in jars on their heads, oxcarts, and a dozen other primitive ways of life that had passed out in the states during the time of our fathers.

We met a group of about twenty vaqueros driving a large band of horses. The riding rigs of these men were worn almost to pieces from plunging through thorny cactus and mesquite brush. Their horses were protected by leather leggings and breast plates.

We needed food to carry with us and stopped at a ranch-house to buy what they had to offer. The only things they had that we could use were dried beef and small sweet acorns they called bellotas. At first we were not interested in the bellotas, but the Mexicans insisted they were the best thing we could carry, so we tried eating them. They were as good as roasted peanuts, so we bought all the Mexicans had, enough to fill about two-thirds of a grain sack. We made almost all of our meals from dried meat and those acorns.

We missed Bob and Emmett at Cananea by only twelve hours and would have given them a close call if it hadn't been for an unfortunate experience. There were five or six American miners in the place. Jim Ford got into a poker game with them and began to lose heavily. At one time he was a hundred and sixty dollars loser, United States money, twenty dollars of which I had loaned him. I had spent almost all of my money and we were about broke. Next day I loaned Jim five more and he won back all of his losses and ten dollars besides.

While Jim was playing poker I found that Bob and Emmett had gone to Fronteras. Some travelers from that town had seen them on the road. So, as soon as Jim could get out of the poker game, we headed for Fronteras.

At Fronteras we learned that Bob and Emmett had found we were in Mexico on their trail and from there I could get absolutely no information about them. One theory was that they had gone over a rough mountain range east of Fronteras. If so, they were undoubtedly heading for El Paso. We had enough of Mexico and decided to travel to El Paso through the States. We went north and out of Mexico to Douglas, Arizona. By going out at this place we couldn't get United States money for our Mexican money at the border and had to sacrifice most of it changing at Douglas.

From Douglas we went to El Paso by way of Deming, New Mexico, and found that both Bob and Emmett had headed for Albuquerque. At Albuquerque we picked up their trail again, sold our horses, took the stage to Santa Fe and from there to Topeka, Kansas, at that time the end of the railroad. There we learned that the boys had headed for Kingfisher, Indian Territory. They had apparently again thought they had thrown us off the trail. We were afraid to ask questions and couldn't let our plans be known, and had to act so slowly and carefully that many times we might have captured the men we were trailing had this not been the case.

I will never forget our experience at Kingfisher. The Dalton home was about four miles from town, on the open prairie, without a tree between it and town. Along Kingfisher Creek back of the house were a few trees, but they were not large and grew on bottom land some distance below the prairie. The prairie was covered with a growth of wild timothy about two feet high. It took us two days to locate the Dalton place. In the early morning we walked to within two hundred yards of the house and hid in the timothy, tying grass around our heads as camouflage and watching the house with field glasses. We observed the actions of everyone about the place.

We found that there were at least three men and one woman living there. The woman was an elderly lady whom we rightly figured to be the mother of the Dalton boys. We were positive that two of the men were Bob and Emmett. The third we couldn't identify.

There were no outbuildings near the house, not a barn or a shed of any sort, except a small open shelter set on posts near the house. The cut wood was stored under this shelter. Four or five horses were staked about the place. Holes had apparently been dug in which posts were placed loosely. In feeding the horses, the posts were removed from hole to hole.

We found that the dogs would run from the house and jump on some objects which were about the height of the timothy. There they would stand and look over the prairie in search of something to chase. After some observation we decided that their lookout was the woodpile, because several times wood was chopped there.

After studying the situation we decided that on the following morning we would hide ourselves behind the woodpile. In staking the horses in the morning the men had passed close to the wood pile and had come out one at a time. We could surprise them there one at a time, disarm them and take them prisoners.

By this time it was past noon and we wanted to get back to Kingfisher. But we were stuck there for the rest of the day. Those dogs kept such a close lookout that we knew we couldn't crawl away. About three o'clock there came a hard thunder shower and we were soaked to the skin and had to lay there in the wet grass until dusk. We finally got back to Kingfisher, dried ourselves and had about four hours sleep before we again started out early in the morning.

We had worried about the dogs, but they didn't show up when we arrived, long before daylight. They had slept inside the house. Daylight found us in readiness. The first person to come from the house was the stranger, who proved to be a young man of about fourteen or fifteen years of age. I now believe that he must have been the youngest of the Dalton boys. He was easily taken prisoner, but assured us that there was no one else in the house, except Mrs. Dalton.

After waiting for at least an hour, and observing that the staked horses were gone, we forced the boy to walk ahead of us to the house and knock on the door, which was opened by the mother of the Dalton boys. She explained to us that the boys had been there the day before, but had left for Guthrie during the night. She invited us in and provided us with a good breakfast, during which time we had quite an extended conversation.

Mrs. Dalton was a very frank and up-right appearing woman and told us what we later found to be the truth about where her sons had gone. She stated that she could not believe that the boys were guilty of any wrongdoing, as they had been officers of the law and had learned to enforce the law, but that we would find them over in Guthrie and for us to go over there and have a talk with them. It was just as simple as that. Jim looked at me and we both laughed.

It is about fifty miles from Kingfisher to Guthrie, but it took us three days to make that distance. In order to travel where we wished and not give away our destination, we found it necessary to buy two Indian ponies and riding rigs.

The intervening country was composed of Indian allotments, each allotment being under the jurisdiction of a different Indian chief. We soon became lost, because of the danger of asking too many questions about directions, and finally came to an Indian. This Indian would give me no directions whatever and would only take us to his chief. This necessitated a trip of more than four hours duration and later proved to return us in the opposite direction to where we wanted to go. The chief sent us back with the same Indian as a guide, but, after traveling about five miles from where we first met him, he came to an abrupt stop and refused to budge another inch. We found the point where he had stopped was the imaginary line between his tribe and the adjoining tribe, into whose territory he couldn't go.

We traveled alone until we found another Indian who also refused to give us information as to how to get to Guthrie. After another delay of about three hours in visiting this second chief we were once again on our way, but were forced within a few miles to repeat the entire performance. At the end of three days of this sort of travel, about two o'clock in the morning, we finally saw the lights of Guthrie in the distance.

One thing happened on this portion of our trip that neither Jim nor I ever forgot. We had trouble getting anything to eat. The wild plums were getting ripe and Jim insisted on eating them. I told him to go easy on them and I ate only a few. I said several times, "Jim, you can't eat those plums like that. They'll make you sick." But Jim kept at them. He must have eaten a gallon of them the first day we were out. By noon of the second day Jim knew what I meant. He had such a terrible dysentery that he had no use for a horse. He had no time to sit on one all the rest of the way to Guthrie. I was sick, too, but nothing like Jim.

We approached Guthrie by a worn trail, which, as it entered the town, became a narrow road with tents and temporary cloth shacks erected on each side. As we came within a few yards of the first tent, the road passed under a large tree, from which three objects were hanging by their necks by ropes. Jim Ford looked at those objects with his mouth open and finally said to me,

"Gene, are those men?" I said, "Looks like it to me, Jim. They've got men's clothes on."

There had evidently been an interesting celebration in Guthrie during the preceding night. We arrived almost at dawn and the entire street was lined for several hundred yards with colored boys and men shooting craps in the street and on the sidewalks. We rode up to the nearest of these groups and asked where the livery stable was. One of the colored boys shot the dice with one hand and pointed over his shoulder with the other to a large tent, saying, "Right over dere, boss."

Almost entirely exhausted from our three days of sleepless wandering, and sick from eating those wild plums, which had been almost our only food during that time, we placed our horses in the livery stable and obtained a bed in the so-called hotel. This was also a large tent with a bar room in the front and the back portion partitioned off with muslin into four or five rooms.

It was a wild place. The bodies of three white men which we had seen hanging from the tree a few minutes before were warning enough to us that the slightest mishap would probably cost us our lives. Our first need was money. Ford made inquiry at the bar about the express office and through some misunderstanding that we never did clear up, the bar keeper became infuriated and started around the back end of the bar with a gun.

At that moment we were closer to disaster than at any other time on our entire expedition. The bar keeper was holding his gun in front of him, pointed toward the floor. Moving as deliberately as I could, I stepped in front of the bar keeper so that Jim wouldn't shoot him.

I met the bar keeper very quietly and motioned behind my back for Jim to keep still. I was soon able to talk the man out of his rage. I induced him to go into our room and have a long talk with us. Taking him entirely into my confidence, I showed him my star and credentials and induced him to go to the express office and send a telegram to Visalia for me. The key word used in our telegrams for money and to identify us was "wheat". The telegram read, "Ship five hundred sacks wheat immediately, Guthrie, Indian Territory."

This telegram was sent at six o'clock in the morning and the bar keeper was given instructions not to awaken us until the money arrived. It seemed to us that we had scarcely gone to sleep when the bar keeper was shaking us by the shoulders. Jim Ford was extremely angry at this, because he was weak and terribly sick, and wanted to know, with a great deal of profanity, what was the idea of awakening him. There stood the bar keeper with a canvas sack containing five hundred dollars in coin and currency. We looked at our watches and saw that it was nine o'clock, A.M. I believe that even today this would be good time for securing money in Guthrie from Visalia by telegraph.

We were absolutely exhausted. Relaxed from our hard, driving ride from Kingfisher, we simply had to have some more sleep. We slept through twenty-four hours and found from the bar keeper that before we had arrived in Guthrie the Dalton boys had quarreled and fought with some local cowpunchers in his place during a poker game and had badly beaten two of them. Then they had skipped the country. The bar keeper wanted to get a couple of cowpunchers to help us run down Bob and Emmett, but we wanted to travel alone.

Before we left Guthrie I met U.S. Deputy Marshal Grimes. He was a fine officer. Through him I contacted two men who claimed to be close friends of Bob and Emmett Dalton and who were suspected of harboring them. One of these was a man named Riley. I had a long talk with Riley.

Riley told me that both Bob and Emmett claimed they could prove an alibi in connection with the Alila robbery attempt and that he believed them. I didn't know whether Riley was bluffing or not, but I put the cards on the table for him. I said, "Mr. Riley, if Bob and Emmett will deliver themselves into my custody I will pay them the three thousand dollars reward offered for their capture. Then they can prove their alibi, clear themselves and be that amount winner."

Riley knew I meant business and he went away in a brown study. I made arrangements with Marshal Grimes to carry out the deal for me should Bob and Emmett show up, but they failed to come in after the reward money.

Although we were still saddle-weary, by horseback and stage we traced Bob and Emmett back to Topeka. Then for a time we completely lost track of them, but found that they had headed west. We tracked them across Oklahoma and into New Mexico and found that there they had sold their horses and had taken the train to Reno without buying tickets, probably by bribing the conductor, as was common in those days.

By this time I had to go to Visalia to get ready for the trial of Grat Dalton. It was due to begin in a few days, but later was postponed. So I returned to Visalia and left Ford to continue trailing Bob and Emmett. I knew he could come as near arresting them as I could. But he was never able to do it. The boys had access to a scope of territory at least a hundred miles square near the Sac and Fox Indian Reservation. There they had dozens of friends to furnish them with horses, guns, ammunition, and provisions. That country was crowded with desperados, and the few well-meaning, honorable people living there were entirely under subjugation, fearing to furnish any information whatever that might lead to the capture of an outlaw.

Jim and I probably saved the middle west railroads several train robberies. The boys had undoubtedly intended to rob trains at a number of places while we were chasing them, but they didn't have time. Within two weeks after I returned to Visalia they did rob a train at Whorton, now Perry, Oklahoma.

A number of accounts have been circulated about my trip to the middle west after the Dalton boys, one stating that I was out a hundred and eight days. That is not correct. Jim and I started on the trail of Bob and Emmett on February 7, 1891 and Jim kept after them for more than four months. I arrived back in Visalia either the day before or the day after May Day, I have forgotten which, a little less than three months. If either of us made a record of any kind, it was Jim Ford.

Early day dray service at Coalinga. This photo shows the primitiveness of the equipment against which the Daltons had to contend in robbing the trains in the San Joaquin Valley during the 1880s.
Photo in Bear State Library.

CHAPTER SEVEN

Grat Dalton's Trial

When I first began work with Littleton Dalton he had been photographed but once since 1896, and that photo was taken for a news story published after Emmett's death. I took a number of still photos of him, and some motion pictures of him and of the places we visited. But I needed a good portrait of him. I suggested that we go to a photographer and have one made. To my surprise he was willing to have this done.

It was Saturday afternoon. The only parking space I found was near the Bakersfield City Hall. Before driving home after the photograph was taken we sat on a bench on the lawn and Lit launched once more into one of his recitals that quietly and easily pictured the days of the Gay Nineties when the Dalton boys were in trouble in the Joaquin.

You know, when I knew Bakersfield this was the County Court House grounds. That fine court house across the street had not been built. Bakersfield was just a little village when I first saw it in the summer of 1878. Frank and I came down here on the train. The country around Bakersfield was the most thinly settled of all the Joaquin. I can scarcely believe that I am in the same country. When I was here last in 1888 there still wasn't a single oil well on this side of the county, and the oil fields of Taft and Maricopa were sheep range.

Well, I was telling you about the boys being arrested. I believe that Grat was arrested three times before he was held for trial. Cole Dalton was arrested along with Grat and Mason, or Bill, so the officers could check his story against the others. Then he was released. Cole told me afterward that he had to lie half the time in order to make his story jibe with the one Mason had told. Mason would tell a wild yarn just in order to have the pleasure of proving it by a dozen more yarns.

Several times a detective came to Clovis Cole's, where I was working, but didn't arrest me or ask me for a statement. The officers also sent a woman detective out to work as a cook and to pump me. I knew she was a detective as soon as she hit the ranch. I watched her and heard a detective coaching her on what to ask me. I didn't do any talking.

As soon as Mason was released on bond he went to Merced and made arrangements for Attorney John W. Breckenridge and his law partner, James Peck, to defend Grat. This was about the fifteenth of March, 1891. They didn't try Grat until the middle of the following June, three full months later. Breckenridge was acknowledged to be the best defense lawyer in the San Joaquin Valley; possibly the best in the state. What Mason didn't know was that he was also a consulting attorney for the S.P. Railroad. He sold us out, lock, stock, and barrel. His procedure through the entire trial proved this. Even Maurice Power, Tulare County District Attorney, referred to it during the trial.

To me the whole thing smelled from the start. Breckenridge was a heavy drinker and was often unable to work for a week at a time. In addition, he wouldn't move a hand until he had all of his pay. Mason turned over to him almost all of his stock, eight head of horses and mules with harness, leaving him only an old driving mare and one old mule. Breckenridge also demanded a thousand dollars in gold coin. Mother raised the thousand dollars and it was paid to Breckenridge two months before the trial began.

Mother mortgaged the Kingfisher home and borrowed money from old neighbors until she had more than two thousand dollars, all in gold, in addition to that paid Breckenridge. Then she came to California, stopping first at Merced to pay Breckenridge and then coming to Visalia for the trial. At that time Breckenridge and Peck were defending a Merced County man for murder.

Mother brought to California with her two of my sisters. In addition, Cole and Mason and I were there and testified for Grat. Father died about the time the boys began to get into trouble. He never knew of any of their horse stealing, or train or bank robbing. Ben Dalton was working on a ranch near Madera at the time of Grat's arrest. He went to see Grat in the Tulare County Jail and then went back to Kingfisher, to help raise money to defend Grat. He stayed there during the trial, while Mother came west. He died at Kingfisher not many years ago, well up in his eighties.

Mother and the girls stayed in a Visalia hotel. The first night after they arrived, Cole, Mason and the rest of us met in Mother's room to talk over plans for the trial. Mother had with her more than two thousand dollars in gold coin. She dumped this out of a little satchel on a table in the hotel room.

Cole's eyes popped when he saw all that money. He moved his chair up to the table, scraped the money up in a pile and said, "If I could just get into a poker game with a stake like this, how I could make things hum." That was the most ambitious thought he had about the money Mother had scraped together from all possible sources, savings, mortgage, and money borrowed from friends.

By the time Mother and the girls arrived back at Kingfisher, almost all of that two thousand dollars was gone. Grat's trial lasted more than three weeks and cost Tulare County many thousands of dollars. I once heard District Attorney Power say that it would cost Tulare County at least twenty-five thousand dollars.

When it came time for the trial to begin, neither Breckenridge nor Peck was there. Jack Ahern, a Bakersfield attorney, and also a Southern Pacific Railroad consultant, appeared for them and at first would not be recognized by the court. He tried to get a postponement of the trial, but there had already been one postponement, and Judge Gray wouldn't grant another. He did grant a recess until afternoon, but the few hours gained were not enough. Ahern said to Mason, "Bill, you get on the train, go to Merced and bring Breckenridge down here right away. Tell him I said to let Peck finish the case they are working on up there."

When Mason arrived at Merced, Peck already was handling the trial and Breckenridge was nowhere to be found. Between trains Mason inquired about Breckenridge and learned that he had been drinking heavily for almost a week and was probably laid up somewhere, drunk. There was nothing Mason could do but go back to Visalia, and admit failure.

After several days Peck arrived, and several days later Breckenridge came down and took charge. The type of witnesses Breckenridge and Peck had to work with did Grat more damage than good. They were almost all bar keepers, gamblers, saloon hangers-on, and pimps. There was no possibility of getting anyone else, because the boys had not been in any other places on their way from Malaga to Delano. Mother and Grat were sure that Breckenridge would free him. I didn't think so. From the first I was skeptical of the whole deal. Grat said, "You're just contrary. There's nothing to this. They can't prove a thing."

But they did "prove a thing" and the trial ended with Grat convicted and Breckenridge and Peck in possession of eight of Mason's horses, mules and harness, and a thousand dollars of Mother's savings.

Here are some of the witnesses for Grat: Dan Armbruster, a bar keeper at the Elite Saloon in Fresno; B.F. Saunders, a bar keeper at the Reception Saloon, and Charlie Worth, a bar keeper at the Hughes Hotel.

Mustang Ed was the worst witness Grat had. You could see that the jury was disgusted with him, to a man. Ed and Joaquín, his gambling and pimping partner, and Johnnie Crawford ran a poker game in Crawford's Visalia bar room all through Grat's trial. They always had from five to six hundred dollars on the table, poker at a dollar an ante.

Ed's last name was Baldonabro, or something similar. Both he and Joaquín were the lowest class of California Spaniards. Ed died from tuberculosis and is buried in Fresno. He was a typical gambler and pimp, good looking, always well dressed, and wore a heavy gold watch chain with a jewelry quartz charm for which he had paid two hundred and fifty dollars. A few weeks before Ed died, down and out, Mahoney, a Fresno dance hall man, paid Ed eighty dollars for the chain and charm.

Johnnie Crawford was another typical gambler and saloon man. Grat had known him for ten years. Johnnie would take in a hundred dollars over the bar in a day and gamble it away that night.

The night before Mustang Ed testified for Grat he had been up all night in Crawford's poker game. I saw him in the game as late as midnight. They actually called him out of the poker game to testify.

Joaquín went from Visalia to Indian Territory. I saw him in Guthrie. He went from there to St. Louis and won two thousand dollars on the horse races and was murdered and robbed the same day.

Well, that was the only kind of company Grat had to prove an alibi for him. There were other witnesses of course, more than fifty of them, but only a few of them testified for Grat.

Soon after the Alila robbery attempt Cole Dalton and Jack Parker were arrested at Paso Robles and put in the jail at Visalia until their stories could be checked. Both testified at the trial. So did Mother and I. Practically all the rest of the witnesses were against Grat.

To Mason and to me Bob and Emmett made no secret of the fact that they were wanted in the east for horse stealing. They talked freely about it. Grat claimed to have come to California to help them keep out of reach of the Indian Territory officers. He arrived at Mason's ranch about January fifteenth of '91. Bob and Mason both told their Estrella neighbors about the eastern trouble. This was related by several witnesses at Grat's trial.

Another thing brought out at the trial was the fact that, while they were at Mason's, Bob and Emmett wore their six-shooters all of the time, when they handled their teams in the barn, when they drove them in the fields, and when they helped Mason's wife wash and dry dishes in the house. They even put them in bed with them when they slept.

At Grat's trial I had a long talk with Loftis McDonald, one of the witnesses. McDonald was Mason's nearest neighbor. He told me about the boys wearing their six-shooters all the time and also told me that in the night he could hear them banging away in target practice with both six-shooters and winchester rifles. There were five-gallon oil cans all about the place, shot full of holes in night practice. It didn't look good to McDonald and he told me he was glad when Bob and Emmett were gone.

From the beginning of the trial, two things began to develop, a complete confidence and trust in Sheriff Kay and his men and a complete distrust and hatred of the railroad detectives and officers, most of all, Bill Smith. Smith was always sneaking around the place trying to job, or proposition, or double-cross someone. His detective work and testimony were absolutely unreliable. I soon came to hate him so much I could scarcely talk to him.

On the other hand, we learned to depend on anything Kay told us. Sheriff Kay was one of the finest men I ever knew. I remember his sharp eyes and his frank, honest way. If the railroad and express detectives had left Kay alone he would have straightened out that train robbery with little or no bloodshed and prevented almost all the trouble that followed.

Kay often pointed out to us Grat's rights when Breckenridge had overlooked them. It was plain to see that Kay knew Breckenridge was letting Grat down. Before the trial was over Grat said to me, "Lit, I would rather have Kay arrest me, try me and sentence me than all the law in Tulare County."

The great pressure on us was the thought that Emmett had killed George Radliff. This was never discussed openly, and was not brought out at the trial by either side. But it made a big difference in the attitude of the jury. All knew, of course, that Haswell, the express messenger, had been indicted for the killing of Radliff. But he had been cleared and we were given to understand that his clearance pinned the killing on the boys. All this time Bill Smith was working hard to bulldoze Grat into a confession. He visited Grat in his cell almost every day. Grat hated Smith like poison, and he stuck to his story.

Breckenridge did two absolutely criminal things. He knew that Radliff was shot by the express messenger, Haswell. He also knew that the freight train Grat must have returned to Fresno on left Alila before the robbery. He at no time presented any testimony about either of these important facts. We pointed out the train schedule evidence to Breckenridge at least a half dozen times. His answer always was that it was too early to introduce it and that, anyway, he was going to ask for a dismissal. We said nothing about the shooting, because we thought Emmett had killed Radliff.

When the trial was almost over, Sheriff Kay, Detective Smith, and District Attorney Power talked with Grat when he was being taken from the court room. Neither Breckenridge nor Peck was present. It was Kay who began the discussion.

"Grat, I know that Radliff was not killed by Bob or Emmett. If we will admit this, will you and Bill tell the straight story of the robbery?" At this point Bill Smith butted in. Grat answered, "I won't discuss anything while Smith is around."

Smith left and then Kay brought Mason to where they were talking. Kay explained what we didn't know about the bullet that had killed Radliff. He stated that the bullet had come from the six-shooter of the messenger and had passed through the door of the express car before it hit Radliff. I believe this to be true, because the express company later paid Mrs. Radliff twenty-five hundred dollars for the loss of her husband.

Kay and the boys talked for an hour. Mason and Grat both agreed to tell all they knew, if they could be shown that there was no first degree murder in the holdup. Breckenridge was called in and the information given him. He wasn't pleased, but could do nothing but agree to it.

Next day Grat and Mason went on the stand and told the truth about the whole affair. But did it clear Grat? It sure didn't. Breckenridge never introduced a witness to prove that Radliff was killed by Haswell. Grat was convicted.

After Grat's trial I went to Kingfisher with Mother. She insisted that I go with her. In a few weeks I came back to California. I had to do something to make a living. I went to work again for Clovis Cole at his ranch near where the town of Clovis is now located. . . . .

> While we were sitting in the City Hall grounds it grew late and too cool for comfort, so we climbed in the car and started home. On the way we planned a trip to San Francisco to see Kay. But before it could be made, a letter came telling that he had suffered a paralytic stroke. It was many months before he was well enough to talk. But I finally did interview him.
>
> During this last visit with Kay we talked over Lit's statement about the trial. Kay agreed with it almost in every detail. He was not able to enter into long discussions, but his mind was perfectly clear. He could make a few statements and could easily give a yes or no answer to Lit's important points. Here is what Kay said:

> From my own investigations I knew that, while Grat had probably helped

Frank Halter, last person living who had any part in the trial of Grat Dalton. Interviewed at his home in Yountville in 1949, Halter furnished an account of how he came to loan his saddle to Bill Dalton.
   Photo courtesy Frank Halter and now in Bear State Library.

plan the robbery, he was not actually at the scene of the robbery when it took place. I learned from a dozen reliable sources that he was really in the Grand Central Hotel in Fresno not later than one-thirty on the morning after the robbery. The northbound freight was the only possible way Grat had to get back to Fresno that soon. Remember, in those days there were no automobiles and no airplanes. The freight pulled off the siding at Alila and went north in the opposite direction to the passenger while the passenger train was clearing the switch to make the stop at Alila. The robbery continued at least half an hour later.

It was well understood to be a fact by both the prosecution and defense attorneys that Radliff had been killed by Haswell. Breckenridge introduced no testimony on that point. None of Breckenridge's default was due to lack of intelligence on his part. He was a brilliant man and one of the most able men ever to practice law in California. He was a son of the famous Kentucky politician, John C. Breckenridge. He told me so himself. He had been drinking at the time, but I believe he was telling the truth.

John C. Breckenridge served as Vice President of the United States under President Buchanan. When John W. Breckenridge argued Grat's case he told me he had a brother and a cousin in the United States Congress. The brother was from Kentucky and the cousin from Arkansas. John W. had also been a delegate to the Democratic National Convention, I believe in 1884, and had nominated Thurman for Vice President of the United States. John W. was the finest appearing man I ever saw and the most flowery speaker I ever heard. He simply sold Grat out to the S.P. Railroad.

Breckenridge also argued Bill Dalton's case and made a good job of it. The jury freed Bill after less than fifteen minutes of deliberation. John W. died from the effects of too much liquor about a year after Grat was tried and was only about forty-two years of age at the time.

When the trial was about over, it looked as though Grat was going to get off in spite of Breckenridge's default in defense, and we would not have a watertight case against Bob and Emmett. So I proposed to District Attorney Power that we tell Grat the truth about the killing of Radliff and persuade him to tell all he knew about the robbery.

The proposition was made and worked out about the way Lit related it. Neither Power nor Smith thought I could get Grat or Bill to tell the truth about anything. They were the most surprised men you ever saw when Grat and Bill had finished their stories and we knew at least three-fourths of their statements to be true.

Yes, I helped to convict Grat, all right, but he didn't get a fair trial, for

Breckenridge didn't clear up the murder point and no one knows how many years he would have been given, for he escaped from the jail in Visalia before Judge Gray pronounced sentence. Grat finally answered sentence for all of his crimes at Coffeyville, Kansas, in October of '92 when the battle of the banks was over, and he and Bob were both shot to death and Emmett crippled for life. . . . .

A number of sensational news accounts influenced the jury at the time of Grat Dalton's trial, and did not end, even with Grat's escape.

On May 18th, 1891, the *San Francisco Chronicle* had received a long telegram from Guthrie, Indian Territory, telling of a long, hot battle between the Dalton Gang and a force of ten United States Marshals under Marshal Calcroft with a troop of fifty U.S. Cavalrymen. Casualties were reported as Bob killed, Emmett captured, and James Eaton, a cavalryman, wounded. The battle was stated to have taken place on the Sac and Fox Reservation near Tishomingo, Indian Territory.

This telegram was the wildest thing ever printed about the Dalton Gang, not excepting all accounts regarding the Coffeyville Raid. Indian scouts and bloodhounds were stated to have run the boys into a cave, where the Daltons shot the dogs. A pitched battle was described as having raged for nineteen hours.

It was a wonderful story, the only fault being that there was not a word of truth in it. The *Chronicle* was handed to Grat and Bill Dalton. They laughed loud and long at the account. Said Grat, "Those boys couldn't have been taken in a battle like that without ten or twelve of that posse were killed." Sheriff Kay agreed with Grat and Bill. He wired Guthrie and received an answer from U.S. Deputy Marshal Grimes, stating that the story was an entire fabrication, circulated by friends of the Daltons in order to relieve the pressure put on them by pursuing officers, including Jim Ford, Kay's deputy.

It is not surprising that train crews and citizens became jittery after news of the Pixley, Goshen, Alila, and Ceres affairs had been broadcast. According to the *Tulare County Times* newspaper, in the latter part of November, 1891, the *San Francisco Chronicle* published a "Full Account of a Train Robbery" that never occurred. Here it is, complete with all the trimmings:

Soon after 8 P.M., the long train pushed into Pixley, Tulare County, and let off a passenger or two, among them a Chinese. The conductor and brakeman were on the platform, and the train was just about started when the Chinese passenger, who had walked on past the engine toward the tankhouse, was seen running back. He was gesticulating wildly, and shouting at the top of his voice.

The conductor held the train for a few seconds to learn what the trouble was, and when he had found out he was in no great hurry to proceed.

The Chinese told in broken English how he had walked into the darkness beyond the tankhouse, where he saw three men crouching in the deep shadow of the tanks. When he saw that they had sacks over their heads and that each of them carried a gun,

The mongol did not tell it so clearly, but his story was enough to make the trainmen understand. They instantly divined that it was a "hold up" and that the three masked men were train robbers. It was impossible to secure assistance in time to meet the bandits hand to hand. Word was passed to the messenger to bar and chain his doors, get his firearms ready and put out his lamps. Then the heavy train was backed slowly down the track three or four times its own length, the throttle of the engine was pulled wide open and the train rushed past the station and the tankhouse where the robbers were hidden at a speed of something like thirty miles an hour.

Meantime the station agent and operator at Pixley had telegraphed the circumstances on to Bakersfield in time to stop the northbound express, number 19. Citizens and constables were aroused and a search was made for the robbers, but they had had ample time to get away and had done so.

> It may have been a genuine robbery in the making, *quién sabe?*

The trial of Bill Dalton for complicity in the attempt to rob the Southern Pacific railroad express car at Alila was begun in the Court House at Visalia, October 5, 1891, and ended with his acquittal on October 10. The Merced law firm of Breckenridge and Peck argued Bill's case, represented by Breckenridge. C.G. Lamberson, Visalia Attorney, assisted Breckenridge. Maurice Power, District Attorney, was assisted by Alfred Daggett. Almost the same evidence was presented as had been used at the trial of Grat Dalton.

Evidently the jury felt differently about *William*, as he was called when an effort was made to be facetious.

The attachment of Riley Dean to Bill and later to Grat Dalton has added a touch of mystery to the Alila robbery. How they became acquainted no one knows, but Bill and Dean were undoubtedly planning a train robbery, or a jail delivery, when arrested at Cross Creek by Kay and

Witty. After his arrest, Dean said to Sheriff Kay, "Don't you remember me? I used to know you up at the French Camp, near Stockton." But Kay didn't remember Dean.

As soon as Bill was acquitted by the Visalia jury, he again was taken into custody under a warrant from San Luis Obispo County.

Although both Dean and Bill Dalton stated that they had met only a few days before they were arrested following the Ceres robbery, it developed that they had been arrested at San Luis Obispo some time before the Ceres affair. They had been charged with stealing a saddle from a Paso Robles farmer and deputy constable named Houston. At the hearing in Paso Robles the saddle was not produced. The remaining evidence was so meager that both Dalton and Dean were released. When they were arrested at Cross Creek both Dean and Dalton were in possession of riding rigs and horses.

After the Modesto hearing, when Dalton and Dean were cleared of the Ceres robbery, Dean was released and took his saddle with him. The saddle used by Dalton was identified by Houston as the one taken from his ranch at Paso Robles. It was upon Houston's complaint that the new warrant was issued and Bill Dalton retained in custody. Sheriff O'Neil took Bill back to San Luis Obispo on the train.

Not even this added petty affliction could dampen Bill's spirits. When the train stopped at Lathrop he met an old Merced acquaintance, a man to whom he owed a considerable amount of money. Said Bill, "As soon as I get out of this trouble I am going east and will send you what I owe you. My brothers have lots of money now."

At Paso Robles Bill slipped out of the saddle deal as easily as he ever slipped out of anything. He said, "Bring in that mule skinner who works on the ranch where that saddle belongs."

The skinner was brought.

"Don't you remember you loaned me that saddle?"

"Sure," answered the skinner.

That ended it. Bill was turned loose.

One of the most illuminating of all news articles concerning the Daltons appeared in the *Visalia Delta* in July of 1891. The article, which follows, gives not only an insight into the character of Grat, and of other members of the family, but also illustrates the loose manner in which the jail at Visalia was operated:

Grattan Dalton, who was recently convicted of participating in the Alila train robbery, was in a violent rage yesterday afternoon. During the afternoon, Mrs. Whipple, the prisoner's sister, called at the jail to tell her brother goodbye, as she intended to go to her home in Oklahoma. After the visit was over Dalton was searched by Jailor Williams before he was taken to his cell. The train robber was indignant and used a good deal of profane language toward Mr. Williams. Whisky had been furnished Dalton by his relatives, and he was in an insolent mood. Dalton was so angry that he cried like a baby, and swore that he would be avenged for the indignities he had undergone. The prisoner has been treated with a good deal of consideration since he has been an inmate of the county jail, and has been allowed liberties not vouchsafed other prisoners.

William Dalton, his brother Lit, and brother-in-law and sister, Mr. and Mrs. Whipple, left last evening for Bakersfield, where they will remain a few days. After their visit there they will go to Fresno. Dalton will be arraigned in department #2 of the superior court on October 5 to answer to the charge of attempted train robbery at Alila last February. Grattan Dalton, who was convicted of participation in the robbery, is still a prisoner at the county jail and no effort is being made to secure his release on bail.

Grat was not interested in bail. He was making definite plans for a permanent leave, without benefit of bail.

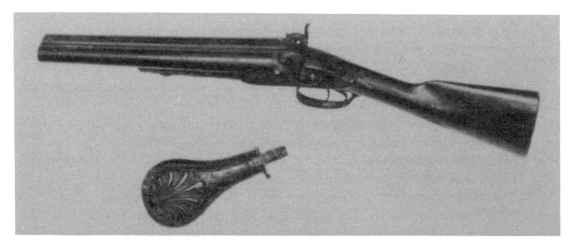

Twelve gauge double barreled shotgun, sawed off and carried to California in a suitcase by Grat Dalton. It was abandoned in Bakersfield just before the Alila robbery because Grat had no money with which to pay the gunsmith for repairs made on it.
Photo by Vesper Dick and now in Bear State Library.

CHAPTER EIGHT

GRAT DALTON'S ESCAPE

The escape of Grat Dalton from the Tulare County Jail at Visalia during the night of September 20, 1891, was one of the most widely publicized events in the history of crime in California. Grat Dalton was hot copy. Magazine and newspaper articles by the hundreds had been published about the exploits of the Daltons. First of the misdeeds credited to the Daltons were the train robberies already described and others in Indian Territory and Arkansas. Next came the pursuit of Emmett and Bob, the arrest of Grat and Bill and their trials in the Tulare County court house at Visalia, and then the escape of Grat. Although two other men, Arvil Beck and Smith, escaped with Grat, the fact was seldom considered or mentioned.

Every schoolboy in the United States knew, or thought he knew, all about the Dalton Gang. They were the topic of conversation on street corners and park benches, in hotel lobbies and bar rooms and about the doors and steps of lodges, schools, and churches throughout the land. Interest continued to mount in regard to the Daltons until after the "battle of the banks" at Coffeyville, Kansas, almost a year after the escape of Grat from the jail in Visalia.

For thirty years Americans were more Dalton-conscious than they were war-conscious in either 1917 or 1941. Such was the exaggerated interest attached to four more or less common, ordinary gun-toting United States citizens.

In Tulare County the escape created a terrific furor. The pursuit, arrest and trials of the four Daltons who were later to be known as the "Gang" had cost Tulare County, the railroad, and the express company about thirty thousand dollars. In addition to this, Sheriff Kay spent more than eight thousand dollars of his own money. Hundreds of other peace officers and detectives had expended hundreds of dollars of their personal funds. Kay once told me that he believed the Daltons had cost the people of Tulare county alone more than fifty thousand dollars, besides the expenses of the express and railroad companies. The entire lives of at least twenty Tulare county persons were thoroughly ruined by the Dalton Gang.

In his book, *When the Daltons Rode*, Emmett Dalton made several statements that for some time were unsupported by anyone else. One of these was to the effect that, through the aid of a Negro trusty, hacksaw blades had been furnished Grat by someone outside. The other was that when Grat escaped he found a winchester rifle and some ammunition hidden in some weeds back of the jail, also that pieces of hacksaw blades and a file were found in the jail toilet.

One of Tulare County's ex-deputies substantiated one of these statements. Billy Russell said, "Grat didn't make a report to us on how he escaped, so I don't know about the gun and ammunition. I heard that he used a file and hacksaw blades. We found pieces of them in the toilet used by the prisoners. The men had broken them up and tried to flush them down the toilet, but there wasn't water pressure enough to carry them through the trap."

I finally contacted Littleton Dalton before I learned any more about the winchester rifle and the ammunition. But Lit disappointed me in one most important thing. He didn't know who had furnished the tools and the weapon. Said Lit:

Yes, I heard from Grat all about the escape, as soon as he arrived at Mother's home near Kingfisher. But I heard about it only that once. It has been more than forty-six years since I heard Grat tell his story, and I don't remember who furnished the gun and ammunition and the hacksaw blade and file. But there was more help than that. There was a horse, and a ladder. The horse, gun, and ammunition were hidden in a pear orchard north-east of the jail. The ladder was leaned against the outside wall of the jail, because it was expected that Grat would come out of the upper story.

Whoever it was that furnished the aid didn't plan for anyone to leave but Grat. When the three of them escaped the one horse wasn't enough for all of them. Grat told me the horse was an old white plug that could be recognized a mile away in the night and wouldn't have carried him twenty miles. He turned the horse loose so it could go home, took down the ladder, grabbed the winchester and ammunition and began to look for transportation. The three of them stole a good double driving team hitched to a buggy. It was tied in front of a church. . . . .

All of this opened a deeper mystery: a horse, a ladder, a winchester and ammunition, a file and hacksaw blades. Who could have been interested enough in the escape of Grat Dalton to go to all that trouble? Later I was to learn who was so interested.

When Grat escaped, Sheriff Kay certainly was on the spot. Criticism of him and his force was extremely bitter. Blackest suspicion was cast on all of Kay's deputies. I talked with two of them forty years later. Even then they had not ceased to smart under the public tongue and press lashings they had received. John Hazen continued intermittently to work in the sheriff's office until his death about 1939. I found Billy Russell in Stockton.

In 1961 only Charles F. Johnson, of Bakersfield, is known to have been left of all the men who worked at the sheriff's office in 1891.

Criticism was precipitated largely by the fact that when the first news accounts were issued, the escape of Dalton, Beck, and Smith was thought to have been entirely an inside job. No damage was discovered done to any of the cells or cages. Only a small window in the basement was found jimmied open. The story was that the prisoners had been furnished with keys for the cell and corridor locks, had unlocked, stepped outside, and locked up after themselves. But it was a fact that no cell door could be opened or closed by means of keys alone. A heavy lever, operating a long, steel safety bar, had to be thrown in the office of the jailor before the doors could be opened. The widespread story was that the night jailor, Williams, with the aid of other officers, had sold Kay down the river. Although it was learned in a few days that there was outside help, the damage had been done and the information came too late to prevent continued unjust criticism of the entire jail force.

It was plain that I was approaching a delicate subject, even after forty-five years, when I asked Gene Kay if he knew who had furnished the outside help that made possible the escape of Dalton, Beck and Smith. It took Kay a short while to come to the point, but he finally told me what I wanted to know.

When I went into office, I promised myself that I would never needlessly injure a man, regardless of how bad a man he was. During my entire term it was only once necessary for me to fire a gun at a man and I never injured anyone. Every man I took was either approached openly and frankly, or was arrested under conditions that made it impossible for him to resist.

One cold winter morning, the day before Christmas in 1891, after climbing for a mile over frozen ground, I stood on a ledge of rock and looked down upon Grattan Dalton and Riley Dean, less than fifty yards from me. Upon my right and left stood deputies with sawed-off shotguns, loaded with buck shot. I held a revolver in my right hand. Neither Dalton nor Dean saw any of us. They were discussing a contemplated hunt and were entirely unaware of our presence.

Grattan Dalton had escaped from the Tulare County Jail, in company with Smith and Beck. Railroad deputies and detectives, Wells Fargo detectives, Deputy U.S. Marshals and others had entirely blamed this escape on me and my deputies, claiming that I was in league with the prisoners.

Determined as I was to take those two men, I saw in a second that one word spoken by any member of our party would cause their instant death. It was useless to command them to throw up their hands, because each would have jumped for cover and each would have been filled with buck shot. The deputy on my left raised his shot gun with the intention of firing. I placed my hand on the gun and pushed it down, motioning with my revolver to the deputy on my right to keep his gun down.

Hurriedly I took in the situation. The trail over which the escaped prisoners were traveling paralleled the ledge of rock upon which we were standing. If we allowed them to go forward approximately a hundred yards, we could detour through the brush ahead of them and surprise them in an open space where they could not seek cover.

A portion of the remainder of this story is well known to the world. Dean was taken prisoner, but Grattan Dalton escaped.

We returned to Visalia in disgust. It was the decision made on that rock ledge that changed my whole subsequent life and which in my own mind has been completely justified only after the passing of forty-five years. It would be useless to tell of the abuse that was heaped upon me because of the escape of Grattan Dalton. One of my deputies, the one who wanted to fire, refused to ride back to Visalia with me. Others were open in their bitter denunciation of my action, and stated that I should have let them shoot the men down where they stood.

The greatest satisfaction of my entire life comes at the present time in knowing that my judgment at that time was better than that of either of those men. The deputy who was willing to shoot them down in cold blood died by his own hand in a San Francisco rooming house. The other deputy, who was just as open in his abuse, drank himself to death in the Bakersfield underworld. Not one of the men who on that morning were willing to take the lives of Grattan Dalton and Riley Dean had any appreciation of the ultimate result of such action.

I knew Grattan Dalton as a brave man. He was a bandit and all that goes with it, but he had in him a strong streak of frank, honest responsibility. Knowing myself as I do, I know that I could never have survived the knowledge that I had backed the shooting down in cold blood of such a man.

All of my efforts to contact Dalton were in vain. Hampered by railroad detectives and officers, every move I made to arrange a meeting with Dalton was blocked. I have always felt that alone, I could have sat down upon the hillside beside that ledge of rock and talked with Grattan Dalton and could have taken him voluntarily back to Visalia, could have cleared him of the charges against him and could have made of him an honest, self-respecting man.

I left that ledge of rock on Dalton Mountain near Kings River with the determination that I would take Grattan Dalton if it took me to the end of the earth, but I was never to realize my desire.

During the time I was in the Sheriff's office there passed through my hands fifty-seven thousand dollars of money, all spent in tracking down and arresting the Daltons, Chris Evans, and the Sontag brothers, and in trying Grattan and Bill Dalton. In addition I spent $18,000 of my own money. I left Tulare County without a cent to my name.

I had almost forgotten. You asked me if I knew who helped Grat Dalton out of the Tulare County Jail. Of course he had help from the other prisoners, but it is also true that his principal help came from outside. At first we thought it was Bob Dalton who furnished the help. We had received word from Indian Territory officers that Bob was making plans to rescue Grat. As a consequence we for some time placed extra guards at the jail. But Bob had nothing to do with the escape. The helpful gentleman was at that time one of our respected Visalia citizens.

It was a year before I knew who furnished this outside help, but I did learn who it was, beyond a shadow of a doubt. I don't ask you to believe me until you have heard my whole story. It was Chris Evans, the train bandit, who sprung Grat Dalton from the Visalia Jail.

How do I know this? It is a longer story than I can tell just now, but it was Chris who furnished the hacksaw blades and gave them to the Negro trusty who took them into the jail. It was also Chris who placed the ladder against the rear wall of the jail, tied his mother-in-law's grey horse in the pear orchard just north-east of the building, and planted the winchester rifle and ammunition.

Most of my information was obtained through Oliver Perry Byrd, brother of Mrs. Chris Evans and one of my most valued deputies. Perry Byrd furnished for me almost every worthwhile clue I ever had concerning the Goshen and Collis robberies. I never knew him to furnish me a single bit of false information. Chris told Perry Byrd that he had sprung Grat, "Because I knew he was not guilty." There was other supporting evidence that Chris furnished the gun, ammunition, ladder, and horse.

In the Goshen robbery there were taken $2,000 in new two-dollar bills. We didn't have the numbers of the bills, but at that time in California a two dollar bill was as rare an article and, when presented as legal tender, created as much comment as would a twenty dollar gold piece today.

The Pixley and Goshen robberies occurred while my predecessor, Dan Overall, was sheriff. From him and his men I learned all I could about both robberies. Billy Russell, Traver Constable, had been a deputy under Overall, and was also my deputy during all the time I was in office. I learned many things from him. I went to Pixley and studied that robbery. Then I went over the Goshen job with Billy Russell and Perry Byrd.

It may be news to many people that one of the few persons ever caught passing those two-dollar bills was Grat Dalton. Don't misunderstand me. Grat didn't perform the Goshen robbery, nor did he share in the spoils. But he passed some of the bills not long after that robbery was performed.

I didn't know Grat, except by sight, but Grat knew all about me. I stopped him on the street and said, "Say, I hear you have some two dollar bills. I haven't seen one since I left Missouri. Let me look at one." He pulled out two or three and showed them to me. They were perfectly new and had consecutive serial numbers. I said, "Where in the world did you get them?" He started to say something about a horse. I have forgotten his exact words. Then he suddenly became suspicious and shut up like a clam. We investigated the horse clue. I knew he must have sold, or hired out a horse. At the livery stable we found that Grat had sold a horse to Chris Evans.

Now, all of the officers knew that two dollar bills had been taken in the Goshen robbery, but Perry Byrd and I were the only officers who suspected that Chris Evans and John Sontag had robbed that train.

George Witty had pointed Grat out to me and it was George I sent to check up on the horse deal. It took him several hours. I kept Grat in sight and talked to him most of the time. When Witty returned he took me to one side and said to me, "Gene, I found where Grat got the money, but it don't mean a thing. Chris Evans says that he bought Grat's horse to use in his Modesto livery stable and Chris got the bills when he cashed a check at Sol Sweet's store." In George's mind that settled it. Chris Evans' word was as good as a bond.

I was perfectly satisfied with the explanation. I apologized frankly and honestly to Grat and sent him on his way. At Sweet's store I found that Chris Evans had cashed a check all right, but that he had been given gold for it. I said nothing about what I had learned. But it meant something to me when Perry Byrd told me what Chris had said about springing Grat out of the jail.

Another fact was that during the summer of 1888, before the Goshen robbery, Chris Evans and Grat Dalton worked together in the grain warehouses of the Granger's Union at Pixley and at Tipton. I know that Grat was supposed to be on active duty as United States Deputy Marshal in Indian Territory at that time. But Grat always circulated around. He told me that he had made two extended trips to California while serving as U.S. Marshal.

Anyway, I was given access to the records of the Granger's Warehouse and was furnished several canceled pay checks endorsed by Grat. The signature on them was the same as one I got from the officers in the Federal Court at Fort Smith, Arkansas. I did this to check the stories I heard that Chris and Grat had worked in the warehouses together. I thought I might be able to connect them with the Pixley robbery.

It was all of these contacts, especially Grat's protection in the instance of the horse sale, that caused Chris to spring him from the Tulare County Jail. Chris was probably afraid Grat would talk about those two dollar bills.

But I have wandered too far from my story of Grat Dalton's escape from the Tulare County Jail.

Grat broke jail while I was in San Francisco. I hurried home as soon as I could get there. At first it surely looked like an inside job. No visible damage had been done to the cells. A hole had been dug in the brick wall in the corridor, but the escapees had been stopped by steel bars embedded in the brick. It surely looked like keys had been furnished and that Grat and his companions, Arvil Beck and W.B. Smith had simply unlocked the cell and the corridor doors, stepped outside, locked them again and then had broken through a window in the basement in order to get outside the building.

J.W. Williams was jailor. I couldn't believe that he had aided in the escape. He was one of the oldest pioneers of Tulare County. During the Indian War of 1862 he had headed a detachment of soldiers and he had done more than his share to whip the Indians. He had been City Marshal of Visalia for many years and was counted one of the most dependable peace officers in the state.

But we had definite word that the escape was done with keys. Bill Dalton was in another portion of the jail at the same time and he told us, "The boys were there when I went to sleep, and when I awakened they had unlocked and gone. Why in the world do you suppose they went away and left me

Col. Jacob Yoes, United States Deputy Marshal at Fort Smith during the time when Frank, Grat, Bob and Emmett Dalton served as marshals and possemen.
Photo courtesy George A. Yoes, son of Col. Jacob Yoes and now in Bear State Library.

behind?" Of course Bill had been known to tell things that weren't true. But this time it looked like his version was correct. It was thirty hours before we knew any different. Jim Wagy, who had been employed as a guard at the jail, and Harry Charters, Tulare newspaper editor, were responsible for the discovery.

In the midst of the furor of criticism that ensued, Harry Charters went to Visalia to see for himself what the situation was. Jim Wagy took Harry through the cells. Harry kept insisting that the escape must have been worked from the outside, that he knew every one of the jail force. Said Harry, "Jim, there isn't a man on the force who wouldn't have lost his right hand before he would have sold Kay out like this."

Bill Dalton had been moved into the same cell from which Grat and the others had escaped. He was playing his guitar when Wagy discovered the place where the break was made. A bar had been cut out and replaced by a smoked broomhandle. Then we began our investigations all over again.

When Wagy discovered the broomhandle, Bill Dalton threw his guitar on the bed, stood up and said, "Now what in the world do you know about that? How did they ever cut that bar out without my knowing it?" Bill was a natural comedian. . . . .

> When I was talking with Kay about the escape, he told me I should see Jim Wagy and Bob Hockett, both of whom he thought were still living. I knew that Jim Wagy was living in Kern County; in fact, for a number of years he had been State Senator from that area. But I knew that Bob Hockett was dead. In the course of my investigations I didn't talk to Jim Wagy until late in 1942. Jim was a find. He had been a deputy under Dan Overall at the time of the Pixley robbery and the Goshen affair. He had been on both posses and had followed the Pixley trail to Porterville and the Goshen trail to a point where the Stokes boys had obliterated it when they drove a band of loose horses over it soon after it was made.
>
> Also, Wagy had been a guard at the Tulare County Jail until the Friday before the escape of Grat Dalton. He had quit because he thought there was going to be an escape and didn't want to be blamed for it when it happened. I talked Jim almost to death that first day, seven hours straight questioning and reading of what data I already had collected from Kay and Lit Dalton.
>
> Here is Wagy's story:

At the time of the Alila robbery I had left the sheriff's office and was operating a little vineyard just north of Tulare. When Dan Overall heard of the robbery he drove in his buggy to my place and picked me up. We drove to the scene of the Alila robbery.

It is true that most of the men at the scene thought the robbers had gone to the east. Both Overall and I thought so, although I now don't know why. When Kay returned from tracing the tracks of Bob and Emmett, we decided to go west, as he advised. A number of horses and riding rigs had been shipped to the place in box cars. Pat Murray of Tulare had been allotted a big buckskin horse with a black line down its back. Pat was not used to riding a horse, and he couldn't handle the buckskin. So I took it, and Pat rode in the buggy with Dan Overall.

The ground was alkaline and very soft and the horses we were following had left good, deep tracks. They had been running hard and continued almost due west from the scene of the holdup completely across the plains to the Kettleman Hills. The country west of Alila was rough and cut with small washes and gullies and the buggies could not keep close to the saddle animals that were following the tracks. Sometimes Murray and Overall were out of our sight.

When we had passed through the Alamo Mocho gap in the Kettleman Hills, Dan learned from a sheepherder that a couple of riders had gone north over the Kettleman plains. Dan took my horse and sent Pat Murray and me on their trail in the buggy, with instructions to follow them as far as necessary and, if the trail proved to be a false alarm, to go on to Huron and take our stock and buggy back to Visalia on the train.

The first night we ended up at the home of a sheepman who had a big adobe house with a big fireplace in it. We spent the night with him. The men we had been following proved to be two of his hired men who could have had no connection with the robbery. So we drove to Huron and rode home on the train.

When Grat Dalton was awaiting sentence after his trial in Visalia, word was received that he was to be liberated. Bob Dalton was going to get him out of the jail, and they were going to rob another train in the San Joaquin Valley. Bob Hockett and I were hired by Wells Fargo and Company to guard the jail until Grat was sentenced and sent to San Quentin. I had the day shift and Bob Hockett the night shift.

We had been on guard for several weeks when a number of things happened at the jail that did not seem to me to be good business. Bob Hockett didn't get in until late at night, sometimes after midnight. I had to do extra duty until he came in. I rigged up a cot in the jail office and used to lie there and sometimes sleep until Bob came. Then I'd go upstairs, where I had a bed, and go to sleep for the rest of the night. The result was that I was on duty about sixteen or eighteen hours a day.

As a result of this there was a good deal of tension between me and some of the jail force, including Williams, whom I didn't think was careful enough in handling the prisoners.

One night I heard a noise in the basement room below the office. This room was used for the storing of wood for use in the jail kitchen. On the outside wall was a window about thirty inches square through which wood was thrown into the room. It was guarded by a hinged grating of heavy bars held shut by a chain and a Yale lock. It sounded to me as though someone was trying to open that grating. My only idea was that the opening was being attempted from the outside.

In reaching for my shotgun, which I kept at the head of my cot, I knocked it down and it made a loud noise. I knew there would be no use in going below after that, so didn't investigate.

Next morning I examined the grating and saw that someone had been hammering and pecking at the lock. I told Bill Hall about it. I said, "Bill, there is something funny going on here." Bill was a man who at that time didn't drink to amount to anything, but attended to business, so I thought he would thoroughly investigate the happening. The jail was searched and nothing found, and I was razzed for being a scarecrow. So I decided to watch the outside of the place at night and catch in the act whoever was trying to open that grating from the outside.

Across the street to the east was the residence of County Recorder Denny. As soon as it got dark I took my shotgun and went across the street and hid in the shrubbery of Denny's yard and lay there all night watching the side of the jail. Toward morning it became very cold and there was some fog, and I took an awful cold. When I went on duty at the jail next morning I could scarcely talk.

That morning Grat Dalton called to me from the cells upstairs and said, "Say Jim, what's the matter? Where'd you get such a cold?" I told him I must have slept in a draft the night before. Grat answered, "Yes, it must have been pretty cold in the yard over there last night."

What Grat said worried me. How did he know I had been watching from across the street? I had told no one I was going to watch anywhere, and Grat couldn't see Denny's yard from his cell. It made me suspicious of the jailor. I decided to quit. I felt certain there was to be a jail break, or a deliberate liberation that I couldn't prevent, and I didn't want to be mixed up in it. So I told Bill Hall to send word to Kay that I couldn't stay.

The next time I came into the jail Grat called to me. He said, "Come up here Jim. I want to talk to you. How is Attorney Lambertson coming along with my appeal?" I told him I didn't know. Then he said, "I hear you are going to leave. It's too bad you're having trouble. Don't bother about that appeal. I don't care anything about it."

I knew from Grat's statements that he was confident he would escape. But I could do nothing about it. No one would listen to me. I was surprised, however, that Grat knew that I was going to leave. I decided that Williams had been keeping him informed of everything I did or said.

Kay was in San Francisco on business, but he came down to Visalia and put Perry Byrd in my place and I went back to my ranch at Tulare. I was replaced on Thursday, and Grat, Beck, and Smith escaped the following Sunday night.

The second morning after the escape I was walking along the north side of Tulare Street in Tulare when Cicero Zumwalt called across to me, asking me why I had given Dalton and the others the keys to the jail. I asked him what he meant and he explained that the story was being circulated that I had furnished the keys they had used to let themselves out of jail.

At just that moment Harry Charters came along on his way to take the little dinkey train to Visalia, so I went with him to the train at the S.P. right of way and we rode over to Visalia together. When we crossed the Courthouse grounds in Visalia we saw a crowd of men at the northeast corner, near the jail. Jailor Williams was talking to the group. We walked up to the crowd and listened.

Williams was telling them that I was the only outsider who had access to the keys and that undoubtedly I had let them out. I shouldered my way through the crowd and asked Williams how he figured it, when no one could possibly get out of the cages unless the long locking bar was thrown by means of the lever in his own office. Then Charters and I went on across the railroad to the jail. Bill Hall was on duty in the jail office.

I told Hall I wanted him to show me the cell where Grat had escaped. He said, "I'm busy here now, Jim, but there are the keys and you can go and look for yourself." Charters asked Hall if he could go, and Hall said that it was all right if I was willing. So we both went into the cells.

Until Grat had escaped, Bill Dalton had been confined upstairs in a cell used for crazy persons, but he had afterward been moved down stairs into the cell from which Grat had escaped. Bill was an agreeable, humorous sort of person and a great guitar player. He said to me, "Jim, the birds have flown."

When we went into the cell Bill got out his guitar, took a soap box as a seat and putting it against the bars of the corridor, sat down and began to play. He played a popular tune to which he had set words of his own and titled, "You'll Never Miss My Brother Till He's Gone." We laughed at this and went on with our investigations.

We worked around the cell until we came to Bill. He didn't move, so we could look at the rest of the bars, and appeared to be very busy. He kept strumming away at his guitar. Right then I knew he was trying to cover up the place where the prisoners had got out. I didn't bother Bill. I looked around and said, "Well, it sure is a conundrum to me." Then we went outside and I locked up again. Going to the outside, back of where Bill was sitting, I looked at the bars. I immediately saw the whole thing. The other prisoners had blackened a broom handle with soap and soot and put it in the place where a bar had been taken out. The bar had been used to pry open the grating in the wood room, and they had taken it with them rather than take the chance of going back to replace it.

Near the top of the broom handle, where they had pushed it in place, their fingers had removed some of the soot and I could see the grain of the wood. I said to Harry Charters, "Here is your hole." I kicked the broom handle, and it clattered across the cell in front of Bill Dalton.

One thing came out during our investigation that amused me. The jailor had insisted that the men could not have gone without keys. He had evidently been worried about the safety bar I had mentioned in the Court House yard. The parts that fastened each door were held by a large bolt, the nut of which had been secured by riveting the end of the bolt. Every one of these bolts showed fresh signs of having been sprung loose with a heavy wrench. After the truth was known about the escape, that was a perfect exposé of the clumsy attempt that was made to pin on me the responsibility for the escape.

Well, when Kay got back from capturing Beck, and after Riley Dean was captured, we learned the whole story of how the escape was engineered. It was very interesting to me.

The sawing was screened from the jailor by a large box in the corridor which the boys had been using for a table. They put a blanket over it and played cards on it. Each time they quit sawing, the cut was plugged with soap and soot. The prisoners sang and talked in order to drown out the noise of the sawing.

Dalton and Smith were out of their cell the night I heard the noise below me. The night I hid across the street in Denny's yard, Dalton and Smith were out of the cell and in the wood room looking over the lay of the land. They saw me go across the street and hide in the shrubbery. That was how Grat knew I had been over there. No one told him, as I suspicioned. After they saw me they went back to the cell and joined the other prisoners at the morning unlock.

Thursday and Friday nights they stayed in their cells. Then Saturday night they came out again and looked the situation over, but went back again and waited until Sunday night, when they decided to go. Beck had expected to be released from jail on Saturday. He was disappointed about being released, so he left the corridor Sunday night. He hid outside his cell under the large box they used as a table for card playing. He was a larger man than either Dalton or Smith, and, when he finally did decide to go, they had to pull him through the hole in the bars. The sawed ends of the bars cut deep gashes in his hips.

Billy Brewer, a trusty, had aided from the inside. He was an habitual drunk who spent most of his time in the Tulare County jail. Williams used to have him help lock up. Williams would yell to the prisoners, "Everybody inside." When he could see no one in the corridor he would throw the lever, barring the doors, and send Brewer in with the keys to lock the cells. Williams didn't know whether the men were in their cells or not. If he saw no one in the corridor he took it for granted that they were in the cells. On Sunday night all three men were hidden behind the box on which they had been playing cards. They put no dummies in their beds and didn't need any, as Williams never came in to lock the cells.

CHAPTER NINE

Captured: Bill Dalton, Dean, Beck, And Smith

The month of September, 1891, was an eventful one in the Joaquin. On September third a train was stopped at Ceres. The robbers were beaten off, but officer Len Harris was wounded. Sheriff Kay was called to the scene. Many of the officers who collected at the site, including Sheriff Cunningham of San Joaquin County, thought the job had been done by Tulare County men. Kay at first suspected Chris Evans and John Sontag, but was unable to trace their actions through an investigation at Modesto, where they were operating a livery stable. The railroad detectives and special officers clamored for the arrest of the Daltons.

"The Daltons did it", said Bill Smith.

In a few days Kay arrested Bill Dalton and Riley Dean, but they soon established a clear alibi, although Bill was held in the Tulare County Jail at Visalia for his part in the Alila affair.

Only a few days after Bill Dalton and Dean were cleared, Grat Dalton, together with Arvil Beck and W.B. Smith, escaped from the Tulare County Jail at Visalia. Then the chase was on after Grat, Beck, and Smith. In two of the most difficult and successful manhunts on Tulare County records, Sheriff Kay arrested both Beck and Smith and later was almost successful in arresting Grat Dalton.

Nothing could be more thrilling than the following firsthand story by Kay, describing the arrests of Bill Dalton and Dean, Beck, and Smith. It is a delightful contrast to these days of vote-conscious, swivel-chair sheriffs with two hundred and fifty dollar suits of clothes, manicured fingernails, two-way radios, TV's and multitudinous deputies in squad cars:

At Ceres we went over the clues that had been found. Most important of these were tracks where the horses had been tied, and a man's coat, found on the ground beside the horse tracks. The coat had apparently been dropped when the bandits left the scene. It had one cleaner's mark in it.

Cunningham said to me, "Gene, it looks to me to be another one on your Tulare County boys." He didn't know that I had already checked on the only two Tulare County boys we suspected.

But railroad detectives demanded the arrest of the Dalton boys. Bill Smith said, "There has been nobody holding up trains in the San Joaquin but those Daltons. When we get them all under cover the robberies will stop." Smith and Hume claimed to have dug up watertight evidence against two of the Daltons, including Bill. I said, "All right, Smith, you swear to the complaints and, if the boys are still in existence, I'll serve the warrants."

Back in my hotel in Modesto I studied the situation for some time. I knew that Grat Dalton was accounted for, and I felt certain that Bob and Emmett were in Indian Territory. Bill, Cole, and Lit were the only Daltons left to check. I telegraphed Witty to check Bill Dalton and to immediately let me know what he learned. I didn't hear from him until I arrived in Visalia.

Before I left Modesto I made another check-up on our Visalia boys, Chris Evans and John Sontag. They had been running a livery stable in Modesto and were still living there. All investigation I was able to make indicated that they had been at home during the Ceres attempt. As they were clearly innocent of the Alila job, I at that time was even becoming skeptical of their connection with either the Pixley or Goshen robberies. I didn't know what to think.

On my way back to Visalia I stopped off at Fresno and checked on Lit and Cole Dalton. They were accounted for satisfactorily, which left me with no definite clues whatever, only the possibility that something could be figured out of the lost coat. When I arrived at Visalia I was worn out from three days of hard work and no sleep, so I turned in. It was almost noon next day before I awakened. After I had dressed and eaten, I walked downtown to the only cleaning establishment in the place. I showed the cleaner the copy I had made of the mark in the coat, found at the scene of the Ceres attempt. He recognized it as one of his marks, but didn't have a record of his work farther back than a month. He thought he might be able to recognize the coat if he saw it.

Thinking I surely had the one clue needed to solve the robbery attempt, I rushed out and telegraphed Bill Smith to bring the coat immediately to Visalia. Bill got in that evening. We took the coat to the cleaner, feeling sure that he could recognize it and tell us who had brought it to him. He remembered the coat, but, try as he would, he couldn't remember who had brought it in. He did remember that some girl called for the coat when it was cleaned. We worked from time to time for three days with that cleaner, suspecting that he was trying to cover up the robbers, and I still suspect that he was, but we got nowhere with him. Our only clue was worthless.

While I was talking to the cleaner, George Witty completed his investigations about Bill Dalton. He was not around Estrella or Paso Robles, so telegrams from the coast assured me. Neither was Bill around Merced or Livingston, and he hadn't been there for some time. But Witty did have a clue from Billy Russell and it was worth running down. Up until a few days before the Ceres affair, and now again after dark, two strange men had been seen hanging around the Traver country. No one had seen them during the day and we had no description of them, except that one was tall and the other was shorter and heavier. It sounded like Bob and Emmett Dalton were back in the Joaquin again to make good Bob's threat to liberate Grat.

I decided that if the men were in the Traver country they would be at the old Cross Creek Station on the old Overland Stage road. This place had been abandoned for some time and had become a hangout for robbers, cattle thieves, and questionable characters in general.

Late in the afternoon I instructed Witty to bring my driving team and buggy to the jail. About four o'clock we started west toward Goshen and from there went across country on the old, little-used Overland Stage Road to Cross Creek Station. When we were about four hundred yards from the station we saw two objects cross the road from the old stage barn to the station. The setting sun, which we were directly facing, was casting its red rays into our eyes and made it impossible for us to definitely determine what the objects were. They might have been large dogs, or men, crouching as they ran. Just as they disappeared behind the trees beside the house I thought I saw them straighten up. I was then sure they were men.

As we drove behind some willow trees where the road curved, I gave Witty the lines and instructed him to drive past the house, passing close to the door, and then turn around and drive back. I climbed around the buggy top to the rear, with my revolver in my hand, balancing myself on the rear axle by holding to the top of the buggy.

The road passed within a few feet of the house. When the buggy came opposite the front door, I dropped to the ground and quietly stepped to the door, which was standing on a crack. I pushed the door a little farther open with my foot. . . . .

It will be necessary to leave Kay for awhile with his foot in the door. This writer has encountered more difficulty in obtaining an accurate account of the arrest of Bill Dalton and Riley Dean than of any other single incident concerning the Dalton Gang. Tulare, Visalia, and Fresno newspapers each published detailed accounts supposedly obtained directly from Sheriff Kay. But they did not check with several indisputable known facts.

As soon as Kay was found, the newspaper accounts were discussed with him. He soon explained the situation. The newspaper accounts were not obtained from either Kay or Witty, but from Jailor John Williams, by Harry Charters, Tulare newspaper editor, after the two officers had gone home and to bed. Williams was confused on several points and probably intended to protect the work of the officers by deliberately misleading Charters on others. Because the accounts were printed as though related by Kay, it was natural that confusion resulted.

Kay continued his statement concerning the arrests, dictated in 1936 as a correction to the contemporary news accounts mentioned above:

Maggie Rucker and a girl were sitting alone in the front room, calmly working on some dressmaking, as though they didn't know there was an officer nearer than Visalia. I quietly asked Rucker if there were any men about the place and she answered in a low tone that there were not. The very manner in which she answered made it plain to me that she was lying.

As soon as my question was answered I heard someone rush across the floor of an adjoining room. The door leading to this room was almost closed, but not latched. As I remember, the old cast-iron rim-latch had been broken and the door wouldn't latch. Through the crack between the door and the jamb I saw a man take up a position at a window.

Slipping quietly across the floor to the door, I pushed it a little farther open with the muzzle of my revolver. Standing directly in front of me and about six feet distant, I saw my friend, Bill Dalton. Bill was standing with his back almost squarely toward me. The forestock of his winchester was lying on the window sill. He was watching the horses and buggy I had just left, and was nervously working the lever of the rifle as if he was undecided whether to shoot or not.

We must keep Bill there at that window for a minute or two until I explain the situation, for this was actually the most ticklish arrest I ever made, and when I looked at Bill I said to myself, "Gene, here is where your non-shooting record is apt to end."

Bill Dalton was a short, heavy-set fellow with very dark hair, dark grey

CAPTURED: BILL DALTON, DEAN, BECK, AND SMITH

eyes, and a florid complexion. He was clever, and smart in a way. He could make a plausible talk any time, on anything, whether he knew anything about the subject or not. What was more important, Bill could make himself believed. When he began to talk, the alibis rained down like snowflakes. He could tell you what you knew to be an absolute piece of fiction and make you believe it. It might take him one minute or thirty, but he could do it, if given time. He was almost a hypnotist. Bill was an insatiate notoriety hunter. Notoriety of any kind was agreeable to him. He didn't care what happened, as long as people saw him and talked about him.

Bill was the best winchester shot of all the Dalton boys and was twice as fast as any of them. He could snap-shoot as accurately as Bob could shoot with deliberate aim. Grat and Cole, and Bill's neighbors had all told me this.

Now, when I looked at Bill Dalton through that crack in the doorway, it was plain as day to me that Bill had at last jumped the line and was beyond the law. He might have been one of the Ceres robbers. If not, he was undoubtedly out to rob something, somewhere, and was a dangerous man.

A man like Bill was actually far more dangerous than Bob or Grat. I realized that at the first word I said, in spite of anything I could do, Bill would swing that winchester around in a flash, point it at my middle and pull the trigger as he did it.

The buggy had gone about forty yards beyond the house. Witty would soon turn the team. My advantage would then be gone. I knew that my first word would touch off the fireworks. It flashed into my mind that if I called Bill by his name it might throw him off his guard. I pushed the door open with my elbow.

I intended to say, "Hello, Bill", but as I opened my mouth, I thought that wouldn't work, either. What I actually said was, "Bill! Hello!" It sounded strange to me as I said it, but it did the work.

Bill turned his head and then went through the quickest mental reaction I ever observed in anyone. He wanted the worst way to swing that winchester around, but he realized that it was too late. He saw that I had taken up the slack in the trigger of my revolver. Parrot-like, he yelled, "Kay! Hello!" in the funniest, startled imitation of my greeting, and dropped the butt of his rifle to the floor. It was really as funny as could be. We stood there laughing at each other for ten or fifteen seconds.

Witty had turned the team while this was happening and was tying it to a tree beside the house. I told Bill to lean his rifle against the wall and to back into the room.

That newspaper account about me grabbing Bill by the collar and jerking him away from his gun was pure fiction. Old John Williams was loading Charters up with a good story. If I had done that to Bill Dalton he would probably have overpowered me, for he was a powerful man and quick as lightning in his actions. He wasn't afraid of anything that walked.

After Bill backed away from his rifle I had him turn his back to me. Then I slapped his sides and hips to see if he carried a revolver. I had him walk ahead of me into the front room where the women were still sitting as quietly as mice. They had expected me to be killed, so Mag Rucker told me a few days later. It was then that I met Witty coming in.

I told Witty to go back into the other room and get Bill's rifle. I supposed the second man had escaped through the rear door. As George entered the adjoining room and picked up Bill's rifle he heard a noise. He couldn't tell just where it came from, but he was certain it came from that room, so he called to me to come in. I herded Bill in ahead of me.

As I entered, I thought to myself that it must have been Bill and Bob Dalton who had been seen around Traver, as Bob was several inches taller than Bill, and the robbers had been described as the usual tall man and short man.

I asked Bill where Bob was. He stated that Bob was not in the country. I told him, "Bill, I know better. Bob is in this house. You tell him to come here and to leave his gun behind. If he refuses to do this, Bill, he will never leave this place alive."

Bill again denied that there was anyone else about the place. He said, "I just stopped here alone to spend the night." I knew this was not true, as we had seen two objects, both of which I was then certain had been men.

Witty and I stood still and looked the place over closely. Maggie Rucker was in the midst of moving out of the house at the time and there was no furniture in the room where we were standing. Near one wall was a worn place in the carpet, caused by some square, uneven object beneath. I decided that this was a trap door and that Bob Dalton was hiding under the house. You must remember that we were expecting Bob to appear any day to liberate Grat. We had received word from the officers in Indian Territory that he was on his way to California for that purpose, and at that moment we had a guard around the jail to prevent just such a thing from happening.

Perhaps I was thinking of the trap door Bob had cut in the ceiling of the closet in Bill's house on the Estrella River. The floor was laid on sleepers directly on the ground and I felt sure that there was no way to get in or out of the place except through the trap door. I told Witty what I suspected. As I mentioned the place, I looked squarely at Bill and saw him change

CAPTURED: BILL DALTON, DEAN, BECK, AND SMITH

Bill, or Mason, Dalton (left) and Bob Dalton from very early photographs in Detective John B. Hume's private rogue's gallery notebook, now in the historical museum of Wells Fargo Bank and Union Trust Company, San Francisco, California.

Photos courtesy Wells Fargo Bank and Union Trust Company and now in Bear State Library.

countenance, but he quickly recovered his composure and said that there was nothing there.

It was now plain to me that, at last, Bob Dalton would soon be under arrest. I told Bill to pull up the carpet, which he did. Then I had him lift the trap door. From where I stood I could see the muzzle of a winchester rifle just below the level of the floor. Bill looked around as unconcerned as could be and said that there was no one there.

I called to Bob, telling him to come out, but there was no answer. It was sundown and I knew we had no time to lose. There were some old papers and packing material lying on the floor. I told Witty to light these and throw them in the hole. While Witty was preparing to do this, the winchester rifle was slowly slid out on the floor and out crawled, not Bob Dalton, but Riley Dean, a hanger-on of the Visalia and Traver Saloons. It was immediately plain to us that when I first spoke to Maggie Rucker Bill had been busy hiding Dean or he would have heard me and this would then have been a different story.

We made a search around the house, but found no one outside. The story that we discovered Dean in a dugout outside is wrong. His capture was made as I have described. However, at the time, I did think that Bob Dalton had escaped us by hiding under the hay in the barn or among the willows along Cross Creek. I later learned that I had been mistaken in this.

Within a few days Dean was able to prove an alibi, so he was turned loose and we didn't see him again until after the escape of Grat Dalton from the jail in Visalia.

There has been a lot of confusion about why Bill Dalton was in jail when Grat escaped. It was really because after his arrest for the Ceres job his former bondsmen withdrew. From the circumstances under which Bill was arrested at Cross Creek it was plain to everyone that Bill had been preparing either to liberate Grat, or to hold up a train. It was particularly plain to Bill's bondsmen that he was a poor risk.

It was John B. Hume, Wells Fargo officer, who persuaded Bill's bondsmen to withdraw and leave him in jail, where he wouldn't require so much watching. Hume first talked with Bill's bondsman, Adolph A. Zirker, a Merced merchant, who immediately withdrew. The other bondsmen soon fell in line. So poor Bill had to languish in the jail at Visalia until after his own trial for the Alila job.

In the same cell with Grat Dalton were Arvil Beck and W.B. Smith. Smith was being held for the robbery of a box car in the railroad yards at Tulare, and Beck for stealing a horse at Traver. Beck had fled to the home of his parents near Cleveland, Washington, after the horse affair took place. He was arrested there and extradited. My deputy, Billy Russell, brought Beck back, arriving at the jail in Visalia in September of 1891. In the latter part of September Beck had his hearing before Justice Boone at Traver and was held to answer, bail being set at one thousand dollars. He couldn't secure bondsmen, so was returned to jail, escaping the next night.

My first act in determining the whereabouts of any of the three escaped prisoners was to arrest Arvil Beck. I took the train to Portland and from there went by boat up the Columbia river to the landing nearest Cleveland. The place was just a little hamlet a few miles north of the Columbia River. Beck's parents lived in the country.

Taking lodgings in Cleveland, I laid my plans to surprise Beck. Going to the livery stable, I hired a livery man to drive me through the country rabbit hunting, telling him that I was in the locality for my health and wanted to hunt rabbits for pastime. He told me I could go through the country hunting without the permission of the land owners, but I said I was not willing to do this and wanted him along to vouch for me.

By this method I got to know the people in the locality. Finally the liveryman pointed out the Beck place. Next morning I drove the team myself, leaving Cleveland early in the morning and driving to within a half mile of the Beck home. From that point, by means of a good pair of field glasses, I watched the place. I found that young Beck was at home and that in the morning at five o'clock he made a habit of going to the corral and barn to milk the cow. During this time he wore two six-shooters outside his coat and seemed to be very much on the alert, approaching the barn by a detour and being suspicious of any unusual happenings.

There was a high shock of corn within a small fence just a few feet from where the cow was tied. While the cow was being milked, the calf was tied to a post not three feet from this corn. After he finished milking, Beck untied the calf and turned it loose with the cow. I planned to conceal myself in the shock of corn before Beck appeared in the morning. This was easily done.

But this morning proved to be the first of winter. An extremely cold and icy snow and sleet storm set in. Probably that was the reason that Beck did not come to do the milking until almost an hour later than usual. During this entire time I stood hidden in the corn with my revolver drawn, ready to surprise Beck at the moment he stooped over to untie the calf.

All of my plans almost came to nothing because a dog followed Beck from the house to the corral. The dog scented me and began to bay at me. This scared the cow and made Beck angry. He threw a rock at the dog. It missed the dog at least six feet, and almost hit me on the head. The dog ran to the house, barking all the way, but it never did occur to Beck to see what he was barking at.

When Beck chased the dog away I was almost frozen. My gun was so cold I was actually afraid it would freeze to my hand. By the time Beck was halfway through milking, I knew that if I waited until he came to the fence in front of me and only three feet distant, I would never be able to hold the gun, or to disarm him.

I decided that something had to be done and done immediately. As I started to step from the corn shock it occurred to me that the cow was scary and would jump or kick at the slightest movement. I jumped out and yelled. The cow kicked Beck over backward into the slop of the corral and I had him covered before he could draw either gun. Rising at my orders, with his hands above his head, Beck approached me at the fence. I reached through with my left hand and unbuckled his belt, allowing the guns to fall to the ground. Then I forced Beck to back away several feet, while I picked up the guns and buckled them around my own waist under my coat.

Forcing Beck to walk ahead of me to the house, I had him knock on the door. At first no one answered. Then I had him knock again. A man's voice called out, "Come on in. What is the matter with you?" Young Beck answered, "I can't come in. Come and open the door." Immediately the father, an elderly and kindly old minister, opened the door. The son explained that I was the Sheriff of Tulare County, in California, and that I had just arrested him.

We were invited in to breakfast. Beck's mother was still in bed, and when she heard that her son was under arrest, she began to scream and carry on at great length. Her husband quieted her, telling her that this was the best thing that could have happened. The mother arose and prepared breakfast.

During this time the father read a lecture to his son, who had apparently explained to them something of his trouble in Tulare County, but had refused to return and make amends for his horse stealing. The father said, "Now, my son, if you will do so, you have an opportunity to learn the lesson of your life. We have tried to have you do right, but you have insisted upon wearing those guns and have told what you would do when anyone tried to arrest you. Where are the guns? I do not see them any more, but I do see this officer, who is a very inoffensive and kindly looking man, driving you around and telling you what to do, and you seem to be doing it."

Continuing, Mr. Beck said, "This man has you in his power and from now on the law is going to tell you what to do. You have finished your breakfast now. I will give you some blankets to keep you warm while you drive to Cleveland. Go with this man and take your medicine, and, when you are through, come back, and we will welcome you."

I had Mr. Beck go out and bring in my livery team, and young Beck and I started to Cleveland through a blinding snow-storm. During the trip I had a heart to heart talk with Beck and finally succeeded in inducing him to tell me the straight story of all of his misdeeds. I became assured in my own mind that he was repentant of it all.

We arrived at Cleveland at night and put up at the hotel. My guns, as well as those belonging to Beck, I checked with the hotel clerk and we went upstairs to bed. Occupying the same bed with Beck, I immediately went to sleep with the certain feeling that he was chained to me by a hand stronger than handcuffs.

When I awakened in the morning Beck was already awake and looking at the ceiling. We both lay in silence for a while. Finally I reached to the chair beside my bed and took a five dollar bill from my trousers pocket. Handing this to Beck, I gave him these instructions. "Take this money. Go down to the

CAPTURED: BILL DALTON, DEAN, BECK, AND SMITH 157

clerk and pay our bill and have the liveryman drive you home. When you get there tell your father that I sent you and have placed you in his care and that he is to report to me by letter once a month as to how you are getting along."

This was the beginning of a correspondence which continued for more than fifteen years and was one of the most satisfactory experiences of my life. I was able to accomplish for that boy what I was certain I could have done for Grattan Dalton, because I knew he had the right kind of stuff in him.

Beck gave me a great deal of information about the Daltons, also the clue I wanted about Smith, that he had planned to go to relatives in Tulare. He also told me all the details of the escape from the Tulare County Jail.

Beck had separated from Dalton and Smith at Goshen, taking a train north. The others planned to go to the home of Joe Middleton near Hanford. The only other information of any value about either Dalton or Smith was that Dalton expected Middleton to hide him and that Smith had relatives in Tulare who were to hide him. Beck didn't know the name of Smith's Tulare relatives.

The finding of the stolen buggy and run-down team along the old Hanford road west of Tulare fitted into the story told by Beck. Grat and Smith had undoubtedly continued to Middleton's, where Grat dropped out and Smith continued to Tulare with the team.

In a few days I located the ranch where Smith had hidden and learned that only a few days before he had left there on a grey horse, going north, probably to a point north of Sacramento. A grey horse sounded like easy trailing, so I took my team and buggy and started after him. I picked up the trail a short distance east of Sanger and followed it to the San Joaquin River. Smith had skirted the east side of the San Joaquin Valley and, traveling day and night, I followed him to Minturn and on to Merced.

At Merced I was entirely exhausted, so I secured the aid of Deputy Sheriff Ed Stockird, who drove while I slept, and we followed the scent. It took some time to pick up the trail out of Merced. We could get no trace of a grey saddle horse and it was some time before we found tracks and received descriptions that revealed to us that Smith had shifted from horseback to a cart and horse. We followed the tracks of the cart to Snelling, where we found that Smith had made a camp. We were about twenty-four hours behind Smith at Snelling, but were gaining on him. We traced the horse and cart to Farmington, in San Joaquin County, and immediately found a boy who had not only seen the horse and cart, but could give a good description of Smith, which reassured us that we were on the right trail.

From Farmington we traced the horse and cart to Bellota, where Smith had inquired for the ranch of a man named Vance. Crowding our team all they could stand, we drove to the Vance ranch. Vance told us he had known Smith for a number of years and had hired him to cut wood on another ranch of his, six miles away. It was about nine o'clock at night when we talked to Vance. Both of us were exhausted and so was our team. But I knew it would never do to wait a minute, or Vance would tip Smith off.

I nudged Stockird in the ribs with my elbow and said to Vance, "My partner is unable to travel any further. You put him up for the night and I will drive on and see Mr. Smith." As Stockird climbed out of the buggy I whispered to him, "Watch Vance or he'll get word to Smith ahead of me."

I pushed my team on to the wood camp as fast as they could travel. I almost broke them down, but I knew our hard driving was about over and that they could take it easy from there on. Smith and another man were camped in a tent set over an old header bed. It was about ten P.M. but there was a lantern burning inside the tent. Smith's companion came to the door when he heard me drive up. I motioned him outside and asked him his name. He told me he was a woodchopper and that his name was McCarty.

Under questioning, McCarty told me there was a man inside who had arrived only a few hours before to help him cut wood. Going in ahead of McCarty, I found Smith asleep in bed, a loaded shotgun standing at the foot of the bed, and a loaded revolver on the bed within six inches of his hand.

I was worn out from travel and loss of sleep after having been on the go day and night for five days. Smith looked so comfortable I felt like crawling in beside him and going to sleep, too. But I picked up the guns and awakened him.

Smith didn't know me. I was really not surprised. I would probably have not known myself if I had looked in a mirror. My clothing had been slept in every night since I left Visalia. I had almost a week of beard on my face, and I was about as dirty and ragged as any hobo who ever beat his way over the Southern Pacific. Until he saw my watch charm, Smith seemed likely to give me trouble. Then he said, "You are Sheriff Kay, of Visalia, aren't you?" I assured Smith that I was no one else and he hadn't another word to say.

Putting a handcuff on one of Smith's wrists, I snapped the other to the bed and ordered him to dress. He did so without making a false move.

In searching Smith's effects, I found a mask made of black cloth with holes for eyes, mouth, and nose. We hadn't heard of his robbing anyone on the way from Tulare to Bellota, but he was undoubtedly planning something of the kind.

McCarty hitched Smith's horse to the cart and I led him behind my buggy, driving back to the Vance ranch. There I picked up Stockird and we started to

Stockton, where we arrived about four o'clock next morning. We lodged Smith in the San Joaquin County Jail, went to a hotel, bathed, shaved, and slept the clock around. I have never been any more tired in my life than I was when we got into Stockton.

We hired a man to drive my buggy team and lead the horse and cart to Visalia. I brought Smith back on the train, Stockird dropping off at Merced.

Smith claimed that no outside help was given when Grat, Beck, and he escaped; that the bar was cut through with an ordinary kitchen case knife which had been nicked to form a saw. I knew this portion of Smith's story to be untrue, for Beck had told me differently and we had already found pieces of a file and hacksaw blade in the prisoner's toilet. I told Smith about this and showed him that he was headed for a long prison term unless he came clean. We were on the train south of Fresno at the time. Smith looked out the car window at the Sierra skyline a long time and then promised to tell me the truth about everything.

According to Smith's "true story", the opening was made several days before the escape was effected and he and Dalton had the run of the corridors, the kitchen, and basement for several nights. The last night they dug a hole in the brickwork of the outer wall, intending to go down the ladder that had been placed for them, but found heavy iron bars imbedded in the wall and couldn't get between them.

On the night of the escape, Beck, Smith, and Dalton were all in the corridor, hiding behind the box used for a card table. The trusty was in with them and locked their cell by stepping over their bodies. Beck was the largest man of the three and when it finally came time for him to squeeze through the hole in the outer corridor wall, his hips were deeply cut on the sharp ends of the sawed bar. He was still suffering from these wounds when I arrested him at his home in Washington.

Lerdo Station as it appeared in Dalton Gang Days. Except for the power poles, this is a typical scene on the combined Southern Pacific and Santa Fe. This site was little changed until about 1930.
 Photo courtesy Paul Robinson and now in Bear State Library.

CHAPTER TEN

Dalton Mountain Battle

It was the opinion of most California peace officers that Grat Dalton left California within a week after he escaped from the Tulare County Jail at Visalia. For the second time, Sheriff Kay disagreed with all of them. During the weeks which went by while Kay was recapturing Beck and Smith, no trace was obtained of Grat in Indian Territory, where Bob and Emmett were busy robbing trains.

Beck knew little of Dalton's plans at the time of the escape. In fact, Beck had not decided to leave the cell until the last afternoon, when he found he could not get bondsmen. The hole in the bars hadn't been cut with the idea that he would go, and it finally took the combined efforts of Dalton and Smith to pull him between the bars, gouging deep cuts in his hips, as described by Kay.

Kay did not expect that Grat had given out any of his plans, even to Smith, and was surprised to learn from Smith that before he left Grat and Middleton they told him what they expected to do and invited him to join them.

From the following account of the trailing of Grat Dalton to his hideout on what is now known as Dalton Mountain, on Kings River, related by Sheriff Kay shortly before his death, it will be seen that Smith probably misled Kay on only one point; that Middleton was to take Grat west to the Coast Range of mountains, instead of east to the Sierra. However, this may not have been deception on the part of Smith, as the original plans may have been changed:

It took me three days to get out of Smith what I needed to know about Middleton and Dalton. But he finally talked freely and told me that Middleton had planned to take Dalton to the Coast Range Mountains and that he could be followed to Dalton's camp when he carried in supplies. This all sounded very reasonable to me, as Grat knew the Coast Range country quite well, and it seemed to me that he would hide out where he was best acquainted.

At that time Kings County was a part of Tulare County. It wasn't separated from Tulare County until 1893. Frank Griffith was my deputy at Hanford, so I went over and put him on the job. Frank set a man to watching Middleton's place day and night. One night I got a telegram urging me to come over, that Middleton had purchased a large order of groceries and ammunition and was making preparations to travel. I hurried over and arrived soon after he had left the place, headed east. We were unable to see in the darkness and soon lost him. We thought he had gone east in an effort to throw any trailers off his track. We hurried back and guarded the roads to the west until after midnight, but without seeing Middleton again.

Griffith continued to have Middleton's place watched and found that he didn't return for almost a week. It was almost another month before Middleton again left, after stocking up in Hanford with enough groceries to last him three months. Griffith followed him to Sanger, where he spent the following day. The second night Griffith lost Middleton at a point about three miles east of Sanger. Next day he learned that Middleton had cut a barbed wire fence and had gone across fields to another road. He evidently found he was being followed. Griffith was unable to track Middleton, so he hurried to Visalia and reported to me.

It was plain that we had to move very soon, or Grat would escape us. The Sanger back country was in Fresno county, so I telegraphed Sheriff Hensley and he began an investigation from Fresno. Griffith hurried to Hanford and immediately telegraphed me that Middleton was already at home. Witty and I drove to Hanford at once, picked up Griffith, and we all three went out to Middleton's place.

We didn't waste a moment. We told Middleton we knew he was harboring and supplying Dalton and that he was headed straight for San Quentin Prison. He could either tell us what he knew about Dalton's hideout or we would slap him in jail at Visalia.

Middleton had a bad record and was surely in a quandary. He had just been threatened by Dalton for not getting him out of the country sooner and was badly frightened before we arrived. We talked with him more than four hours. He insisted that we could never find the place alone without being killed; that it was a natural fortress on the side of a steep, heavily wooded, rocky mountain and that Riley Dean was with Dalton. They guarded the trails during the day and had a watch dog to keep a lookout during the night. We thought that Middleton was trying to scare us out, but when we finally found Dalton's hideout we knew he had been telling the truth. We could never have located the camp in a week, even with Middleton's most accurate description.

Finally I promised Middleton secrecy, and a horse and riding rig if he would guide us to within a half mile of Dalton's camp. He agreed to this, more because he had been abused by Dalton for not bringing horses on his last trip in, and was afraid to have Dalton loose any more, than for any other reason. We didn't let Middleton out of our sight. We took him to Visalia with us and I telegraphed Sheriff Hensley that we planned an immediate assault on the Dalton camp.

I started a posse horseback for Centerville on the Kings River and drove to Fresno with my buggy team to pick up Hensley. Hensley sent one of his deputies with two saddle horses toward Centerville and rode with me in my buggy. About noon, Hensley and I met the two posses in the old hotel at Centerville. It was the twenty-third day of December, 1891, and one of the coldest days I ever experienced in the San Joaquin Valley. It had been raining, and, while we were on the road, the rain turned into sleet. Our buggy and harness were actually covered with ice.

We stopped at Centerville only long enough to get our combined posse into motion. We then proceeded to the Elwood ranch on Kings river. Middleton was with us, already mounted on the horse that was to be his as soon as he had led us to within a half mile of Dalton's camp. We avoided the Elwood house and secreted our posse in the timber at the foot of what now is known as Dalton Mountain. Middleton pointed out to us the exact location of the camp, turned his horse and left. I have never seen him since that moment.

Hensley and I decided to do some exploring that day, although it was then late in the afternoon. We wanted to plan an approach and surround the camp. I was wearing a long, heavy bearskin overcoat. In order to climb better, I took it off and went up the mountain without it. Even with the exercise of climbing, I was blue with cold and almost helpless when we returned. But we accomplished our purpose. We found all of Middleton's descriptions to be accurate and planned to return before daylight next morning.

There has been considerable disagreement about who was in my posse and who was not. Only a few months ago I heard it stated that Perry Byrd was not with us. I distinctly remember that he *was* with us, and that he did as much running up and down Dalton Mountain as did the rest of us. As I recollect at this late date, Hensley and Ed McCardle were the only officers who came direct from Fresno. Jim Mead, a Fresno man and Southern Pacific railroad detective and special officer, was in Visalia and went with my men to Centerville, returning with them to Visalia in order to question Riley Dean. Besides the four mentioned, there were George Witty, Bob Hockett, Cal Burland, Fred Hall, Jim Ford, and Bill Hall. Fred and Bill Hall were not related, although both lived at Visalia for a number of years, and both died in Bakersfield.

We drove to the home of Judson Elwood at the foot of the mountain. The Elwoods had no facilities for housing so many men, but Jud put our horses in his barn and fed them. Mrs. Elwood prepared a fine meal for us and we bedded down as best we could on the floor of the living room in front of a large fireplace, which was roaring with a fine oak fire. In my bearskin overcoat I kept warm during the night and was as comfortable as could be. But the bare floor was a hard, cold bed for most of the men. They kept rolling about looking for a warm, soft spot in the boards. I did what I could to keep up their spirits.

Amusement was scarce in Dalton days. We provided most of our fun. We made use of anything that could be turned into something funny, however tragic it was. As we lay on the floor there in the Elwood home, I told the posse of a funny thing that had happened a few days before. I remember this portion of our trip better than anything else that happened. Maybe I ought to tell this story. I believe it should be a part of the history of the battle of Dalton Mountain.

I took my revolver and an accomplice, went into R.E. Hyde's bank in Visalia, robbed the place of three thousand dollars in gold, walked out, put it in my own safe, and next day walked back into the bank and deposited it in my own name with no questions asked. At least that is the way the story was told around Visalia as long as I was there.

Tulare County had elected a County Tax Collector and the Tulare County Supervisors had purchased a new vault and installed it in the Court House. Previous to 1890 county funds had been collected by the Sheriff and Tax Collector and deposited in the bank of R.E. Hyde. About the first of October, 1891, I had to transfer the county funds, seventy-odd thousand dollars, all in gold coin, from Hyde's bank to the new tax collector, Duke Lipscomb, for placement in the new vault.

R.E. Hyde was a fine pioneer banker, but with no more humor in him than a redwood fence post. Once, when a touring troupe of comedians arrived in Visalia at the depot about a block from Hyde's bank, we told them that the bank was a hotel. They piled inside with all their baggage and noise and, before they found they were in the lobby of a bank, tried to register. Hyde's dignity was badly damaged and he tried to have them arrested for disturbing the peace. The comedians cracked jokes about Hyde all through their stand at Visalia.

Hyde was noted for his hair-splitting concerning money. He had, among other rules, an inflexible law about handling money at the cashier's window. All mistakes had to be corrected before you picked up your money. Briefly, R.E.'s rule was "no mistakes corrected after you leave the window." And he had never been known to break that rule.

Billy Russell helped me transfer the money, which was in canvas bags, $3,000 to the bag, Hyde counting out the contents to Billy. Billy put the money back in the bag and tied it, while Hyde opened another. I acted as guard. By noon we hadn't transferred a third of the money. We hadn't found a single variance from the three thousand dollars in any of the bags, so, after dinner, I told Hyde we would take his bag count. By closing time the money had all been carried across the Court House lawn to the new vault. I stood around as guard while Duke put his accounts in order, rendered me a receipt and locked the vault.

When Duke had finished, a bag of gold remained on his counter. I said to him, "Duke, lock up the rest of your money so I can go home." Duke assured me that all of *his* money *was* locked up. Now, Duke was the most noted accountant and mathematician in Tulare County. If he had said that twelve dozen was a hundred-and-sixty I wouldn't have questioned him for a second. I would have known that all other mathematicians had been wrong, back to the beginning of time.

I said, "Well, it isn't mine."

"Now", said Duke, "If it isn't yours and it isn't mine, it shouldn't take you very long to figure whose it is."

There was only one answer. It belonged to R.E. Hyde. He had turned over to me $3,000 too much. We both thought of that window rule of Hyde's.

Between us we decided to have some fun with Hyde. I took the bag of gold on my arm, threw my coat over it, carried it to the jail and locked it in my safe. Next morning, as soon as the bank opened, I sent Billy Russell over to get change for a twenty dollar piece. Every day or so we had been getting change, so this was nothing unusual. Billy had the gold piece in his hand, folded in a piece of paper.

Hyde thought Billy had a note from me. When he was nervous, Hyde had a habit of rubbing his hands together like he was dry-washing them. Billy talked for about ten minutes about one thing and another, while Hyde washed his hands. Then he took out the twenty and asked for change. Billy told me he could see Hyde shrink about three inches in disappointment. Next I sent Witty, just before noon, and he was gone an hour; Hyde forgetting dinner and washing his hands all the time. When he came back Witty told me, "Gene, I think that fellow is going to have heart failure unless you get that money deal settled pretty soon."

After dinner I went to the bank with the bag of gold. When Hyde saw me come in I thought he was going to wash all the skin off his hands. He bowed and scraped and said, "Good afternoon, Mr. Kay, I mean *Sheriff* Kay. You're surely looking fine this afternoon." You would have thought I was Little Red Riding Hood.

I walked up to the window, put the bag of money on the counter, leaned against the wicket and began talking about the first thing I could think of. I talked for fifteen minutes.

In those days customers never wrote their own deposit slips. Ordinarily Hyde would have taken a slip, emptied the bag, counted the money and written me a deposit slip. But he just stood there washing his hands and saying, "Yes sir, Sheriff Kay" and "No sir, Sheriff Kay," with less enthusiasm all the time, until at last he said to me, "You wanted to deposit this, Sheriff Kay?" I answered, "Yes," and went on talking.

It took at least ten minutes for Hyde to make out that deposit slip. First he wrote across the top of it, *Eugene W. Kay*. Then he untied the bag, fingers trembling like I was Grat Dalton holding a revolver in his face. He counted out the money, wrote the total, *three thousand dollars, gold coin*, on the slip, put the bag of gold behind the wicket, handed me the slip and leaned forward with his elbows on the counter, hands clasped. His coat looked like an empty grain sack.

I folded the slip without looking at it and twisted it around in my hands while I continued talking. Hyde had lost all interest in anything I had to say. Finally I unfolded the slip, read it and said, "Mr. Hyde, you have made a mistake."

Hyde actually grabbed the slip from my hands. He thought to himself, "Good Lord, another mistake!" He jerked the slip open, almost tearing it in two.

"Why, Sheriff Kay, there is no mistake here."

"Yes, there is," I answered, laughing. "I expected to deposit that money in your name."

Hyde was himself again. He said, "Now, Mr. Kay, I knew all the time you would never take that money." But Hyde misstated himself. He had *hoped* all the time I wouldn't take it.

Most of the posse knew Hyde and they laughed an hour at that story.

[Then Kay got back to his main narrative.]

We all arose about three o'clock in the morning and started afoot up the side of one of the roughest, steepest mountains in the Sierra. I remember that some of the men were nervous, and, in order to relieve the tension, several of us began to joke. Bill Hall was behind me about fifty yards and remarked that, in my coat, I looked and climbed like an overgrown brown bear. I then told everyone to remember that we were not on a bear hunt and not to shoot anything that looked like a bear.

We would climb a short distance and then stop and puff. It was bitter cold. It had been impossible for some of the men to keep warm during the night and, in spite of the violent exercise, they were almost paralyzed with the cold.

The plan was to surround the camp. Our party was split. Hensley took one group and I took the other. Hensley went to one side of the camp, and I took a rock ledge that Middleton had told us would permit us to approach to within a few feet of the camp, which would be directly below us. We expected to find the two men in camp. We knew we had to work very quietly in order to surprise both them and the dog.

It had broken full daylight and the men were proceeding according to schedule, when we heard voices. We figured that we were within a hundred yards of the camp. The rock ledge along which we were traveling overhung, and left below us a corridor of protection that we could not reach with our guns.

We were then about a mile from Elwood's and it was about nine o'clock. George Witty and Ed McCardle, who were about a hundred yards above me, and Fred Hall and Bob Hockett, who were the same distance below me, discovered the smoke of the camp at about the same time. Witty motioned for us to come up, and by the time we got to them, Dalton and Dean were right where we had been before we started to climb up to Witty. If we had remained where we were at first they would have walked right into our arms. Hall and Hockett were within forty feet of them at one time, but couldn't see them because of brush and rocks.

We stepped to the edge of the rock ledge, stopped, and watched through the brush. There, inside of fifty yards, Dalton and Dean had stopped and were discussing a hunt they were planning, to provide fresh pork for their Christmas bill-of-fare, pork from Jud Elwood's herd of hogs that was feeding on acorns at the foot of the mountain.

A deputy stood on each side of me, so close that I could take them by the arms. Each was armed with a ten gauge, double barreled shotgun, loaded with large buckshot, at that range one of the most deadly weapons in existence, then or since. Both deputies raised their guns and leveled them at Dalton. The deputy on my left wanted to fire. I put my hand on the barrel of his gun and forced it down. With my revolver I forced down the other gun. I saw that it would be necessary to shoot Grat Dalton dead in order to capture him where he then stood. We couldn't see Hall and Hockett and there was also danger of shooting them. Besides, at the first sound of any kind, both Dalton and Dean would have jumped out of sight under the rock ledge below us.

As Dalton and Dean started on I motioned my men to move back from the ledge and hurry ahead of them. My plan was to surround them below, where they wouldn't have cover. But they traveled too fast for us and we came in behind them. Knowing they would return to camp as soon as their hunt was over, I gathered the two parties and planned a reception for the bandits.

We planted men all about the approaches to the place. I sent Hensley, McCardle, and Perry Byrd directly west, diagonally across the mountain. Fred Hall, Witty, Hockett, and I followed the trail clear to the foot of the mountain, about a mile and a half away. We had no opportunity to intercept Dalton or Dean, so began to climb back toward the camp. From the camp Hensley and McCardle saw Dalton and Dean heading up the mountain, so they sent Perry Byrd to hurry us up.

It was about eleven-thirty when I received the signal from Perry Byrd that both of the men were returning. We climbed as fast as we could and were completely exhausted when, in about twenty minutes, I heard two rifle shots. Just as the shots were fired, Hensley appeared at my elbow with Riley Dean, already captured. Hensley asked me for my handcuffs. We handcuffed Dean and ran across the gulch in the direction from which the sound of the shots had come.

Of course the world knows that Grat Dalton escaped us, but few people know how it was accomplished. So many garbled accounts of this escape have been given to the world that I want to give the reader in a few words an accurate statement of what I learned within two minutes after the escape.

Hensley and McCardle were guarding a trail which led up the summit of a small, narrow ridge. Dean was walking some distance, probably a hundred yards, ahead of Dalton. He was allowed to approach to within twenty feet of the officers. Hensley stepped from behind a rock and motioned to Dean to put his gun down, which he did. Hensley had no handcuffs with him, so he started to me with Dean so he could secure him with my handcuffs before Dalton appeared.

In about one minute Dalton appeared over the same trail that Dean had used. McCardle was alone. He watched from behind an oak tree and saw the upper part of Dalton's body appear. He was about forty feet away. In another fifteen feet he would be in full view. McCardle had his gun leveled and his mouth open to command a halt, when the dog, which was ahead of Grat, saw him and barked.

McCardle and Grat fired almost together. Grat threw himself behind the ridge and ran down the mountain. The bullet from his rifle struck the tree within six inches of McCardle's face and filled his eyes with powdered bark and stung his face as badly as though he had received a charge of birdshot.

I have heard McCardle criticized for standing behind the tree. If he had been in sight he would never have seen more than Dalton's head. Grat was a brave man, but even he took cover in the fraction of a second, just as he would have done had we commanded him to halt when we first saw him that morning. He charged down the mountainside, tearing a path through the brush that would have done credit to a thousand pound bear, commandeered a horse from Elwood's plow team, and rode over a faraway ridge, shooting his revolver into the air.

Since we have been talking about these old days, I have read in Emmett Dalton's book his description of Grat's encounter with our posse. Certainly all of his information came from Grat. I believe that Grat must have told him the truth. But Emmett's account has almost no truth in it. He states that six men, the sheriff and his posse, strode toward Grat's tent with leveled rifles and riddled the canvas with a volley.

None of us saw Grat's camp. We saw no tent. There was no firing until after Grat fired. The only other firing done at Grat was as some of the posse caught glimpses of him charging through the brush half a mile or more away.

Emmett also stated that Middleton lived in the camp with Grat, which is not true. He made no mention of Riley Dean.

Well, the posses went back to Visalia and Fresno, hungry, worn out, and without Grat Dalton. We had eaten but three meals since leaving Visalia, and, in addition, I had to suffer the most severe criticism for not allowing both Dalton and Dean to be shot down in cold blood.

Grat Dalton had good stuff in him, but was entirely under the influence of Bob. I always felt I could believe Grat. He was one of those men who hesitated to tell you anything unless he told you the truth. His big failing was whisky. He was a heavy drinker, and, when drinking, always quarreled and generally fought.

Bob was a light-haired, sandy-bearded, grey-eyed fellow, at least six feet tall. I remember having seen him on the streets of Tulare long before they got into difficulty, and I held at least two conversations with him. We had a good photograph of Bob as an exhibit at the trial of Grat. It was easy to see the resemblance between the photo and the man I had known. I believe that Bob was the tallest of all the Dalton boys I knew. He was also a heavy drinker and also very quarrelsome. Both Bob and Grat were known throughout the length of the San Joaquin Valley for their poker games and fist fights.

At Grat's trial all of the train crew were certain that Grat didn't take part in the robbery. He could not be mistaken for either of the other boys. He was about five feet nine or ten inches tall and very strong. He was not fat, but was heavy limbed. His shoulders were rounded and carried slightly forward and his arms hung forward of his body in an aggressive position. He also had an unmistakable gruff voice. Maybe I have overestimated Grat, but I liked him and I am still glad I didn't allow him to be shot down in cold blood at Dalton Mountain. . . . .

> The brush with Grat Dalton at the Elwood ranch marked the end of the active career of the Dalton Gang in California. Only Bill Dalton's trial remained to be settled, and he was freed by a jury October 15, 1891, after fifteen minutes deliberation.
>
> The Elwood affair caused intense bitterness among the members of both Hensley's and Kay's posses. Many impossible stories have been told and some preserved in print about what happened that day on the side of Dalton Mountain. Emmett Dalton's book misrepresented almost the entire affair. This has been proved by various members of the posses; by Kay, Fred Hall, and Ed McCardle. McCardle prepared a detailed account of the entire expedition. Leonard Elwood, son of the man who owned the ranch where the encounter took place, was seven years of age at that time and saw Dalton leave the place. He is also the only known living person who visited the Dalton camp before it was disturbed. Leonard dictated a detailed account of the visit of the posses and of Grat's ride on the grey plow-horse.
>
> Fred Hall was in Kay's posse. His account agrees in every detail with that given by Kay, whose story already has been told.
>
> Here is what Ed McCardle wrote about the Elwood ranch battle.

On the night of December 22, 1891, I was preparing for bed in the Treasurer's Office in the Fresno County Court House, when George Moore came to me and said, "I am going to take your place tonight, Ed; John [Hensley] wants to see you down in the sheriff's office."

It was just after several days of big collections at the Treasurer's office, and one of us unmarried deputies had been sleeping in the office during such times, as large amounts of money were held in the treasurer's vault.

I went down to Sheriff John Hensley's office and there met Sheriff Eugene W. Kay and Hensley. Kay had just got in from Visalia.

Hensley said, "Ed, go down to my barn and get your saddle horse and mine and take them to Centerville. You will meet Sheriff Kay's posse there. Wait there with them until Sheriff Kay and I get there with his buggy and team." I started out horseback, leading Hensley's horse. Kay and Hensley followed later in the buggy.

About the time I left Fresno it began to rain. It was as cold as I ever knew it to rain. Within a few hours it began to sleet, and kept it up every step of the way to Centerville. How I suffered! I was wet to the skin and my clothes and riding equipment were covered with sleet.

I arrived at the Caldwell Hotel at Centerville just as Kay's posse arrived. All eleven of us sat in front of a fireplace and a big oak fire for almost two hours, and partly dried out our clothes and recovered from the exposure we had suffered. Then we started out again on horseback.

With us was Joe Middleton from near Hanford. He had been scouting provisions for Riley Dean and Grat Dalton, whom he had secreted on what is now known as Dalton Mountain, near Kings River above the Judson Elwood home, now the Pierson Dude Ranch. He agreed with Sheriff Kay to guide us to the hide-out in return for a saddle horse and riding rig.

We rode through the hills toward the high mountains pointed out by Middleton. When we had finally arrived at a point a mile or two from where the camp was supposed to be, the whole party halted. Middleton described the hiding place, just over the brow of a ridge in our sight and under a big oak tree. The ridge was a massive ledge of out-cropping rock.

All of this time it was bitter cold and all of us were chilled to the bone. It was about four o'clock in the afternoon of December 23. As soon as Middleton finished giving directions as to how to get to the hide-out, Hensley made him a present of a six-shooter. He put spurs to his horse and that was the last we ever saw of him.

Sheriff Kay and Hensley started out to reconnoiter and get the lay of the land, leaving the rest of us, eight in number. Kay was wearing a fine, long bearskin overcoat. Before he left he took it off and laid it on the frozen ground near me. I immediately put it on and was soon the warmest I got on that entire trip. I have always since wanted a bearskin overcoat.

About six P.M. Kay and Hensley came back. It was then too late to go to the camp and make an arrest. But plans had been laid for a return in the morning, and Kay and Hensley took us down to the Judson Elwood home to spend the night.

The Elwoods had no room to bed us for the night, so we all lay around on the living room floor in front of a big oak fire in the fireplace. But that floor was as cold as the ice on a pond of water. We rolled over and over, always freezing on one side. Mrs. Elwood did the best she could to feed us and make us comfortable.

About two o'clock in the morning we all piled out and made ready to climb the mountain to the place where the hide-out of Dalton and Dean was located. It was a bright moonlight night. The moon must have been full the evening before, because it was almost as bright as day as we made the climb up the mountain. Just after daylight we had arrived within one quarter of a mile of the camp. I can remember that we all halted for a rest while Kay and Hensley completed their instructions to us. We were to spread out and approach the ledge of rock from several angles. The camp was almost directly under the rock ledge, and in that way we could approach within about one hundred yards of it.

I remember that I was as scared as a rabbit just then, but as I looked at the faces around me I could see that all of the rest were as badly scared as I was. Hensley told us, "Boys, those fellows are not going to be arrested without a fight. Some of us may not come back from this venture. If any of you do not feel that you want to go ahead, now is the time to drop out." Not one fell out of the procession as we started for that rock ledge.

Early as we were, fortune was against us. Dean and Dalton were starting out on a hog hunt. A yellowish-red bird dog was following them. As we came in sight on top of the rock ledge we could see them with their guns on their shoulders. There were perhaps twenty or thirty seconds when they could have been called upon to surrender and then be shot, for they would never have done anything but dive for cover.

Several of Kay's men wanted to shoot them at first sight, but Hensley and Kay would not allow it and in a few seconds they were out of sight. This action on the part of Kay and Hensley in not allowing the Visalia deputies to shoot Dalton and Dean down in cold blood was resented ever after by some of the party, but it was the means of saving the lives of several of them, including those of Sheriff Hensley and myself at a later time during the Evans and Sontag affair. Chris Evans and John Sontag had an opportunity to shoot both of us dead from ambush. Sontag wanted to shoot, but Chris said, "No, they would not kill Dalton and Dean and we will let them go."

Well, it was about six-thirty on the morning of December 24, 1891, when

Dalton and Dean disappeared into the brush and left our posse standing there in the cold. But none of us felt the cold just then.

About ten o'clock we could see that they were drifting back toward camp. To meet them to advantage and surround them so they could not get away, Kay and Hensley split the posse into three groups. Part of the posse went on each side of the gulch and trail, and Hensley and I covered the trail they were almost certain to use in approaching the camp. Hensley and I were close together.

At eleven A.M. Hensley and I could see one of the men coming directly toward us. He was then about two hundred yards away. Hensley said, "Keep out of sight and let him come as close as he will." Hensley hid behind a pile of rocks and I behind an oak tree a little apart, until he was within thirty feet of us. He was a tall man with a heavy brown beard, and must have weighed at least two hundred and thirty pounds. He was Riley Dean.

In a low, but determined voice, Hensley said, "Drop that rifle." Dean dropped the rifle. Hensley said, "Come here." Dean walked to within fifteen feet of us. Hensley said, "Unbuckle that revolver belt." Dean unbuckled the belt, and the revolver, cartridges, and belt all dropped to the ground.

During all of this time both Hensley and I had our rifles cocked and aimed directly at Dean's middle. If he had made a false motion of any kind we would have shot him instantly. When we had Dean safely separated from his guns, Hensley hurried over the brow of the ridge with Dean to get a pair of handcuffs from Kay. He wanted to handcuff Dean to an oak tree so we would be free to capture Dalton.

Almost as soon as Hensley was out of sight I heard the sound of footsteps in the same direction in which Dean had approached. Before I could do a thing, except step behind the oak tree again, I saw the head of a man appear over the steep brow of the hill about thirty feet from me. It was Dalton. I waited about four seconds until he was about twenty feet away. I could see to a point about at his belt-level and was ready to call to him to drop his gun, when the dog saw me and barked sharply.

The dog was about ten feet ahead of Dalton and came into view at about the same time as Dalton did. The rest of it was over in two seconds. Dalton was carrying his winchester rifle over his shoulder. He threw it forward and to his shoulder in one quick motion, and fired instantly. I fired at almost the same instant. My bullet went over Dalton's head and whistled over the heads of the rest of the posse down the hill. The bullet from Dalton's rifle entered the oak tree about six inches from, and above, my face.

Dalton's action was the most instinctive, involuntary motion I have ever observed. From the time the dog barked until Dalton disappeared in the brush two seconds did not elapse. In one continuous motion he drew and fired the rifle, dropped flat on the ground and rolled into a gulch about ten feet away. Down that gulch he went like a frightened deer.

I ran a few steps toward where Dalton had stood and saw that he was gone. Then Hensley came back with Dean. When I told Hensley how it happened, Dean said, "He never shot at you; he can shoot the head off a quail at that distance." But I guess both of us were somewhat startled, because I should have hit him and he surely did shoot at me.

When Hensley understood what had happened, he said, "Well, I am glad he didn't get you, Ed, but I am sorry you didn't get him." Soon the entire posse had assembled, but no trace of Dalton could be seen. We found afterward that he had followed the bottom of the gulch directly to the valley below.

Judson Elwood was plowing with a six-horse team and gang plow in a field about two hundred yards above his house. While we were still on the mountain we saw Dalton approach the plow team. Elwood unhitched a white horse from the plow. Dalton jumped on it bareback and started along a trail over the side and brow of the hill in the distance. As he rode away he yelled and fired two shots from his revolver. The dog was still with him. They soon disappeared over the hill on the trail. That was the last we ever saw of Grat Dalton in Fresno County.

When Kay came up he said, "Ed, you couldn't have given me a better Christmas present than Grat Dalton!" But Kay was never to capture Grat again, Christmas or no Christmas.

We returned to Elwood's and heard Judson tell of how Dalton at the point of a gun had ordered him to unhitch the horse. We got our horses, concealed during the day in Elwood's stable, and started for the valley.

Soon after we reached the edge of the plains, Hensley and I proceeded to Fresno. Kay and his posse went south toward Visalia, taking Dean with them.

While Leonard Elwood was only seven years of age when Grat Dalton escaped the posses on Dalton Mountain, day before Christmas, 1891, he did observe many things, and he had direct from his father and mother many other facts about the affair. The wildness and inaccessibility of the Dalton camp may be appreciated when it is understood that Elwood is probably one of only two persons who have been able to readily find the place since Dalton left it. Here is his account:

DALTON MOUNTAIN BATTLE

I was about seven years of age in 1891 when the posse came to the ranch of Judson Elwood, my father, in search of Grat Dalton and Riley Dean. I lived on the place for many years after the encounter between Dalton and the posse and know intimately every inch of the country involved.

The Elwood ranch where Dalton and Dean were hidden was located about sixteen miles east of Centerville. None of our family knew that they were there. Joe Middleton frequently came to the locality hunting and generally stayed overnight at our house. We did not know that he was hiding Dalton and Dean and taking supplies to them.

It was late in the evening of a day shortly before Christmas in 1891 when a posse of about ten men came to Father's house and wanted lodgings for the night. The posse consisted of Eugene W. Kay, Sheriff of Tulare County, John Hensley, Sheriff of Fresno County, Edwin McCardle, a Fresno County deputy, Fred Hall, Jim Mead, and several others from Visalia and vicinity. Kay and Hensley were in a buggy. The rest were horseback.

Of course my parents knew that the posse was probably on the trail of Grat Dalton, but no one asked any questions and no explanations were made.

Our accomodations were not sufficient to do justice to such a crowd of men, but father and mother did the best they could. Father put the animals in our corral and barn and fed them. He built up the oak fire in our big fireplace and the men lay around on the floor and made themselves as comfortable as possible. I remember that Sheriff Kay was wearing a big bearskin overcoat. He took it off and spread it on the floor in front of the fireplace for a bed.

Although the hunting season was closed, the mountain people considered that the wild game was theirs and killed what was necessary for their table. Father had a couple of fine deer hanging from a tree in the back yard. After talking about it with Jim Mead, Father went out and cut off a ham of venison and Mother fried steaks for the posse. She also had beans, bread, and other common foodstuffs of the day for them.

Early in the morning the posse left afoot for the mountain, and we neither saw nor heard anything more of them until the forenoon, when we heard shooting high among the rocks and oak trees above the ranch. My Father had hitched his six horse team and was about a half mile south and a little east of the house, plowing with a Stockton Gang plow.

After the shooting, Father was walking behind his plow when he felt something jab him in the ribs. He looked around and saw a tall, dark man threatening him with a winchester rifle. He appeared to mean business. He said, "I want that white horse out of your team and I want it in a hurry."

Father did not argue. He stopped the team, untied the horse, unhitched it and led it from the team. He stripped off the harness, including the halter and bridle.

Dalton stood quietly by, watching every move Father made. The horse he had selected was a flea-bitten white horse we called Darby. He was the only horse in the team fit for a saddle animal. Dalton had probably seen us children riding Darby after the cattle and other stock and knew that he was a good saddle animal.

Darby was extremely hard to bridle. When you tried to put the bit in his mouth he would clamp his teeth shut and it was all you could do to force the bit between them. Father was afraid he would have trouble getting the bridle back on Darby, but he didn't. He jammed the bridle over Darby's head and he took the bit like a good fellow.

Dalton jumped on Darby and away he went. He rode up by the house and along a trail through a field to where a wire fence joined an old rock fence. There he jumped Darby over the rock fence and rode over the brow of the hill, firing his six-shooter in the air.

As Dalton rode toward the house I heard the horse running and saw him coming. I did not know the dog and thought it was someone chasing one of our hogs. I called to Mother and she came out. We watched him ride by, the red bird dog running ahead of him. Until they disappeared over the hill I saw everything that took place. We afterward decided that Dalton fired the six-shooter as a signal to let Dean know that he was clear.

In an hour or so the posse came in with Dean as a prisoner. They saddled their horses, hitched the team to the buggy and left. When Father went out to feed and harness his plow team the next morning, Darby was standing at the gate, waiting to be let in. He did not appear to have been hard ridden.

As I remember Dean, he was a large man, about six feet three inches in height, weighed about two hundred and twenty pounds and had a heavy, brownish-black beard. He was a very quiet man. He returned to our place when he was released from prison. By that time Father had found two saddles that Dalton and Dean had hidden in a cave across the canyon and several miles from Dalton Mountain.

When Dean returned, he told us where he and Dalton had camped. Father and I went up there with Dean and found the camp just as they had left it. It was an open camp, sheltered only by the overhanging rock. They had no tent of any kind. The only protection from the outside was a blanket, which they had hung in front of their fireplace, so that the glow of their camp fire could not be seen in the valley. The camp was in a narrow place between the rocks and just back of a large granite boulder. They could have stood off a half dozen posses from the place. They had been keeping the bird dog as a watch dog. Just in front of the granite boulder they had dug a hole in the ground for the dog to sleep in and had covered it with a blanket.

Everything was in the camp just as Dalton and Dean had left it. We found blankets, some grub, and a good pair of field glasses. Afterward Father found a long dirk knife that Dalton had lost during his run down the mountainside.

I am familiar with Emmett Dalton's story about the encounter between Grat and the posse. It is not true. He claimed that Grat and the dog were alone in the camp, which is not so. Dean had been staying with Grat. Dean told us about this himself when he returned to get the blankets and other personal effects left in the camp. The posse captured Dean a few yards from Grat when the shooting scrape took place between Dalton and McCardle.

The posse did not encounter Grat sitting in camp, as Emmett wrote. He was some distance from the camp and walked up on them.

None of the posse ever saw the camp used by Dalton and Dean. If they had they would at least have carried away the field glasses. The camp was entirely undisturbed when we went to it, a month or more after the battle.

No officers fired any volley into their tent for two reasons; one that I have mentioned, that they never got to the camp and the other that there was no tent there and never had been one at the place.

Grat had no horse at the place. Neither did Dean. The men had been taken in there by Middleton and left there until horses could be taken to them, when they expected to use the cached saddles on them. Middleton had probably also provided Dalton and Dean with the dog. I doubt if he ever "wandered into Grat's camp", as Emmett wrote. He would never be wandering around that kind of country at Christmas time. Anyway he was a long way from being a "half starved greyhound."

Most of Emmett's other statements about the Dalton Mountain battle were also not true. There were no magpies, chipmunks, or pine trees near the Dalton camp on Dalton Mountain. The growth there is almost all live oak. Large, slaty granite boulders cover the mountainside. Grat was not run off Dalton Mountain during a "summer afternoon." It was on the morning of the day before Christmas and was cold and freezing where they were camped.

Isaac C. Parker, the "Hanging Judge" of the Federal Court in Fort Smith when Grat Dalton was serving there as a Deputy U.S. Marshall and later when he was jailed there.

Photo courtesy former U.S. Marshall George Yoes and now in Bear State Library.

CHAPTER ELEVEN

Grat Dalton's Ride

There always has been deep mystery about the route taken by Grat Dalton after he escaped from the posse at the Elwood ranch, and about his "one hundred and seven" day ride from California to Indian Territory. In his book, *When the Daltons Rode*, Emmett Dalton was very dramatic concerning this famous ride of Grat's, but was quite vague as to facts. It was a thrilling experience to hear Littleton Dalton tell in detail just what happened. According to Lit, Grat went direct from the Elwood ranch to the home of Charles Owen, a short distance west of the present town of Clovis. After a short stay there he rode eighty miles to the home of ex-supervisor W.W. Gray, seven miles south of Livingston, in Merced County. From there, almost a month later, the ride was begun to Indian Territory.

Charles Owen had passed away before material for *Dalton Gang Days* was being assembled, so we have no first-hand account from him of the stay of Grat Dalton at the Owen home. But his son, Roy Owen, has furnished the following interesting account:

Yes, Grat Dalton stayed at our house a week or more just after his escape from the posse headed by Sheriffs Gene Kay and Ed Hensley on Dalton Mountain, above the Elwood Ranch, now the Pierson Dude Ranch. I was about thirteen years of age at the time. Grat made his getaway on a grey plow-horse which he turned loose before he arrived at my father's home, three-quarters of a mile west of present Clovis. Grat hid in the wild sunflowers near the barn and finally got my father's attention about nine P.M. This was the second evening after his escape and the weather was freezing.

Grat was suffering from pneumonia. Father took him upstairs and put him to bed in a spare room and kept him there until he could travel. During the night I heard someone coughing in the spare room, which was generally vacant. The cough was low and muffled, but went on through the night while I was awake.

When I came downstairs in the morning I went to my mother, who was at the cook stove, and said, "Mother, who is it I heard coughing last night upstairs in the spare bedroom?" She answered, "Hush. That is someone we are taking care of. He is sick. We don't want anyone to know he is here." That ended the matter as far as I was concerned.

Cole Dalton was working nearby for my uncle, Tom Owen. When Grat recovered sufficiently, my father outfitted him with a horse and an old saddle, and he and Cole started out for the West Side, planning to hit the Coast Range at the Cantúa. I did not know that they finally went north to Merced County.

Arch Turner and Mrs. John W. Breckenridge furnished more details concerning the stay of Grat Dalton at the home of their sister, Mrs. W.W. Gray, but it was from Littleton Dalton that the detailed story of the ride to Indian Territory was obtained:

After the battle with Kay's posse at the Elwood ranch, Grat came to Charlie Owen's. The officers were watching Cole Dalton at Tom Owen's, and me at Clovis Cole's, but they didn't think of watching the Charlie Owen ranch. Grat didn't come to me after the jail break, because I had told Bob and Emmett I wouldn't help any of them again; for them not to come to me for money, horses, riding rigs, ammunition, or guns. They had told Mason what I had said and he had told Grat. So Grat went to Owen's. He knew that Charlie would take care of him.

Cole Dalton was working for Tom Owen at the time. As soon as he could get away, he rode with Grat to the home of Merced County ex-supervisor, W.W. Gray, seven miles south of Livingston and west of Merced. Gray's wife was Ellie Turner, a sister of Arch Turner, and also a sister of Mrs. John W. Breckenridge, wife of the attorney who defended Grat. Gray had a large two-story house with a cupola on top of it. He put Grat in the cupola with a spyglass to watch the plains for posses and had his Chinese cook carry food to him during the most of a month. Grat was sick from exposure incurred at the time of his escape from the posse at the Elwood ranch and couldn't travel any sooner. Cole left Tom Owen and went to work for Turner on the San Joaquin River west of Gray's place while Grat was in the cupola.

When Grat was ready to travel, Cole agreed to get a horse and riding rig for him and to accompany him to Indian Territory. One afternoon Cole was helping the Turners load hogs on the cars at Livingston. When the loading was done, Arch Turner was to ride to Turlock on the train and Cole was to lead Arch's horse back to the ranch. The horse Arch had been riding was a fine, large, powerful pinto called Commodore.

Cole had hinted several times that Commodore would be a fine horse for Grat to ride back to the Indian Territory. So Arch knew what Cole meant when he asked if he could use Commodore. Arch said, "You take Commodore home, unsaddle him and put him in the barn." Arch said this in the hearing of several persons so he could not be directly accused of furnishing Grat with a horse. Of course Cole didn't take the horse home and Arch didn't expect him to. Cole took the horse direct to the Gray home where Grat was hidden.

About the middle of February, 1892, a little more than a year after the Alila robbery attempt, Grat and Cole started together horseback for Kingfisher, Indian Territory. They crossed the San Joaquin River to the West Side at Hills Ferry, and headed for San Luis Gonzaga at the east mouth of the Pacheco Pass. From there they skirted the Coast Range foothills from water hole to water hole until they reached the San Emigdio ranch. They took this deserted route in order to avoid the many settlements east of the river.

The boys stopped at San Emigdio to have their horses shod, and then cut south through San Emigdio canyon and east, crossing the present 99 Highway near Gorman Station, to Antelope Valley, where they skirted the desert to San Diego County. There they hit the old trail to Yuma.

When they started from Gray's, Grat wanted Cole to take the lead, but Cole wouldn't do it. He said, "You go ahead and I'll follow and stand guard at night. If you run into any trouble, I don't want you to say that I led you into it."

Cole told me that they avoided Yuma and swam their horses across the Colorado River about eight miles downstream. They had quite an experience crossing the river. Commodore was a fine swimmer, but Cole's horse was not, and almost drowned. The boys undressed, tied their clothing to the saddle horns and tied the stirrups together across the saddles. Then they started their horses into the water and held to their tails.

About half-way across the river, Cole's horse tried to turn around and swim back to the California side. Cole circled him in midstream three or four times before he could get him to follow Commodore. Both Cole and the horse were exhausted when they climbed out of the river in Arizona.

It was a hard trip. Cole told me afterward a dozen times that he would never try such a ride again. He said that they would have been just as well off to have disguised themselves and ridden the brakes. Cole lost twenty-five pounds of weight between the time they left Gray's place and their arrival at Gila Bend, Arizona. Most of the time they had to hide out in the daytime and travel at night. They had to avoid every habitation and steal food for themselves and feed for their horses all the way. Once, on the Arizona desert, they escaped pursuit by a posse which probably mistook them for other hunted men. After that they hid in the Gila River bottom for three days, afraid to move.

It has been stated a number of times that Grat was on the road a hundred and seven days on his forced ride to Kingfisher. That is not entirely true. When they had almost reached the big bend in the Gila River, they stopped for two weeks. They were skirting the south bank of the Gila when they saw ranch buildings ahead, almost on the very bank of the river. It required a long detour to avoid the place by taking to the plains. So they rode along the river bottom near the water.

Opposite the house, they couldn't resist riding up the river bank and peeking over the edge. Not seventy-five yards from them was a man cutting firewood at a ranch woodpile. Grat said to Cole, "Seems to me I have seen that fellow before." Cole studied the man closely. Then he spurred his horse up the bank and let out a war-whoop. The rancher was an old Missouri neighbor of ours.

Grat and Cole worked for the old fellow for two weeks. Then Grat went on to Kingfisher. Cole and Grat had been quarreling, and Cole wouldn't go on. He had been trying to talk Grat out of joining up with Bob and Emmett. He kept telling Grat, "You're not in serious trouble. If you go in with Bob and Emmett you'll stretch rope. They are going from bad to worse and will either be shot or hung."

They were over the worst part of the journey, so Grat went on alone. Cole worked for the old neighbor for several months and then came back to Turner's on the San Joaquin River. He arrived at Turner's only a few weeks before Grat and Bob were killed in the Coffeyville raid.

Commodore, the horse Grat was riding, gave out at Cantonment, Indian Territory. There was a gathering of Indians there and their stock was running loose on the nearby plains. Grat roped a fine buckskin horse out of the Indian caballada, turned Commodore loose and rode on into Kingfisher.

Nothing was heard from Cole or Grat by any of us during the time they were on the road to Kingfisher. Mother wrote me repeatedly, trying to get me to come home. I finally had to quit my job with Clovis Cole and go to her.

When I arrived at Kingfisher, Bob and Emmett had returned from Florida, where they had hidden while Grat was in jail, and were again hiding up in the

Cheyenne and Arrapohoe country, eighty miles west of Kingfisher. Grat hadn't arrived from California. Ben and Simon were the only boys home. Mother was almost exhausted from worry. I comforted her as much as I could and waited.

I noticed in looking over Emmett's book that he didn't tell of the trip he and Bob made to Tampa, Florida. He gives the idea that they were somewhere on the way south when they read in a newspaper that Grat had been convicted at Visalia. Then, according to his story, they immediately set out for California to break Grat out of jail. A day or so later they read in the papers that Grat had escaped and was probably headed for Kingfisher. Emmett didn't account for about three months between the time when Grat was convicted and when he escaped. It was this time that Bob and Emmett spent in Tampa. They told me about this themselves, just before they hid out in the Cheyenne country. I don't remember just what it was, but they pulled some kind of a robbery in Florida. So, in his book, Emmett didn't want to admit they had been there during that time.

Mason was acquitted at his trial in Visalia, California, sold the lease on the Cholame ranch, and moved his family to the home of his wife's parents near Livingston, California. He then went to Indian Territory. Just before Grat arrived from California, Mason took two horses, grub, and a sack of cartridges out to where Bob and Emmett were hidden, west of Kingfisher.

One night I was awakened by the slamming of the yard gate. I could hear someone coming up the walk, spurs raking on the gravel. In an instant I knew it was Grat. I would have known his walk anywhere. Ben and I were sleeping in the same bed, Ben on the outside. I jabbed Ben in the ribs and said, "Get up. Open the door. Here comes Grat." Mother came in and could scarcely believe it was Grat. He was simply skin and bones. He had lost forty pounds of weight between Gray's place in California and Kingfisher.

A day or two after Grat arrived at Kingfisher, I went down to Cantonment and got Commodore, the big pinto horse Grat had ridden away from California. I put him in the pasture at Kingfisher, but he never recovered. He soon died. The ride had been too much for him. Later, when I saw Cole, I learned how Commodore had been broken down. He had been abused the same as were the horses Bob and Emmett started out to ride to Ludlow.

Regardless of the fact that they had practically been raised on horseback, none of the three boys had any mercy on horses, or any sense about putting them through a hard ride. They'd run them down at the start and then spur and quirt them the rest of the day. Cole told me that he quarreled with Grat all the way to Gila Bend about the treatment of their horses. If it hadn't been for Cole, Commodore would have broken down before they crossed the Tehachapi Mountains.

Grat stayed with us two or three days and then went up to join Bob and Emmett. Mason came in the day before Grat left and told him just where to find them. When Grat went away it was like seeing him being led away to the gallows. The three began planning robberies right and left.

Bob and Emmett headed the gang that had robbed the train at Whorton, now Perry, Oklahoma, on the Santa Fe, in the Neutral Strip. [Now central Oklahoma.] With the money from that robbery they financed the trip to Tampa. Then they came back and robbed a train north of Waggoner, on the M.K. & T. Bob planned the first robbery and he planned all that followed: Red Rock, Adair, and Coffeyville. . . . .

CHAPTER TWELVE

OKLAHOMA TRAIN ROBBERIES

It was to be an *estancia* in the Argentine, with endless, rolling, grass-covered range; thousands of fattening cattle; *gauchos* and *mozos* galore with prancing steeds, gold and silver mounted saddles and bridles, bits, and spurs; with Spanish costumes trimmed with gold braid and gold coin buttons — all of these; and with United States deputy marshals, Pinkerton detectives, and sheriffs all things of the past. This was the picture that both Lit and Emmett Dalton assured me the outlaws painted for themselves — when they made the big haul. And who knew how much that haul might be, twenty-five, fifty, perhaps a hundred thousand dollars apiece and worth five times as much in the Argentine. When the land payments were being made to the Cherokee Indians several millions might have been taken. It was such loot that the boys had hoped to bag. Emmett looked me calmly and coolly in the eye and said, "It would have been just as easy to have knocked over an express car that was loaded, as one that was carrying chicken feed."

I asked Littleton Dalton about the chances of the Dalton Gang having intercepted the shipment of money intended for the Cherokee payment. He laughed dryly and said, "I don't know how the money was shipped from the Treasury to Indian Territory, but it would have been the quickest kind of suicide for the boys to have tried to lift any of it after it reached the Cherokees. The Cherokees had about twenty-five Indian guards around the payoff tables, armed with winchester rifles or with army muskets loaded halfway to the muzzle with buckshot. I never saw so many at one time in my life. A half dozen or so of those guards were of the famous Starr family and related to Henry Starr, who ran an outlaw gang of his own. No, the boys didn't want anything to do with that Cherokee money." Lit continued to look me in the eye, just as calmly and coolly as Emmett.

Although they became world famous, the realities of the dreams of Bob, Emmett, and Grat and later, Bill, seemed with each succeeding robbery to fade farther and farther into the distance, and the law began to cast darker and longer shadows across the cedar brakes of the North Canadian River. The picture was best painted by the California newspaper editor Ben Maddox, in his *Tulare County Times*, September 10, 1891, when he published the following:

The Daltons robbed a train and the lawyers' fees were so high they had to rob two more to get out of the scrape and still two others to get out of that and so on. The impossibility of their ever getting away with the game led the state legislature to prescribe capital punishment for them — if they are caught, in order to let them down easy.

Regardless of all the stories told concerning the robbing of Oklahoma trains by the Daltons prior to the attempt at Alila, California, this writer is convinced that the Alila robbery was their first attempt. That affair showed an entire lack of experience and the careful preparation that such experience later brought about.

After Bob and Emmett had unsuccessfully attempted the Alila robbery in the Joaquin, they decided that they could do better by patronizing their home country. As soon as Sheriff Kay and his deputy, Jim Ford, gave up the chase of Bob and Emmett, there began a series of robberies, each following the other in close order. All of these were recognized as having been performed by the same gang.

But it must be understood that the California responsibilities of the Dalton Gang didn't end. Train robberies continued in the Joaquin, one at Ceres, and then one at Collis, now called Kerman. The Dalton Gang continued to get credit for them. As late as August 11, 1892, less than two months before the Coffeyville raid, the following news item appeared in a Visalia, California, newspaper:

California is getting up a reputation as notorious as Oklahoma and Indian Territory regarding train robberies. Those Dalton boys must travel on the fastest trains to be able to bury their treasure in Indian Territory one week and rob a train here the next. If a company of trappers were to be robbed at Hudson Bay tomorrow the Daltons would get the credit. While officers are chasing the Daltons, other highwaymen are committing robberies and stepping aside to watch the officers hunt the Daltons.

Meanwhile the gang was minding its own business, little caring whom California credited with her robberies.

The Dalton Gang, as it existed in Oklahoma, in the summer of 1891, included about eight men, most of whom had grown up together in the nations. Some of them had been saddle companions of Bob, Emmett, and Grat when they worked on cattle ranches. Several of them were well known to Littleton Dalton. Here is what Lit had to say about them:

I had known almost all of the fellows who ran with the boys in the nations. They were just kids when I first left home, but I saw them afterward when I visited at Kingfisher.

Bill Doolin was a tall, straight, likable fellow. When I knew him he had not gone bad. He was just a good-natured, red-headed kid, always up to some practical joke. The last time I saw him he was married and had a child. There was talk then about his having to keep under cover, but I never knew what it was all about. He later robbed a bank in Missouri and had to go on the scout, and was finally ambushed and killed.

Dick Broadwell, who was killed at Coffeyville, was a slender man, about six feet tall, with fair skin and black hair. When I knew him he was the finest kind of a boy, good looking and from a fine family in Hutchinson, Kansas. After the Coffeyville raid his family claimed his body and had it buried at their home.

Bill Powers was not tall, about five feet seven inches in height. He was a stocky, powerful man, wore a dark mustache, and had black hair. When he was killed at Coffeyville, there was talk about his being Tom Evans. I never did know where he was born, but when I left Belton, Missouri, in 1878, his family lived not many miles from us. The Powers family had Bill's body buried at Coffeyville beside Bob and Grat. How Powers came to be identified as Tom Evans I could never understand. I never knew of anyone by the name of Tom Evans to run with the boys. Some people thought he was a brother of Chris Evans, the Visalia train bandit, but that was not true. I had known an old guerrilla by the name of Tom Evans. He had run with Cole Younger and the James boys during the Civil War, but he was twenty or more years older than Grat, being about sixty years of age at the time of the Coffeyville raid. He could not have been the man killed at Coffeyville.

At least a dozen other men ran with the boys from the time they started stealing horses until Mason was killed down at Poolville. I knew many of them. There were probably more I didn't know. Most of them went by nicknames. Few people knew these outlaws personally, so they were easily confused and at least two different men were known by most of the nicknames. Dick Clifton was the original Dynamite Dick, but George Newcomb was also called Dynamite Dick by many people. I have heard Arkansas Tom Jones described as being almost every possible complexion and height, and the same about Six Shooter Jack, whom I never could identify, unless he was the same man as Tulsa Jack. A lot of people called Dick Clifton the Slaughter Kid. Bob Yokum was called Bitter Creek. Charlie Pierce, whom Emmett mentioned in his last book, was known as Cockeye Charlie. He, along with Newcomb, was killed about a year after Mason was killed.

A number of other men were mentioned in connection with the boys, but I knew little about them. I got my information from my brothers Mason, Cole, and Simon, and from neighbors I visited while in Kingfisher, Oklahoma. These other outlaws were Lee Killian, John Ward, Nate Sylvia, Felix Young, and Bill Raidler. John Ward was killed near Duncan, Indian Territory, about the same time that Mason was killed. Nate Sylvia and Felix Young were captured by Deputy U.S. Marshals at about the same time that Ward was killed. Raidler was shot up and captured about a year after Mason was killed. Killian was captured about two years after Raidler. He was the last captured of the Dalton Gang.

I know that some of the above names were assumed. Maybe most of them were.

That about winds up the gang that ran with the boys. I don't know of one of them that was not killed or sent to the penitentiary for a long term. . . .

Due to the great amount of fiction published about the Daltons there have been unending questions as to who composed the final Dalton Gang, the one that robbed trains in Oklahoma just prior to their windup at Coffeyville, Kansas, October 5th, 1892. After consulting with Emmett and Littleton Dalton and with ex-U.S. Marshals George A. Yoes and Chris Madsen, I have come to the conclusion that the following nine are all that ever will be definitely connected with the final gang: Bob Dalton was the leader. With him were Emmett and Grattan Dalton, Dick Broadwell, Bill Powers, George Newcomb, Charles Pierce, Charles Bryant, and Bill Doolin. They are well identified, with the exception of Powers, Bryant, and Newcomb. Bryant was often known as Black-faced Charlie, because his face was black from powder burns, "caused", said Lit Dalton, by being too close to a muzzle loading, black powder shotgun when it was fired by a United States deputy marshal. According to information furnished by Deputy U.S. Marshal Chris Madsen, Newcomb was known by two aliases, Bitter Creek, because he had punched cattle on the Bitter Creek Ranch and The Slaughter Kid, because he had worked for a cattle man by the name of Slaughter.

The Dalton Gang, as led by Bob Dalton, prior to Coffeyville, was accused of only one bank robbery, that of the El Reno, Oklahoma Territory, bank, which took place July 27, 1892. Most persons who are informed of the activities of the Dalton Gang have doubted that they had anything to do with this robbery. Many have claimed that it was an "inside job." This was the opinion of Littleton Dalton. The following letter from Mr. Claude E. Hensley, of Oklahoma City, is illustrative of the opinions encountered:

Replying to your letter relative to the bank robbery at El Reno, July 28, 1892, will state that this bank was known as the Bank of El Reno with S.W. Sawyer, president, and E.J. Sawyer, cashier. It was generally referred to as the Sawyer Bank.

I arrived in El Reno August 5, 1892, a few days after the alleged robbery. Although the Daltons were accused of the crime, no one saw any of the bandits and it was openly alleged by the depositors that the robbery was an inside job. One of the depositors, a gambler and saloon man, took his six-shooter, it is claimed, and forced the bankers to give him his deposit.

Concerning the alleged El Reno robbery, the best news account discovered appeared in the *Cherokee Advocate* under the following heading:

Bold Bank Robbery

El Reno, O.T., July 28 — El Reno was thrown into a fever of excitement at 10:30 yesterday morning by the screams for help emanating from the bank of El Reno. The screams were from Mrs. S.W. Sawyer, wife of the president of the bank, who was held up by two robbers who robbed the bank of $10,500. At 10:30 a stranger entered the bank, stepped up to the cashier's window and made inquiry about some town lots, then stepped to the desk and commenced writing. In a moment another stranger stepped to the cashier's desk and presenting a gun at Mrs. Sawyer's head, demanded that she hand over all the money in the bank. The lady was so frightened she could not move, but the robber threatened to shoot her if she did not accede quickly, and in a dazed way she stepped to the vault and handed him all the bills in it and what was in the daily change drawer, aggregating about $10,000, and less than $100 in silver.

The man who was writing at the desk turned quickly, grabbed the money as Mrs. Sawyer handed it through the wicket, and disappeared out of the door, the one holding the pistol following quickly. Mrs. Sawyer screamed several times and fell in a swoon. The robbers mounted the horses standing at the edge of the pavement, unhitched, and rode out of town as fast as the horses could go. Mrs. Sawyer was the only person in the bank. It is believed to be the work of the Daltons on account of the manner of execution. A hundred citizens on horseback and in buggies, fully armed and with ropes, are in pursuit and capture is only a question of a short time, as the robbers had only about fifteen minutes the start. They headed for the Dalton rendezvous in the Granite mountains in the Wichita reservation.

It is significant that the robbers were seen by no one but the bankers. It also is significant that in less than two weeks after Sheriff Kay arrived back in Visalia after his long chase of Bob and Emmett Dalton, they and their associates held up a train at Whorton, now the town of Perry, in what was then known as the *Neutral Strip;* now central Oklahoma. In discussing this event with me Emmett stated that when Kay left, and Ford went to Guthrie to plan a new campaign with Marshal Grimes, he and Bob slept for three days and nights without a break. He stated that while he lived he never again expected to be so exhausted. Emmett also stated that both had been broke for a month and had borrowed more than four hundred dollars from friends scattered all over Kansas and Indian Territory. As soon as they were rested they looked up George Newcomb and Charlie Bryant and laid plans for a train robbery. This resulted, as already stated, in the robbery at Whorton.

According to Emmett, only the four mentioned had any part in the Whorton robbery. But Littleton Dalton stated to me that two others held a change of horses about twenty miles northwest of Whorton. This was verified by Chris Madsen. Emmett also stated to me that Bob's sweetheart, Eugenia Moore, rode from near Vinita in northeast Oklahoma, to their hide-out in the cedar brakes of the North Canadian to inform them of a large shipment of money soon to be made through Whorton. According to Emmett she obtained this information from a relative who was an employee of the railroad.

Bob Dalton, as he appeared May 9, 1889. He was killed at Coffeyville, Kan., Oct. 5, 1892.
Photo courtesy N.H. Rose, and now in Bear State Library.

Emmett laid great stress on the help Miss Moore had been to the Dalton Gang throughout the remainder of their train robbing career. No one whom I have interviewed has known of such a person. Littleton Dalton felt certain that she was pure fiction, placed in Emmett's story to add some badly needed romance. Madsen felt that there was no truth in the story that any woman had read any telegraph messages concerning the shipment of money by banks, as had been claimed by Emmett Dalton in his book, *When the Daltons Rode.* But Madsen did know of several women with whom Bob Dalton had associated. His story of this phase of the robbing of trains will be presented a little later.

In running down the facts about the Oklahoma activities of the Dalton Gang, I always came back to Chris Madsen and George A. Yoes. Newspaper accounts were not reliable: Emmett Dalton would not talk, except to quote his book, *When the Daltons Rode,* and many of the statements in it were entirely unreliable. Littleton Dalton was in California during the time when the trains were robbed in Oklahoma. George Yoes could tell of the activities out of the Fort Smith office of his father, U.S. Deputy Marshal, Col. Jacob Yoes. United States Deputy Marshal Chris Madsen was in the field chasing the outlaws most of the time and knew more about the robberies than all other informants. In 1938 I visited him at his home in Guthrie, Oklahoma, went over with him Emmett Dalton's book and a sheaf of newspaper items, and took many pages of notes. Plans were laid for him to continue furnishing data by mail. This he did, although he was more than ninety years of age. During the time when he was engaged in preparing a full written account of Dalton activities in Oklahoma he fell and broke a hip. The work was finished from his bed just prior to his death at the age of ninety-two years. The material in the remainder of this chapter is from data furnished by Madsen. Here is his account, which for the first time gives to the public the true facts as to the inner workings of the Dalton Gang in Oklahoma:

In western Oklahoma the Dalton Gang holed up near Jim Riley's ranch. It was about eight miles from where the village of Taloga is now located. When officers referred to the Dalton hideout in the Sac and Fox country, or Emmett referred to his dugout among the cedar brakes of the North Canadian, they were referring to Jim Riley's ranch.

Jim Riley had driven a stage between Caldwell, Kansas, and Fort Reno, and had married an Indian woman. He had taken his wife's allotment near the Canadian river, where the country was covered with dwarf cedars and blackjack oaks and crisscrossed by deep canyons that carried the waters from the plains to the river, an ideal place for an outlaw hiding place.

Jim was absolutely honest in his personal business, but he had either to leave that country or be blind to what was going on. He would feed the outlaws and would do the same for the officers. But if one party would ask about the whereabouts of the other Jim would become mum. A brother-in-law of his, who served with me in the army, was different. He would write to me and tell me what he could learn about the outlaws.

The outlaws, at times when they were not out to prey on the railroads, or banks, dug out large rooms into the steep banks of the hills in the cedar brakes. There they spent their time, probably much as Emmett described in his book. But whatever money they obtained was soon used up. So they decided on a holdup of the Santa Fe train at Whorton, now known as Perry. According to Emmett the gang got $14,000 in the Whorton holdup. That should have left enough to carry them through for a while after expenses had been paid. In his book *When the Daltons Rode,* Emmett Dalton attached much importance to a woman informant whom he identified as Eugenia Moore and a sweetheart of Bob Dalton.

The only woman Bob Dalton ran with and who carried grub and information to the gang was well known to me. She was a heavy drinker and a dope fiend. It was dope that killed her. She was known as Mrs. Mundays and sometimes by the alias of Tom King. Of course, I can't state that this was the woman Emmett had in mind, but I had her in jail several times and she caused me more trouble than all the other women I ever had anything to do with. Once I had to deliver her at Oklahoma City for trial. I took her over in a buckboard, taking all of one afternoon. She cursed and swore at me and called me all the vile and obscene names in existence all the way to the city. She didn't stop more than ten minutes all the way. When we got there she was so hoarse she couldn't talk so you could understand her. I will tell you more about her later on. It was a hard gang that the Daltons ran with. I knew many of them, as well as the people who put them up. Few of them were trustworthy. It was always my belief that most of them got a cut out of the robberies.

According to Emmett, Eugenia Moore and other outsiders had also to be provided for from the proceeds of the robberies. So those who actually took part in the holdup received very little. And there was where Emmett began to stray from the facts. He stated that Miss Moore understood telegraphy, had been listening to the messages going over the wires and had ridden more than a hundred miles to tell the robbers that a large shipment of money was going to be sent to a bank in Guthrie on a certain date, also that the express company had only been fooling them by telling the public that the big safe could only be opened at certain places. Emmett stated Miss Moore said that this was nothing but a way to fool would-be train robbers and that the messenger could open the through safe at any time.

The idea that Emmett would either believe such statements, or think that others would believe that the express company would wire ten days or two weeks ahead of sending money to banks, is so ridiculous that it casts a doubt on all of Emmett's statements. However, the plan to rob the train was carried out early in May of 1891, but the large safe was not opened, regardless of Emmett's story, and even all the money carried in the small, or wayside safe, did not get into the hands of the robbers. The expressman concealed some of it before opening the door and was given a gold watch by the express company for saving quite a sum of money.

After their failure to get into the express car at Alila, in California, Bob and Emmett decided to take along reinforcements when they went to Whorton. Bob and Newcomb went to the station. Emmett and Bryant held the horses at the cattle loading corrals a short distance south of town. Newcomb and Bob boarded the engine just as the engineer was opening the throttle to pull out. But they were seen by the expressman, who hurriedly opened the way safe and hid most of the money that had been in it, as I have described. According to information furnished me by the express company, the loss at Whorton was less than twelve hundred dollars. It had to be split six ways. Although Emmett stated that only four of them had any part in the robbery, two others accompanied them to within twenty miles of Whorton and held fresh horses in readiness for the return of the four who went to Whorton. I had this on good authority from several sources, one being the man at whose ranch the fresh horses were held. Anyway, Whorton was a quiet affair and a real disappointment to the Dalton Gang.

After the robbery, Emmett and Charley Bryant went to their dugout near Jim Riley's place. About the first of August, 1891, Bryant started out to visit his brother at Mulhall, but on his way stopped at Hennessey to get medical aid. He was identified by some citizens and they informed Ed Short, who was too eager to make a big catch all by himself, and did not notify either Marshal Grimes or me, although both of us were working with him. He made arrangements with the waiter girl, who was carrying meals to Bryant, to follow her into his room when she went there with his dinner. Short took off his boots so as to make no noise, until the door was opened, when he stepped in and covered Bryant with his gun. That talk by Emmett about promising Bryant that he would not handcuff him is all hot air. The prisoner was taken to the train about four o'clock in the afternoon to be committed to the jail at Wichita, Kansas, where the territorial prisoners were kept, as Oklahoma had not yet built permanent jails. Acting against the advice of the people, Short took the prisoner without a guard.

When the train was nearing Waucomis, the first station from Hennessey, some mounted men were seen coming across the country towards Waucomis at a fast gait, as if they were trying to get there before the train. Fearing that it was some of Bryant's friends coming to release the prisoner, Short took him back and placed him in charge of the baggage man in the combination mail and baggage car, and handed him his revolver to use should the prisoner try to make trouble.

Short then went out on the rear platform of the car with his rifle. The baggage man carelessly stuck the revolver in one of the letter pigeon-holes and went to work in the other end of the car. The prisoner, without making any noise, went to where the revolver was put by the baggageman and secured it, after which he ordered the man to go back to his work, and then opened the door, and, while Short had his attention directed at the mounted men, noiselessly stepped up behind him and fired the gun point blank into his back. Short turned and the two both emptied their guns into one another.

Conductor Jim Collins had caused the train to be stopped and came back to where the two were lying on the platform. Bryant was slipping down the steps and Short was trying to hold him. Collins spoke to Short, who in a weak voice replied: "Jim, he got me, but I think I got him too. I would like to see my mother." But the wish could not be complied with, for he drew his last breath, and the two combatants lay, side by side, dead on the platform.

Waukomis was only a small way station, the last one in the country opened for settlement, and the bodies were taken to the first town in Kansas, where they were claimed by friends or families. The first battle between the outlaws and the law had ended in a draw.

In the mean time I had received a telegram from Marshal Grimes, asking me to come at once to Hennessey to assist Short, but the train had already left El Reno, so I had to travel by horseback to Kingfisher, where I met Marshal Grimes. He informed me that Short had already arrested Bryant, but that both had met their death, and I was ordered to go to the place to investigate whether anyone else could have been implicated in the killing. When I arrived at Waukomis I found that the killing had been as reported above, and that no one else was a party to it.

The band of Dalton Outlaws now had only seven members, as Bryant had been killed. Grat had escaped from jail in California, but had not yet joined the outfit. Bill Dalton was making his home with his mother at Kingfisher, Oklahoma. He did not participate in any of the holdups with his brothers, but acted as an outside spy and advisor for them until after their outlaw work ended at Coffeyville. Then, from the remains of the original Henry Starr, Dalton, and Doolin Gangs, he and Bill Doolin organized the Dalton-Doolin Gang.

But they were again nearing the bottom of their treasury box and something had to be done to replenish it. According to Emmett, Miss Moore, or Mrs. Mundays, as I knew her, the "expert telegraphist", after a meeting with Bob at Woodward (which was then not in existence) went to Wagoner to read the messages coming over the wires about big money shipments.

Miss Moore must have gone to Wagoner at just the right time, for a few days later she was back at the dugout near Jim Riley's after riding two-hundred miles through the Indian country. She returned with George Newcomb, Charlie Pierce, Bill Doolin, Dick Broadwell and Bill Powers. That made a four hundred mile roundtrip ride by Miss Moore, while the express people were idling their time away, waiting for the robbers to be there to grab the money.

What a story, and what a remarkable woman Miss Moore must have been! She was suffering with consumption and other diseases, but she was back in time to beat the express people, who were stowing the money away in the safe, and she had her army with her. She must also have made arrangements that they should not be molested while gathering up the money.

The second train robbery performed in Oklahoma by the Dalton Gang was at a small station about three and a half miles north of Wagoner in northeastern Oklahoma. It is often referred to as the Wagoner robbery, although the train was actually stopped at Lelietta, the little way station at the location I have mentioned.

There was some gunplay during the Lelietta robbery. The gang fired along the train at passengers and at people who had been hanging around the station. But no one was killed, or even wounded, that I ever knew of. In his book, Emmett Dalton stated that their haul amounted to more than nineteen thousand dollars, three thousand of which was in silver dollars. From data given me by the express company, I believe his statement is about correct. We traced the gang for some time by the trail of new silver dollars they strung about north-central Oklahoma.

Emmett complained that their share of thirty-five hundred dollars each was far from being sufficient for their needs, and probably, on that account, was much to the dissatisfaction of the other members. Another version given me by Bill Doolin was that Bob squandered the money on women and gamblers, and did not divide the spoils fairly. In particular were Doolin, Newcomb and Pierce dissatisfied. Doolin told me that they themselves quit on account of mismanagement of financial affairs.

It is almost impossible for a reader of today to understand the conditions under which we peace officers had to work during Dalton Gang Days. Before going on with the story of my work with the Daltons, I must relate my experiences with some of their associates. This will show the type of people the Dalton boys ran with and how far Emmett's story comes from the actual truth about them.

I will first make you better acquainted with the notorious female horsethief and outlaw of Oklahoma, Mrs. Mundays, whose supposed husband was running a butcher shop here at Guthrie at the time. She was rather a small woman, good looking, and could be very pleasant. She used to dress up in a buckskin suit trimmed with fancy beads. She would wear a cowboy hat, ride a fine horse and live very stylish. When she was out on business she used to travel around with a horsethief named Chappel, wearing a common suit of men's garments. At these times her name was Tom King. That of course was at the time when Guthrie was the Territorial Capital, and gamblers and loose women were in the saddle.

I got acquainted with Mrs. Mundays one evening when the city marshal from Guthrie and I called at the police station at Oklahoma City and the chief there asked me to take two prisoners to Guthrie, as they were wanted in Logan county for stealing horses. They were brought into the office and our marshal identified Tom King and called her by name. She denied being a woman, saying that she did not know what she was, a man or a woman, but that she was not Mrs. Mundays. The Guthrie city marshal then took hold of one of her ears and showed the scars where her husband had bitten her in one of their frequent fights.

I took her to Guthrie and placed her in the jail, as I have already described, but a couple of days later she had taken "French Furlough" and was gone. A few days later she was seen near Yukon, Oklahoma, in company with some suspicious looking fellows. Sheriff Fightmaster from Oklahoma City went after the outfit with a posse, including his own brother. They thought they had the outfit surrounded in a cornfield, and before they could see who was on the other side, some of the party commenced to shoot at what they thought was the horsethieves and mortally wounded the sheriff's brother. During the time the search was made by the officers, Tom King was getting a drink of water from a well near a house and was watching the men in the cornfield.

After she was recaptured the sheriff of Canadian county claimed her on account of her connection with the supposed horsethieves, and I was glad to get rid of her, as we had nothing sure about her other connections.

I told her she would be turned over to the Canadian county officers. She did not object, but just asked me what kind of a jailor they had at El Reno. I asked her for her reason to want to know, and she laughed and replied: "I just wanted to know so I could fix the right medicine for him."

She must have made the right kind of medicine, for in less than two weeks she was out, and the two jailors were gone too. One of them returned a few days later, claiming he had been hunting for the prisoner, but the other never returned. It was reported that he had been seen in company with the woman in the Indian country. He had a brother living on my farm and went there after leaving the jail and borrowed a buffalo coat which I had left with his brother. He had a wife and two children living close to my place, but none of them ever heard from him again.

Tom King, however, was again caught by the Oklahoma sheriff and was in the Oklahoma county jail when the notorious Christian brothers were also in that jail. A sweetheart of theirs played sweet on the jailor and was allowed to bring meals into the jail for them in a basket, which the jailor failed to search. The girl, Jessie Finley, was later arrested for bringing revolvers concealed in the basket into the jail. Two other desperate brothers — the Casey boys, were also confined in the jail, and so was Ernest Lewis, the husband of Julia Johnson, later Julia Dalton. Lewis had been arrested as a member of a gang that held up a Santa Fe train at Whorton (now Perry). He had been arrested by Deputy Shadley at Pawhuska, and had been sent to Oklahoma City for safekeeping. This I will explain later.

Having had a chance to distribute the guns, when the jailor opened the door to their cell to let them get water, the prisoners overpowered him. They reached the street, and met City Marshal Jones, who tried to stop them. He was shot and instantly killed by one of the Casey boys, who in turn was shot and killed by a policeman. The other prisoners, including Tom King and Lewis, escaped.

A short time thereafter an attempt was made to hold up the Santa Fe train at Black Bear in the strip. A man by the name of Manuel Herrick entered the train some place before the strip was reached and when Conductor Glazer came through the car, Herrick uncovered a gun he had wrapped up in his overcoat, and made the conductor stop the train, after which he ordered him to go ahead of him and have the express agent open the door. The train had stopped on a high embankment. On their way to the express car, Herrick ordered the conductor to stand with his back to the car so he could pass him and get ahead. The conductor was a powerful man, and as Herrick was passing him, hit him with his fist and knocked him off the embankment.

In addition to the gun, Herrick had also armed himself with a Knights of Pythias sword, which he carried with straps fastened to a belt. When he tumbled down over the embankment, he got himself wrapped up in the belt straps, and before he could get up Glazer was on top of him and had tied him securely with his own straps. Glazer was the conductor on the afternoon train for Wichita, and the superintendent also happened to be on the train. The passengers and the whole train crew gathered around, but could find no trace of anyone who might have been waiting to assist in robbing the train. So the superintendent decided to take the man arrested to Wichita to interview him, and bring him back the next day to Guthrie.

When they arrived at the next station, they wired to Guthrie and asked the marshal to go to the place and try to find out if anybody had been seen loafing near the place. They then wired the railroad officers at Guthrie to furnish without delay an engine and a car for the marshal and such men as he might desire to take with him.

It was one of the last days of June, and Marshal Grimes had been in Guthrie to turn his job over to the new marshal, who was to take over the office on the first of July. The deputy who would be out of a job on the next day had left, so Grimes and I were the only two to go. We got on almost at once, as there was a freight ready to leave for Arkansas City, and we were unloaded at the place where the attempt to rob the passenger train had taken place.

There was nothing there except the wide open prairie, and our investigation was limited to finding, if possible, some tracks of men or horses. Finally we found a freight teamster going towards Guthrie, and he told us that he had seen a man and what he thought was a boy, looking for a camping place, and told us where there was a water hole they had started for. We went there and found the tracks of two horses and of two persons — one set of footprints looking like they had been made by a man, and the other tracks looking like they had been made by a small woman or a boy.

We had no horses and were fifteen miles from the nearest place where we could get food or beds, so we just bedded down in the long grass and waited for the train from Wichita, which would bring the outlaw, and which had orders to pick us up the next morning.

The superintendent was on the train, and the bandit, Herrick, was turned over to me, as I had already been appointed a deputy under the new marshal. He was the hardest looking outlaw I have ever seen. He was wearing an old hat with his hair sticking out on top, and an old pair of plowshoes. He also had on an old necktie and a dirty shirt and that sword buckled on the wrong side. The superintendent had secured a good pair of handcuffs, which were fastened on Herrick's wrists.

Old Heck Thomas was one of our best deputies, but he liked to be seen strutting along with a "bad" man, so I wired for him to meet me at the Guthrie station, and take the prisoner to the jail. Heck was there, but refused to be seen with a "scarecrow", and got another deputy to take him to the jail.

Later I found several persons who gave me a good description of the parties who had been at the scene of the robbery. I also found the owner of the two horses. They had been stolen near Oklahoma City, the day after the jailbreak there. From the circumstances, Ernest Lewis and Tom King were the two who had been waiting for the train, and probably had other helpers to step in if things went right. I told the woman about my suspicion before she escaped from El Reno, and she did not deny that they had picked up the crazy fellow to stop the train so they could rob it.

The man Herrick was given a hearing before the federal court and declared insane. He was sent to an asylum in the east, from which he later returned as cured. He then settled at Perry after the opening of the strip, and became a candidate for Congress. The incumbent, Mr. Morgan, died a few days before the election. So Herrick, the only other candidate for the office, was elected. He made himself conspicuous in Washington by starting beauty parlors for women and taking lessons in flying, and was a disgrace to the voters who had sent him there. I do not know what finally became of him.

Ernest Lewis is the same person who killed a man in the Chicasaw Nation and escaped to Oklahoma, where he lived with the Indians in the Osage country. As I have mentioned before, he there organized an outfit for the purpose of robbing the Wells Fargo Express. An Indian, a cousin of Henry Starr, was one of the gang. The other two were young men of no account. Lewis himself did not enter the express car, but took charge of the loot, consisting mostly of express guns.

The robbery took place on the night of Cleveland's election in 1892. I had been informed that Mrs. Mundays (Tom King), had been seen going north with a bunch of horses, supposed to be a relay for some outfit bent on mischief. Later Three-Fingered Jack, one of our spotters, informed me that the Santa Fe train was the object of their maneuvers. The Santa Fe had given the employees orders to furnish a special train for the United States Officers at any time when it was reported that an attempt would be made to rob any of their trains. I had arranged for the train to be ready by the time the regular train would leave Arkansas City, and also told the telegraph operator to wire the conductor at Arkansas City to be prepared for a holdup. I then had five horses saddled, ready to be put on the train if any suspicious characters were seen near any of the stations.

But it was election night. The operator had forgotten all about train robberies, and was busy receiving election news, for which he received extra pay from the saloons. So it was not until the train was held up at Whorton station, in the strip, that he took time to receive the message in regard to the holdup. It was first reported that the conductor Wilcox had been killed and that the Chief Justice of Oklahoma, who was a passenger on the train, had been badly wounded. In a few minutes we had the horses and men loaded, and were rolling out of the yard. Suddenly the engine took a switch track, and we landed in the ditch and upset the car with the horses, two of which were badly hurt.

Before we could get another outfit, the train that had been held up arrived, and it was then learned that the report about the conductor and the judge were pure fabrications, but that the train had been held up all right.

It had been snowing all night and there was not the least chance that there would be any trail left, nor that the robbers had been identified.

From the express messenger I learned, however, that one of the parties was an Indian. With a couple of men I took the next train to Whorton, to find out if there was any clue left by the robbers. But neither at the station nor from the other employees could we learn anything, and so far as finding out from anyone traveling on the wagon road, that was also impossible, as the country for miles around, which had not been opened for settlement, was just a snow-covered plain without any habitation. So we returned to Guthrie.

A day or so later, I learned that the men, or someone answering the description of the bandits, had stopped at an Indian camp, and after much inquiry I learned that the party had gone to Pawhuska. Lafe Shadley, who was later killed in the Ingalls fight, was a former sheriff at Independence, Kansas, and at the time of the robbery was Chief of the Indian Police in the Osage nation. He was an excellent officer, and knew all the Indians, so I wired and told him to try to find out if any Indians had been away on the night of the robbery.

In a few days Shadley had the three men in jail, after shooting one arm off Jackson, who was one of the robbers. It was not until later that they confessed and told me that Ernest Lewis was the one who had plotted the hold-up, and had the guns taken from the express car. I secured a warrant for Lewis' arrest and sent Heck Thomas to arrest him. Thomas found Lewis in a hotel at Pawhuska, but Lewis was quicker with his gun than Thomas was with his, and would have killed Thomas had it not been for Charley Petit, a colored deputy, who grabbed Lewis and disarmed him.

Petit had been a policeman in Arkansas City, and was a great friend of Bill Doolin, who had worked with him for Halsell. Lewis was taken to Guthrie and confined in the jail there, but I learned that some of his friends were planning to try to get him out. This would not have been a hard matter, as the jail there had not been finished. I decided to take him to the jail in Oklahoma City, and on the way there, he abused me and threatened me with death and destruction as soon as he got out of the jail. Some of the passengers told me to kill him for the vile language he was using, and I felt like doing it, but I could not do that to a handcuffed prisoner. He made his escape from the Oklahoma City jail with the Christian boys and other prisoners, Tom King among them, as I have already related.

After the attempted robbery at Black Bear, Lewis and Tom King disappeared, although I heard from both of them occasionally. Lewis went to Colorado, killed a man there, but got off with a short time in the Colorado State Prison. He returned to his old haunts in the Indian Territory, and married Julia Johnson at Bartlesville after one or two of her former husbands had been killed. Lewis was killed in a fight with a policeman on the 16th of November, 1906. Because a newspaperman referred to the killing as a duel between the policeman, and Lewis, both of whom died, and said that they had both gone to hell where they could start it again, she horsewhipped the newspaperman in the streets. Then she married Emmett Dalton, to whom she had been true for the fifteen years he had spent in jail and the Kansas penitentiary — according to Emmett's own statement in *When the Daltons Rode*.

Tom King, according to reports, died at Tombstone, Arizona, but I do not remember the date.

After Grat rejoined the Dalton Gang in the spring of 1892 the three dissatisfied members also came back, and new plans were formulated. That Bill Dalton knew of these plans can be read between the lines of the following conversations he had with me on the night of May 31st and the morning of June 1st, 1892, when the United States court was in session at Kingfisher, Oklahoma.

After supper, Judge Burford, United States Attorney Horace Speed, and I, representing the U.S. Marshal, were sitting in the hotel lobby, talking about the cases to come up the next day, when Bill Dalton entered the room and started to talk to me. Bill did not whisper any secrets to me, but talked in a rather loud voice, so my companions could hear.

At ten o'clock Bill looked at his watch and spoke out loud: "It is ten o'clock and my bedtime, but I will be down in the morning and have breakfast with you." And sure enough he was there for breakfast. After Bill left for home at ten o'clock the night before, the judge asked me who the man was that had been talking to me, saying that he appeared to be a man of education, and well posted. I told the judge that the man was Bill Dalton, a brother of the notorious train robbers, and the judge asked me to introduce him when he came for breakfast, which I did. The four of us then took the same table, Bill and I sitting opposite one another and the judge and the attorney occupying the other two seats in the same manner.

A short time after eight o'clock the telegraph messenger handed me a telegram from Mr. Fred Dodge, the Chief Special Agent for the Wells Fargo Express Company. It read: "The Daltons held up our car at ten o'clock last night and secured about fifty thousand dollars — please attempt to capture the robbers. They went west from Red Rock".

After I had read the telegram I handed it to Judge Burford, and he read it out to the audience. Bill spoke up as soon as the judge had finished, and exclaimed "Well, I can prove that I was not there", to which I added, "And not by accident either", for I was satisfied that he had been waiting all night for the news, and had purposely made his arrangements to be with the court, and particularly with the marshal, who would most likely be informed if his brothers carried out their plans to rob a train that night. Telegraph service was at that time dependent on the railroad wires, and messages were not delivered until the day shift arrived at the offices, so Bill had no earlier way of learning the news.

The robbery had been performed about June 1st, 1892, at Red Rock, a small station on the Santa Fe about fifty miles south of the middle of the north boundary of Oklahoma. It was also about seventy-five miles north of Whorton, where the Daltons had robbed a train a few months before.

The Santa Fe had set a trap for the boys at Red Rock. They had word that a robbery was to be attempted. They ran a dead-head a few minutes ahead of the regular train. It was loaded with heavily armed officers. But they made a mistake by leaving the train dark. Emmett Dalton was suspicious of this, so they allowed the train to go by. When the regular train pulled in a few minutes later, they robbed it with no trouble. Emmett wrote that not a shot was fired and I believe that is correct. His statement that their haul came a little short of eleven thousand dollars is far above the facts. Much of what they did get was in silver dollars, as had been the case at Lelietta.

As soon as I could take leave of my breakfast companions, I made plans to take the trail. There was no train going north on the Rock Island until after five in the afternoon, and I was unable to get to where I could make connection with the Santa Fe going west, so I did not reach Woodward station until the next day. I then learned that a party from Purcell had gone through there the day before, and was on the trail of the outlaws, who had been reported to have been at Amos Chapman's place and also at McKinley's place. So I had no chance to follow them, even if I had been able to obtain a posse and horses at Woodward station. This was impossible, as there were neither horses nor men there to give any assistance. So there was no way for me to do anything, and I took the first train back to Winfield, Kansas.

The story by Emmett about Bob meeting Miss Moore at Woodward, where she was staying with friends, and of their taking a walk around town to look at the stores, is all hot air. The Strip, or Cherokee outlet, was not opened for settlement until fifteen months later, and Woodward was only a way station where the freight for Fort Supply and Indian Agencies and some mail were delivered to a Quartermaster's Agent. There were neither hotels nor rooming houses.

I was tired and worn out, and when I found that I could not get out on a train for Guthrie until about three o'clock in the morning, I went to a hotel and to bed. I had hardly gone to sleep when I was called and told that I was wanted at Guthrie. A telegram was handed to me and I was informed that the police had Bob Dalton in jail, and wanted me to come at once to identify him so that a reward offered for him dead or alive could be collected.

It was possible that Bob could have left the other members and returned to Guthrie, where one of his old sweethearts was living, and also where a number of his band had their headquarters in the so-called Cowboy Flat, on the Cimarron River near Guthrie. So I took the first train and arrived at Guthrie, where I was at once taken to the city jail to identify the prisoner.

Now, I had not seen Bob Dalton for a long time, and then only when he and Emmett would stop at a camp near the Kansas line, where I had charge of a military supply outfit before the opening of the country. Here Bob and Emmett, and some other travelers from Pawhuska and the Osage reservation would occasionally stop on their way to Wichita. But when they brought the monster they called Bob Dalton before me, I could not help to laugh. Bob Dalton was a well built man, taller than most men, but the Bob they had was at least six inches taller than our Bob Dalton, ungainly, stoop shouldered and awkward in his moves. Bob Dalton was as near a perfectly built man as could be found, and quick in his moves.

It was no trouble for me to decide that neither the police nor anyone else would get the reward, and at the request of the bogus Bob I wired his father in Kansas to come and get him, which he did.

After Bill received the good news about the hold-up at Red Rock he wrote to his wife and told her not to worry about him, that he had been with the U.S. Judge, the U.S. Attorney and the U.S. Marshal during the night of the hold-up, and that as soon as he could see his brothers he would send her the $130.00 they owed to the bank at Visalia. He must have seen them, or at least have been in touch with them, for another letter a few days later stated that he enclosed the $130.00 for the bank and something for herself. The letter did not state how much. Those and many other letters, which she had kept until they were taken from her by the deputy marshals when they killed Bill near Loco, were turned over to me by Shelby Williams, U.S. Marshal for the eastern district of Texas. They had been written in a back room in the Silver Dollar Saloon at Guthrie, but mailed on the train, so the writer's location would not be known.

But Bill was disappointed in the amount of money the boys got at Red Rock, for instead of $50,000 it dwindled down to $1,800 after drafts and other securities had been thrown out.

That was not a great deal of money for eight men, for the whole band had a hand in the game. They included Bob, Emmett, and Grat Dalton, Bill Doolin, George Newcomb, Charley Pierce, Dick Broadwell and Bill Powers.

By the time all of the outside spotters, the Dalton family, and the many loose women were paid off, the treasury box was nearly empty again, and it was necessary to levy another assessment on the railroads. This time it was the Katy, or M.K. & T., railroad that had to dig up. It was at first intended to make Pryor Creek the place for holding up the train, but for some reason the hold-up was changed to Adair. One of our spotters had informed me that the Daltons were planning to hold up a Katy train either at Pryor Creek or at some point near there about the middle of July, 1892. I had wired the Chief Detective of the Katy, giving him what information I had received, but he did not even answer the telegram, so I paid no more attention to the matter.

Adair was a small station on the M.K. & T. railroad about ten miles north of Pryor Creek, now the town of Pryor, in Mayes County, Oklahoma. It was about fifty miles south of the north boundary of the state and about forty miles west of the east boundary. It was also about thirty miles north of Lelietta, where the Daltons had robbed a train some time before. The gang had two locations where they were protected and had cover. From these they could launch a robbery and then dodge quickly back after the robbery was over. One of these was northwest of Wagoner and the other southwest of Whorton. All of the Oklahoma robberies were performed within easy reach of one or the other of these localities.

Emmett stated in his book that on the afternoon before the robbery their presence was reported to the station agent at Pryor Creek and that the agent made arrangements for a posse to be on the train. The details were never known to me. I was not notified of any trouble until after the robbery. But I am inclined to believe that Emmett's statement is correct. In the posse which boarded the train were a number of able peace officers, all well known to me. They included U.S. Deputy Marshal Sid Johnson, Charlie Le Flore, L.L. Hinnery and ten others, making thirteen in all. They were armed to the teeth with shotguns, rifles, and revolvers and should have wiped out the entire Dalton Gang to a man.

But Bob Dalton changed his plans at the last hour. Instead of boarding the train at Pryor Creek, he led his gang northeast and performed the robbery at Adair. When the guards did not meet anyone at Pryor, they thought they had scared the outlaws away. They were in high glee when they arrived at Adair, but were soon faced by the whole Dalton gang. Three of the leaders of the guards, Kinney, Le Flore and Johnson, were wounded. The balance of the guards made little attempt to resist the robbers, who took what they wanted and left without having received a scratch, but, contrary to Emmett's story, after having killed a local physician. The Dalton Gang made their largest haul at Adair, about eighteen thousand dollars. Again a large amount of the booty was in silver dollars. But it did not last them long and it was the last successful robbery attempted by the Dalton Gang.

CHAPTER THIRTEEN

THE BATTLE OF THE BANKS

The town of Coffeyville, Kansas, may exist for thousands of years as an important municipality, but it is doubtful if it ever will be noted for anything so much as it has been for the "battle of the banks." All of the notoriety and sensationalism that had grown up about the Dalton Gang finally was focused at Coffeyville that October morning in 1892 when the Daltons tried to outdo their cousins, the Youngers, by holding up two banks at one time. Bob and Emmett were to rob the First National Bank, and Grat, Broadwell, and Powers, the Condon. In the fifteen minute battle that followed, when all of the Gang but Emmett was exterminated, all of the publicity ever afforded the Gang was localized at Coffeyville. During more than seventy-five years that have followed, whenever the Dalton Gang has been mentioned, there has been a responsive interest and the comment, "Oh yes, they got cleaned out at Coffeyville." The interest still is growing.

In the Gang at the time of the Coffeyville raid were Bob, Grat, and Emmett Dalton, Dick Broadwell, and Bill Powers. These last two had taken part in two of the train robberies performed by the Gang in Indian territory.

Concerning the Gang and their last visit to the home of their mother at Kingfisher, Littleton Dalton has left the following description:

On their way to Coffeyville, Bob, Emmett, and Grat came to Mother's house at Kingfisher one night and stayed until the next night. They slept in the dugout bunk house about one hundred yards west of the house. I carried water from the well to both the boys and their horses each night.

While the boys were in the dugout, several people came to the place. Some neighbor girls came to visit and to sew with my sisters. Several other persons visited. They didn't know the boys were there and if they suspected anything, they said nothing. Until dark, Simon or Ben or I was walking around the house all the time on the lookout for officers. We knew that the boys were doomed. The time for talking was long past. All we could do was to try to keep them from stretching rope.

After dark the three boys got on their horses and rode across the field to a fence, which they took down. They then cut across the wild grass of the prairie until they were many miles from home, meeting Powers and Broadwell near Guthrie. . . . .

> In discussing the Coffeyville battle with me, Emmett Dalton spoke freely of the preliminary preparations for the robbery, as well as of his own part in the affair. He stated to me that he was not in favor of attempting the Coffeyville job; that Bob planned the entire affair.
>
> The citizens of Coffeyville, including some of the bank forces, always had been friendly to them. There might be shooting and some of their old acquaintances might be injured.
>
> But Bob ruled out all objections with the one argument, "There won't be any shooting. It will all be over and we will be on our way into the Nations before they know what has happened."
>
> It had been several years since any of the three Dalton boys had been in Coffeyville and a number of changes had taken place. In addition to other changes, several buildings had been constructed, where in the days when the Daltons lived nearby there were vacant lots. Emmett proposed the evening before the robbery that he ride into town and see if there was anything to interfere with the plans. But Bob said, "No. Someone may recognize you." No one can say what would have been the outcome if Emmett had been allowed to visit Coffeyville before the robbery.
>
> The most important change of all had been brought about by a contract let to install city sidewalks and curbs at uniform levels. In this work the streets were torn up. Worst of all, every hitching rack near the banks had been taken down.
>
> It had been Bob's plan to tie the horses to a hitching rack in front of the Opera House, the back of which adjoined the back of the Condon Bank. This spot was completely protected from the center of the town by brick walls. The hitching rack had been less than one hundred and fifty feet from the door of the Condon Bank and less than two hundred feet from the First National Bank. But, along with the others, this hitching rack was gone.
>
> Bob knew that in an alley just west of the city jail, and adjoining a livery stable, was a fence to which farmers often tied their horses.
>
> Coming into town, traveling south on Union Street, the Gang turned west on Eighth Street in front of the Opera House. A block west they

The Condon Bank at Coffeyville, Kansas. It was one of the two banks the Dalton brothers attempted to rob at the same time, Oct., 5, 1892.

It was directly behind this building that Bob Dalton had planned to tie the horses, while the robbery was going on, but was prevented because the hitching racks there had been removed.

Photo courtesy N.H. Rose, and now in Bear State Library.

turned on Maple and tied their horses in what now is known as Death, or Dalton, Alley. From there they could look directly east into the front of the Isham Hardware Store and the corner of the First National Bank.

Little did any of the Dalton Gang dream that before fifteen minutes had passed more than two hundred bullets would pour out of the front of the Isham store, and that the alley would become a corridor of hot lead, holding the dead bodies of City Marshal Connelly, bandits Bill Powers, Bob, and Grat Dalton, and the shattered body of Emmett, alive, but bleeding from fourteen deep, paralyzing wounds.

Dismounting, they hurried through the alley east to the Plaza. Alec McKenna, a storekeeper, was sweeping his sidewalk only a few feet from where the gang emerged from the alley. He recognized Bob and Emmett and even Grat, who had fastened some false whiskers to his face.

Grat, Powers, and Broadwell dropped out of the procession at the Condon Bank. Bob and Emmett hurried on across the Plaza to the First National, expecting their work to be over in not more than five minutes. According to Bob's plan, they were to be back on their horses with the loot at the end of five minutes.

Futile plans.

The citizens of Coffeyville were expecting the Daltons. Many business men and bankers, as well as their clerks, had prepared a course of action. McKenna, the sweeper, skipped into his place of business as soon as the Gang passed. Another citizen yelled, "The Daltons are robbing the bank." Before either bank was entered, half of the business men about the Plaza knew what was going on. Ringing from a dozen throats was the cry, "The Daltons are here," and the battle was on.

The Coffeyville Raid has been written and rewritten numerous times; twice by Emmett Dalton, the only survivor of the bandit gang. As long as Emmett lived, the complete story of the battle could not be told without incriminating him. After the battle he pled guilty to second degree murder for the shooting of Cubine, a Coffeyville business man killed during the battle, receiving a life sentence for that crime. Most writers have avoided mentioning any shooting by Emmett. So have most witnesses of the battle.

Charles Gump, probably wounded by Emmett, stated that when he faced the gang, Emmett was carrying a winchester rifle with a grain sack of currency slung across the crook of his left arm, and that he used his rifle freely. Emmett told me almost the same story, adding that twice during the battle he refilled the empty magazine of his rifle.

THE BATTLE OF THE BANKS

The Dalton Gang horses and the fence where they were tied in Dalton Alley, Coffeyville, Kansas, October 5, 1892, reproduced from an accurately redrawn copy of the damaged original run in the Coffeyville Journal newspaper the day after the battle.

Drawn by Joe Rodríguez and now in Bear State Library.

During the summer of 1938 I visited many scenes of Dalton Days in Missouri, Kansas, and Oklahoma, including the old Dalton homes near Belton, Missouri, and Kingfisher, Oklahoma. A number of pioneers were interviewed and their stories obtained concerning the Coffeyville raid. Among these were Charles T. Gump, mentioned above, and Charles T. Carpenter, both of Coffeyville. Carpenter and Gump looked into the muzzles of Dalton winchesters, and, although Gump was wounded, both lived. They furnish additional details and picture first-hand the impressions of participants on the ground.

Following is the Carpenter account:

Coffeyville in 1892 was a frontier town.

The great frontiers of the United States had already been pushed to the Pacific Coast, but right in the heart of America was the Indian Territory, known as the Nations. Immediately south of Coffeyville it stretched in unbroken, rolling plains, crossed by cattle trails. In it were vast herds of cattle, plenty of wild game: turkeys, prairie chickens, and deer. It was a veritable paradise for hunters, but it was also the hideout of ruthless bands of bandits, train and bank robbers, and murderers.

During the '80s of the last century there was an outbreak of criminal violence in the frontier states of the West akin to the organized criminals of the great cities today. The notorious gangs of the Youngers, the Jameses, and the Daltons succeeded each other in careers of crime. The three families were quite similar in their activities. In 1876 the Youngers were imprisoned for life in a Minnesota penitentiary. Frank James retired to his Missouri farm and Jesse James was murdered in his own home in St. Joseph, Missouri by his traitorous companion, Bob Ford.

Then the Daltons rose and kept the entire border in a state of terror. Train robberies were their specialty. Frank was a Deputy U.S. Marshal, never a criminal. He died in line of duty and received honorable burial in Elmwood Cemetery, here in Coffeyville. Grat and Bob, too, at one time held government commissions which they finally used for promoting crime, rather than suppressing it.

The M.K. & T. railroad, after three bold holdups, offered a reward of five thousand dollars for each man participating in the Adair and Pryor Creek robberies. Numerous stories circulated in regard to the activities of these modern Robin Hoods, and every reported holdup from Missouri to California was charged to the gang.

THE BATTLE OF THE BANKS

It was universally admitted that the extraordinarily bold attack on the two Coffeyville banks in broad daylight October 5, 1892, with its thrilling battle and the undaunted courage displayed alike by bandits and citizens, forms the most wonderful story the border ever furnished. Bob was the leader, although younger than Grat. He planned to rob both banks simultaneously, an exploit amazing enough to eclipse the fame of Jesse James and the Youngers.

With Bob were his brothers, Grat and Emmett, Dick Broadwell, a newly-fledged desperado from an honorable Hutchinson family, and stocky, swarthy Bill Powers, who was never definitely identified.

Indian summer was here, with its mild sunshine and purple haze. The bandits, like young Lochinvars, came out of the West, mounted on splendid horses, heavily armed with winchester rifles and revolvers. Grat wore a false beard, but the others were not disguised. Riding in from their camp on Allin's hill, along Eighth Street, they turned south at Maple Street, thence into the alley running through Block 50. The Long-Bell Lumber Company was then where the Columbia building now stands and Charles Munn's residence was where the Kress building is now. They dismounted, tied their horses and marched in close order to the East mouth of the alley, Bob and Emmett leading. They crossed Walnut Street to the Condon Bank. Grat, Broadwell, and Powers entered the southwest door of the Condon Bank while Bob and Emmett continued across Union Street to the First National Bank.

Hearing their clanking spurs, I looked up and saw Grat Dalton level his winchester at me. With an oath he ordered me to hold up my hands. Broadwell took his station at the east door while Powers took the west door. Grat then strode into the back office where Charles M. Ball was seated and ordered him into the front office. He tossed me a two bushel grain sack with the order to put into it the cash in the money drawer. He then asked, "Where is your other currency and gold." Seeing the vault door open, he ordered us to enter and open the safe. Young Tom Babb had dived into the vault at the first appearance of the bandits, and hid behind the book rack. Grat Dalton saw him, and with blood-curdling oaths threatened to kill him, suspecting that he had a gun.

It was then nine-forty o'clock. "Open the safe," ordered Dalton. I took hold of the handle to show that the combination was locked. But Mr. Ball said, "It is a time-lock and will not open until nine thirty." Grat asked, "What time is it now?" Mr. Ball took out his watch, looked at it, and replied, "Nine twenty" although it was really nine forty. Had Grat looked at the clock on the wall he might have seen for himself. However, he cussed and said, "Well, I will hold you for ten minutes until it opens." There were on the floor of the

Dalton Alley, Coffeyville, Kansas, October 5, 1892, reproduced from an old cut run in the Coffeeville Journal the day after the battle.
From the historical collection of Frank F. Latta, now in the Bear State Library.

vault three bags of silver, each containing a thousand dollars. Grat ordered me to put them into the sack, which I did, making the weight of money about two hundred pounds.

During this interval Bob and Emmett had entered the First National Bank, covered the officers and two customers, forced the cashier, Thomas G. Ayres, to open the burglar proof chest of the safe, and put the currency and gold into another two bushel sack, and turned to go out of the front door. They had planned to cross Union Street again and pick up Grat and his two companions at the west door of the Condon Bank, dash through the alley to their horses, and gallop away.

But by this time an alarm had been given. As Bob and Emmett, driving Mr. Ayres before them approached the door, Mr. Cox, American Express agent, opened fire with his forty-four revolver. Leaving Mr. Ayres on the sidewalk, Bob turned back and he and Emmett left through the back door into the alley in the rear, driving before them Will Shepard and Bert Ayres, employees of the bank. Emmett carried the sack of money and Bob his winchester rifle.

Let's return now to the Condon Bank. Hearing the revolver shots, Grat ordered Mr. Ball and Tom Babb to take the sack of money to the front door, and as it was too heavy to carry, they dragged it into the back office, where Grat ordered the silver taken out. He stuffed the currency into his coat pocket. The battle was on. Both the Isham and Boswell hardware stores carried guns and revolvers, which were passed to citizens, who began firing through our windows at the bandits.

The noise was deafening and the acrid fumes of the guns filled the room. Powers was disabled by a shot in his right shoulder and told Grat that he had been shot. Grat replied, "Let's get out of here." The trio huddled at our west door and, crouching low, made a dash to the alley across Walnut Street.

Before leaving the bank, in the midst of the hail of bullets, Grat had told us to go behind our counters and lie down on the floor to escape injury. D.E. James and John D. Levan had entered the bank and been captured by the robbers. Luther Perkins, unaware of events in the room below his office, had seen Bob and Emmett enter the First National Bank. He ran down the stairs to our back door and called to me, "Oh Charlie." Then, seeing us all covered by guns of the bandits, with Grat and Powers aiming at him, he slammed the door shut and scampered up the stairs to his own office, where Joe Uncapher and J.H. Wilcox were watching the battle.

Bob and Emmett had no sooner gained the alley in the rear of the First National Bank than they met Lucius Baldwin, who had snatched a pistol and was watching the back door. Bob ordered him to drop the pistol, but the boy

In the left center is the building occupied by the Condon bank. At the right is the Isham Hardware Store where many citizens were barricaded behind stoves and other hardware. Adjoining the Isham store on the left in the photo is the building (now a grocery store) which housed the other bank, robbed by Bob and Emmett Dalton. Directly to the rear of the light colored car in the center foreground is Death Alley.

Photo by Frank F. Latta, 1938 and now in Bear State Library.

THE BATTLE OF THE BANKS

failed to heed his command, if he heard and understood. Bob fired his winchester and Lucius fell dying, the first victim of the murderous raid.

Bob and Emmett ran out of the north end of the alley into Eighth Street. Going west, they heard the battle already raging around Condon's. George Cubine was standing in front of Rammel's drug store with a winchester, looking north towards the entrance of the First National, awaiting the exit of the robbers he supposed to be within. Bob shot him through the head. By the side of Cubine stood his partner, Charles Brown, unarmed.

As his partner fell dead, Brown stooped down and picked up the rifle. That was his death warrant. Bob sent another bullet from his rifle and Brown, the third man killed, fell dead across the body of his partner and friend.

When Mr. Ayres was driven out on the sidewalk, he ran into Isham's and seized a rifle. He caught sight of the bandit brothers on the corner north at the moment Mr. Cubine fell dying, followed almost immediately by Mr. Brown. Seeing this, Ayres knelt behind Isham's north window to shoot, but Bob's quick eye found him, although he was almost completely concealed.

The distance was about two hundred feet. Mr. Ayres had already aimed, yet more swiftly Bob's winchester blazed and Ayres fell with a bullet through his head. George Pickering placed his thumb over the wound, stopped the spouting blood and no doubt saved him from death. Mr. Ayres slowly recovered, but the frightful scar remained and his face was paralyzed until his death. The brothers continued their flight along the south side of Eighth Street and entered the alley at the rear of the building on the corner of Walnut and Eighth, intending to go where their horses were hitched.

Meanwhile, the three desperadoes in the Condon Bank were waiting for the time clock to open. Bob's first shot was to them the signal to escape, and as they rushed from the bank with what money Grat had put in his pocket, they were in direct range of riflemen concealed in Isham's store.

Bob and Emmett, approaching from the north, met Grat and his associates in Death Alley. John Kloher had run from the south side of the Plaza to the rear of his livery stable. A high board fence shut it from the alley where the Daltons made their stand. Charles T. Connelly, town marshal, followed by Kloher with a rifle, came into the alley west of the robbers. He ran boldly, looking west, not seeing them less than fifty feet behind him. Grat Dalton, although wounded, shot him through the head. Connelly was the fourth citizen to die. Then Grat turned to face the increasing storm.

The firing was so furious the outlaws could not mount their horses. Broadwell shot and killed two horses hitched to an oil tank wagon, because their plunging disturbed his aim.

Looking into Death, or Dalton Alley in Coffeyville, Kansas, 1938. The horses were tied in the alley about fifty feet behind where the auto is parked. In the right foreground appears the front of the Condon Bank. Most of the firing into the alley was from the Isham Hardware Store, almost directly behind the camera.

Photo by Frank F. Latta and now in Bear State Library.

John J. Kloher, Coffeyville liveryman, who did some of the shooting on October 5, 1892.
Photo courtesy N.H. Rose, and now in Bear State Library.

As Bob turned to face Isham's, Henry Isham shot him squarely through the heart, killing him instantly. Grat Dalton, after killing Mr. Connelly, caught sight of Kloher through the fence and lifted his rifle, but Kloher's spoke first and Grat fell dead with a bullet hole exactly in the center of his throat. Shots from the bandits wounded Art Reynolds and Lew Diets in Isham's store.

Broadwell reeled and blood spurted from his mouth, but he mounted his horse and galloped out of town. His body was found two miles away. Powers tried to mount his horse, but a shot from Isham's laid him dead near his leader. Unharmed, and with the sack of money tied to his saddle, Emmett jumped to the saddle on his big bay racer.

And now follows an almost incredible thing; Emmett Dalton, unwounded, with over twenty thousand dollars in cash, mounted on a swift racer, reined his horse before he reached the exit from the alley. Through the hail of bullets, he deliberately rode back to where his brother, Bob, lay dead and tried to lift him into the saddle, that he might bear away his corpse.

Carey Seaman, barber, fired a load of buckshot into Emmett's back and the youth fell unconscious by the side of his brother, an arm shattered, a thigh broken by a rifle bullet, and a dozen buckshot in his back.

The last raid of the Daltons was ended. In Death Alley lay three dead robbers with another fatally (as was supposed) wounded, another dead in the country and Marshal Connelly, who died in the line of duty. Among the dead and dying horses, and through the winchester smoke, the distracted citizens moved the dead citizens to their homes, while the bodies of the dead raiders were placed in the city jail. Emmett, the sole Dalton survivor, found refuge in the office of Dr. Walter Wells.

Coffeyville sat in sack-cloth and ashes to mourn for the heroic men who had given their lives for the protection of their fellow-citizens and the maintenance of law in the old home town.

> The account furnished by Charles T. Gump gives a description of the battle from the street and reveals that it was he who gave the general alarm, even before Bob and Emmett had entered the First National Bank, and brought on the heated battle that followed. It will be noted that, contrary to most printed accounts, Gump has denied that he was shot by Bob Dalton when he first cried that the Daltons were robbing the banks. He stated that he was shot later by Emmett and was holding a shotgun in his hands at the time:

The report that I recognized the Dalton boys when they came into Coffeyville to hold up the banks is wrong. I didn't know any of them. They had lived near Coffeyville for several years, it is true, but I hadn't come to Coffeyville until after they had gone, so I didn't know them. I had seen Bob once, but didn't know who he was until afterward. I saw Bob on the train while we were crossing the Missouri River. He was riding in a chair car a seat or two ahead of me. As the train was crossing the river he decided to do some target practice. He took out his six shooter and began shooting at some object floating on the water. There were several women in the car and they were badly frightened.

One of the women became hysterical. The conductor came in and gave Bob a good lecture. He called him by name and showed that he knew him. He said, "Bob, you know better than to do a thing like that when there are women in the car. If you wanted to shoot out the window you should have told these people that you were shooting for target practice or you should have gone into the smoker." Afterward I asked the conductor who the man was and he answered that it was Bob Dalton. I had heard of him as a U.S. Marshal, but it was before any of them got into any kind of trouble.

When the Dalton gang came into Coffeyville on the morning of the robbery I was standing near the city pump, a long handled fire pump to be operated by four or more men. I was about thirty-five years of age at the time. Old Billy Hughston, constable, was standing beside me. He was about seventy years of age. We were talking about the street work that was being done. The city was having the sidewalks put on an even level and some paving done. They had let a contract for the work. The contract was let to a Mr. Brewster. I had hired my teams to Brewster and was overseeing part of the work.

As we were talking, I saw five men march over from the mouth of Dalton Alley to the Condon Bank. They were hurrying along, almost on a dog trot and were heavily armed. Several of them carried winchester rifles held down close along their legs as they walked. As soon as I first looked at them I was suspicious of them. I told Billy, "Say, Bill, those fellows are the Daltons and they are going to hold up the Bank." Billy laughed and said, "Oh, I guess not." Just then three in the rear cut over to enter the Condon Bank, and I was positive that I had guessed right in the first place.

I yelled at the top of my voice, "The Daltons are robbing the bank." I remember that a number of people were outside their places of business, one man sweeping off the sidewalk. Several of them took up the cry and actually, before Emmett and Bob had entered the other bank, a dozen or two persons knew what was going on.

As soon as I yelled, Billy knew I was right, but he told me to shut my mouth, that they would shoot us and, if not, my yelling would warn them, but I yelled again, anyway. I ran into Isham's Hardware store and got a winchester rifle, intending to shoot the bandits' horses. You know a bandit afoot isn't much of a badman. But George Pickering wouldn't let me kill the horses. He said, "If you kill their horses they'll kill every person in town." Really, I wasn't as brave as this sounds, because I hadn't been in the Dalton country long enough to hear all about their outlawry, so I wasn't as afraid of them as were some of the Coffeyville citizens. But Pickering took the rifle from me. He was a big man and took the rifle from me easily.

I ran back into Isham's store and got a shotgun, about the only thing left by that time, guns were being handed out so fast. I ran out again. This had all taken a lot of time and Bob and Emmett were about ready to come out of the First National Bank next to the Isham store. I hid behind a big, solid looking column between the bank door and Isham's. I could look in and see them coming out, the bankers ahead. I yelled at them to come on out, swearing at them and telling them that I would take care of them.

The bankers came out. Bob stepped out of the door just long enough to fire a couple of shots. I could see Emmett behind him, trying to bang the swinging door open with his gun, a heavy bag of money hanging across his left arm. To this day I believe that Emmett shot me. But he afterward said not; that Bob poked his rifle around the column and pulled the trigger. Anyway, before I could get them where I could fire the shotgun at them without risking hitting the bankers, a bullet took me in the right hand between the thumb and forefinger, knocking the forestock off the shotgun and denting the barrels. I went back into Ishams. Bob and Emmett went back into the bank and out the back way.

I don't know much more about the rest of the fight than anyone else. Broadwell rode out Eighth Street to where the school is now. There, by a hedge, he fell from his horse, dead. The horse was quietly feeding by the roadside when a party came on Broadwell's trail and hauled his body back to town in a wagon.

One other thing was confused at first. A number of persons were sure that there were six of the bandits before they entered Coffeyville. No one saw more than five in Coffeyville. Emmett later told me that only five of them started on the expedition. A posse investigated their camping place on Sycamore Creek. They had fed their horses there during the night. There were only five places where horses had fed. [It generally has been agreed that, because of a lame horse Bill Dalton was forced to leave the gang and retreat into Oklahoma.]

After the shooting was over, Emmett was carried upstairs from the alley directly to the office of old Doctor Wells. Wells knew Emmett. He was from the Daltons' home country. A gang went up the stairs with a rope and were going to hang Emmett. They were going to put the rope around his neck, tie it to a telephone pole outside, and throw him out the window. Doc Wells said, "This is my patient. My patients all die. Don't hang a dead man". In this way Doc was able to talk them out of it. Emmett was kept in Wells' office that day and for some time afterward.

When the crowd was trying to hang Emmett he said he'd tell all about the rest of the Dalton Gang, and all the other gangs in the Nations, if they would spare him. But he changed his mind afterward.

It was common talk around Coffeyville that the Daltons had brought all their trouble on themselves, starting by stealing horses while Bob and Grat were U.S. Deputy Marshals.

> The Carpenter and Gump accounts present illuminating personal impressions of a terrific battle, but the Coffeyville affair was a free-for-all and no dozen persons observed everything that happened. At the time of the raid, A.J. Biddison, later a Tulsa attorney, had an office over the Condon Bank. Until the shooting was well under way, and Luther Perkins rushed upstairs after his brief glimpse of the robbery below, Biddison didn't know that the Condon Bank was being robbed. He saw only the action across the street at the other bank. Biddison snatched a revolver from a desk drawer and fired from a window at every robber he saw, adding his bit to the stream of lead that poured into the mouth of Dalton Alley toward the spot where the horses of the bandits were tied. Although he thought he was unobserved by the outlaws, a winchester bullet plowed through the window casing a foot above Biddison's head. Other unnamed citizens undoubtedly did more such shooting, but, in the general battle, their action was unobserved.
>
> When the raid was over, Coffeyville citizens had written one of the most remarkable records ever made of resistance by laymen against organized bandits. Emmett Dalton was not far wrong when he later stated that it looked as though everyone in Coffeyville had a gun.
>
> One fact missed in most accounts of the Dalton raid is that Coffeyville had been officially forewarned. It long has been a mystery how this warning came about. The late George A. Yoes, of Greenland, Arkansas, who served out of Fort Smith under his father, Deputy U.S. Marshal, Col. Jacob Yoes, finally explained this mystery in a letter to me in 1942, also in a personal interview in 1944. The Yoes statement follows:
>
> I knew all the Daltons. Frank was killed just across the river from Fort

Smith. Bob and Grat had commissions under my father, Col. Jacob Yoes, and Emmett was posseman for them. I am the only man living who knows just how they got put out of business. I have never before told anyone about it, but here is the story.

When they were planning the robbery, one of their bunch came to Fort Smith and told U.S. Jailor W.B. Pope, my father, and me that the Daltons were going to rob either the two banks in Van Buren, Arkansas, or in Coffeyville, Kansas. This fellow had been in jail in Fort Smith and we had treated him well. He knew that father was president of the Crawford County Bank of Van Buren, so he tipped us off. We at once armed all the merchants in Van Buren with 38-56 winchesters and notified the banks at Coffeyville to prepare for the raid; so the citizens and bank officials were looking for the Daltons when they came. Emmett Dalton stated in his book that it looked like everyone in Coffeyville had a gun and I guess most of them did.

I also interviewed Chris Madsen about this tip-off that had been furnished the officers prior to the Coffeyville raid. His statement fully corroborated that made by George A. Yoes. In addition it made clear the fact that Bill Dalton not only knew of the plans to rob the Coffeyville banks, but was in waiting to aid in the get-away. Following is what Madsen wrote about the affair:

About the first of October, 1892, the United States Marshal at Guthrie, Oklahoma, was officially notified that the Dalton Gang was preparing to make a grand raid on the banks at Coffeyville, Kansas, or at Van Buren, Arkansas. The information came from the United States Marshal Jacob Yoes at Fort Smith, Arkansas, who stated that a prisoner, who had been in company with the Daltons, had given him the tip, because the marshal had in former years done the prisoner favors. He had also learned that the marshal was President of the Crawford County Bank, and did not want him to lose his money. Furthermore, he, the prisoner, had been a spy for the Daltons, but after they had found out all they wanted, they had left him without a penny and told him that if they heard of him telling anything about them they would kill him.

After I received Marshal Yoes' information, and in the absence of Marshal Grimes, I notified the deputies near the Oklahoma and Kansas borders to be prepared to take the field at once if ordered by wire. As some of the deputies were too talkative, I did not let them know what information we had from Mr. Yoes. A couple of days before the Daltons started on the trip for

Ex Deputy U.S. Marshal George A. Yoes, of Greenland, Arkansas. George A. Yoes was a deputy under his father, Col. Jacob Yoes, when Franklin, Grat, Bob and Emmett Dalton were marshals out of Fort Smith, Arkansas. He placed Grat Dalton in the same Fort Smith jail cell where Grat had placed many other prisoners.

Photo from the collection of Frank F. Latta and now in Bear State Library.

Coffeyville, I received a telegram from the marshal, telling me that they were ready to make the assault on some of the banks. Hence we kept our office open day and night, waiting for news.

The clerks and office deputy had just left for dinner on the 5th of October, and I was alone in the office, when I received a telegram from the Mayor of Coffeyville stating that the Daltons had attempted to rob two banks in the town, but that they had been repulsed and three of them killed in a fight with the citizens. The message also stated that one of the gang had been badly wounded, and that one had escaped. I at once telegraphed to the deputies to be on the look-out for the one who had escaped. Before I could get the telegram off, I received another message saying that the one who had escaped temporarily, had been found near the edge of the town where he had dropped dead from his horse.

I then called the newspapers and told them if they would come to the office at once, they would get some real news. They came, and a few minutes later extras were on the streets.

Soon a man came to the office and inquired about the telegram — whether it was genuine news or a hoax. I told him that it was genuine. Before I could ask him any questions he was out of the door, and presently Bill Dalton appeared for the same information.

Bill Dalton and this other look-out had both been at Fitzgerald's place, near where the road from Guthrie branches off for Stillwater. As I learned later, Bill Doolin had also been there with them. They had been waiting for the news from Bob's outfit, but had grown tired of waiting and had moved closer to Guthrie. The first man had been sent into town to be near the marshal's office, and ready to inform others if any news was received. I am not sure whether Doolin came with the other two, or went to one of their harboring places in Cowboy Flat, but I am satisfied that Bill and his companion had extra horses placed at some pre-arranged hideout, should the boys succeed at Coffeyville and need re-mounts.

However, Bill did not get much agitated, and asked me to wire the Mayor of Coffeyville and find out if it would be safe for him and his mother to come there to see Emmett, who was not expected to get over his wounds. I sent the telegram, and the Mayor answered that if they would wire him when they would arrive, he would see to it that they be permitted to see him.

As soon as I told Bill, he left to notify his mother, but whether he went direct to Kingfisher, or met his people at some place in Kansas, I do not know, for I never saw him or his mother again, except Bill — after he had been killed and his body shipped to Guthrie for identification.

So far as the fight at Coffeyville is concerned, the main points are as well

Charles Gump at the graves of the Daltons in Elmwood Cemetery, Coffeyville, Kansas.
Photo by Frank F. Latta, 1938 and now in Bear State Library.

stated in Emmett's book as any man, not on the ground, now could do. Most of the details were told in newspapers, and most of Emmett's book is almost a reprint of what was published fifty years ago.

Although sieved by twenty pieces of lead, Emmett Dalton did not die. A rifle ball had shattered his right arm above the elbow. Another had cut through his cartridge belt and entered his hip from behind, passing out through the groin. Eighteen buckshot from Carey Seaman's shotgun had driven deep into his back.

After his recovery, Emmett pled guilty to the killing of George

Headstone at the Dalton graves in Elmwood Cemetery, Coffeyville, Kansas. Photo by Frank F. Latta, 1938 and now in Bear State Library.

Cubine. He was sentenced to life imprisonment and served almost fifteen years at Lansing Prison. Just past twenty years of age when he entered prison, he was soon made foreman of the tailor shop, and fitted some of his old associates with stripes when they drifted into prison. In 1907 he was pardoned. He married soon after. For several years Emmett lectured, exhibited motion pictures, and in 1918 wrote a book about his experiences as an outlaw, the title of the book being *Beyond the Law*. A later book was titled *When the Daltons Rode*. About 1916 he came to Los Angeles County, California, where he became a successful contractor and builder. In discussing his experiences with me in 1935 he stated that he had cleared more money in building the house in which we then were seated than he had from any robbery he had ever helped perform.

Although the years of prison and outlaw life had left their mark, one could not help but admire Emmett Dalton. He was a large man, about the height of Bob, more than six feet tall, and for many years weighed well over two hundred pounds. But the old arm wound, received in Coffeyville, that October morning, never healed. It wore down even his tremendous physique until, when he was last interviewed for this account, he was a shrunken, shaking wreck. He died in 1936. His body was cremated. Before she passed away in 1944 at Fresno, California, his wife placed his ashes beside those of Bob and Grat in Elmwood Cemetery, Coffeyville, Kansas.

This brick building was constructed on Turner Island soon after Turner acquired the property. Turner purchased the island, which lies between the main San Joaquin River and Salt Slough, with gold mined near Hornitos and Mariposa. It first was used as a dairy house, butter and cheese manufactured there and shipped to Stockton on steamboats. During the time when the Dalton brothers worked for Turner, they used it as a bunkhouse. Brothers who slept there included Bill, Ben, Cole, Simon, Grat, Bob (and Littleton very briefly).

Photo by Frank F. Latta and now in Bear State Library.

CHAPTER FOURTEEN

Bill Dalton's Gang

When Eugene W. Kay, ex-sheriff of Tulare County, California, began relating his experiences, it was clear that all previous impressions of Bill Dalton needed revamping. The common picture was of Bill as a jolly, harmless sort of fellow, given principally to telling funny stories and playing practical jokes. This impression was gained from friends and neighbors who had known Bill at the California ranches of Turner and Bliven, and from the fact that Bill was a family man and so could not have been very dangerous. The persons interviewed had known Bill only before he had gone bad.

It will be remembered that when Kay arrested Bill Dalton at Cross Creek in September of 1891, he immediately saw that Bill had "jumped the line". By this Kay meant that Bill had made his final fatal decision; that he had plunged from the position of a highly respected family man and rancher to that of an outlaw. There was no question that when Bill and Riley Dean were arrested, just after the Ceres robbery, they were planning one of three things: to hold up a train, to aid Grat in a getaway, or to do both. It will also be remembered that Grat did escape less than three weeks later and that even before the Ceres robbery he was working toward that end. Here is what Kay had to say about the situation at that time.

By the time of the Ceres robbery, I had thoroughly studied four of the Dalton boys. These were Bill, Grat, Cole, and Lit. I had also seen Ben and Bob several times, but had talked to Bob only a few times. I had heard of Emmett, particularly in connection with the Alila affair, but, even to this day, I have never seen Emmett Dalton to know him.

I got most of my information about Emmett from Clark Bliven, Bill Dalton, and Jim Ford, my deputy. The six Daltons I had known were interesting men, all fine specimens of physical manhood, intelligent, but high tempered, quick to take offense, and, once offense was taken, certain to carry it with them to the grave.

As I have often said, Grat was my favorite of the four outlaws. He had that fibre of responsibility that one found in Lit and Ben. Grat was a heavy drinker and a noted fist fighter, but I could talk to him and be certain what he would do, even if it was only to be certain that he would kill me. He kept only one door open.

Although Bill occupied the respectable position of family man, politician, and rancher, he kept all doors open all the time and I had the feeling that he might disappear through any of them, any time. Bill was a great actor. He posed until the last as a harmless wag and clown, but there was more than that under the surface.

At Cross Creek, when I was arresting Bill and I called him by his first name, he thought I was Riley Dean. Here is what Bill afterward told me: "I thought Riley had heard the buggy go on down the road, had crawled out of the trap door, and was calling to me to know who had passed." That is the reason Bill turned his head, instead of swinging the winchester around and pulling the trigger.

But when Bill dropped the butt of his winchester to the floor and began to laugh, I could see the handwriting on the wall. Bill was saying to himself, "All right, old boy, but it won't be like this very long." From that second on I never gave Bill one-fourth the chance I would have given Grat. This caution was immediately put into effect.

To take Bill Dalton and Dean to Visalia after the arrest at Cross Creek required close work. First I had Witty shackle them, looping the chains through each other. Then I watched them while Witty gathered up their guns and finished saddling their horses. The gun I took away from Bill was a new 45-60 winchester. The packing case in which this gun had been shipped was in the barn where the horses were tied. Witty found the horses were almost completely saddled. We had surprised Dalton and Dean while they were getting ready to travel.

Witty tied the guns to the saddles and I had him throw the ammunition in the creek so Dalton and Dean couldn't recover their weapons in any kind of a break and lay us out. I put Bill and Dean in the buggy and had Bill drive the team to Visalia. When we started, Witty sat on the back of the buggy and led the saddled horses. I stood on the axle of the buggy, directly behind Bill Dalton, with my revolver drawn and the muzzle of it against the back of the buggy top, less than six inches from Bill's back. Witty and I traded places about once a mile.

It was about twelve miles from Cross Creek to Visalia and, before we reached the County Jail, that old buggy axle almost had cut the insteps of our

Bill Dalton, leader of the famous Bill Dalton outlaw gang.
Photo courtesy N.H. Rose and now in Bear State Library.

feet in two. We got there about seven o'clock in the evening and we couldn't walk for two hours afterward.

Jailor Williams was the only one of my force at the jail when we arrived. He swore we were the funniest looking outfit he had ever seen. He said, "Kay, I thought sure Bill Dalton had captured you and Witty and had you tied up in the back of the buggy."

I remember that we sat on the jail steps and nursed our crippled feet and Bill, and Dean, and Williams stood around and laughed their heads off at us. But I could see all the time that the very fact we had given Bill Dalton no chance to make a getaway or to get the drop on us had made him more deadly than ever.

If you will study the rest of Bill Dalton's career you will come to the same conclusion I did about him. He was the most tricky and dangerous one of the Dalton Gang. . . . .

At that time few officers were as familiar as they might have been with Bill Dalton's career. They knew he had been a great entertainer and joker. When Grat was tending bar in Livingston, Bill put a dead cat in a shoebox and set it under the bar among some mops and dust cloths. Before Grat found what was the matter, the odor had driven all the customers from the place. Bill related this joke to anyone who would listen.

At least one of Bill Dalton's jokes at the Turner ranch threatened to lead him into serious trouble. Here is the way Arch Turner told the story:

There was a good looking Irish girl named Nora Coffee cooking on the ranch and a young Irishman doing roustabout work there. Bill and Cole Dalton were skinning mules for my father. Bill joshed the Irish boy about the cook. Some of Bill's joshing was pretty rough and the boy didn't take it very well. This continued for several days and finally came to grief one evening while Bill was unharnessing his team in the barn.

The Irish boy resented something Bill said about his attentions to the cook and attacked Bill with his fists. Bill hit him over the head with the tines of a manure fork, knocking him senseless and cutting a large gash in his scalp.

The roustabout fell under the mules and they began plunging about so Bill couldn't rescue him. Bill called to Cole, who had a team in the opposite side of the barn. Cole didn't come immediately, so Bill ran to get him, swearing a blue streak all the time.

As soon as Bill and Cole got the roustabout out of the barn, Cole carried him to the bunk house and Bill saddled a horse and rode to Hills Ferry as hard as he could go. He got Doctor Miller to come out to the ranch and take care of the injured boy. Bill paid the boy's doctor bill and wages while he was laid off, and was a mighty relieved fellow when he found that the boy was out of danger.

In Dalton Gang Days the vicinity of the Turner ranch on the Merced

River was a picturesque and historic locality. Stretched for a distance of fifteen miles along the banks of the Merced and San Joaquin Rivers were the ranches of John Turner, W.G. Collier, and J.J. Stevinson.

Stevinson settled on the Merced in 1854, taking his bride to a log cabin on the site of the present Stevinson home in 1856. The Stevinson ranch included 25,000 acres of river land, extending along the Merced River to the point where the Merced emptied into the San Joaquin. The town of Stevinson is located on this old ranch. Before Henry Miller, of Miller & Lux, entered the Joaquin, J.J. Stevinson was known as the Cattle King of the Joaquin. In 1934 his wife, Louisa Jane (Cox) Stevinson passed away at the old homestead, aged 94 years; 84 years after she came to the Merced river and 78 years after she had arrived on the old place as a bride on horseback, with her entire personal belongings in a carpet bag. She had sewed and knitted while she watched the elk and grizzly bear pass within fifty feet of her open log cabin window, and stayed until the transcontinental air liners carried their colored lights over the same spot.

On the west bank of the San Joaquin River, directly opposite the mouth of the Merced, was the old San Joaquin River town of Hills Ferry, as late as 1886 the second town in Stanislaus County. Hills was a roaring, wide-open town, born of travel to the mines, reared on the river steamboat trade, and boasting a two story hotel (shipped 'round the Horn), a full-fledged town of sporting and gambling houses, a Chinatown, and a white, respectable population of one hundred seventy-five.

Above the Stevinson ranch was that of W.G. Collier. Collier and wife had crossed the plains to California in 1853. During that winter, in the midst of a blinding snow storm, on the summit of the Sierra Nevada Mountains, their first child was born. She was named in true pioneer fashion, "Sierra Nevada Summit" Collier. "Sierra" later changed this to Emma Summit Collier.

Fleetness of Dalton Gang Days can best be recognized by considering that Emma Collier was born almost ten years before any of the Dalton Gang and outlived all of them, including Emmett, by more than ten years. She lived in Turlock, California, and passed away when more than ninety years of age.

W.G. Collier was a supervisor in Tuolumne County during the mining days and settled on the Merced River in 1857. In the Collier family were ten girls and one boy. In 1942 seven of these "girls" and the "boy" were still living. Five of the "girls", Misses Sarah, Mary, and Lillian, Mrs. Whitworth, and Mrs. Hartman resided on the old Collier ranch.

Mary passed away in 1942. The other four in 1945 were still living on the old place.

In the 1850's Turner settled adjoining Collier upstream. In the course of years he became a prominent stockman. In 1883 the first of the Dalton brothers started work for Turner. This was Cole. He was soon followed by Grat, Bob, and Bill. Littleton and Ben each occasionally worked at the Turner ranch. Frank, Simon, and Emmett were probably the only Dalton brothers who lived to maturity and did not work at the Turner ranch.

The lower Merced River and the territory about old Hills Ferry, which knew the Daltons so well, is unique in California in that a large percentage of the original settlers remained in the vicinity. Besides those mentioned, descendants of many other settlers are still nearby, or own their original homesteads. These include the descendants of Newsome, Hawkins, Steinberg, Mendoza, Ruddle, Barfield, Moreno, Belt, Gorham, and De Hart. It was into this pioneer western society that the Dalton boys drifted during the years from 1883 to 1901. They were entirely at home. They came and went among the best families of the locality. Along the Merced and San Joaquin Rivers they retained many warm friends. Sarah Collier stated:

On a Sunday afternoon in either 1888 or 1889 my Mother and I visited the home of Colonel J.J. Stevinson. There we found Billy Dalton, his wife, Jane, and their little son, Chub, aged about four. They were very nicely dressed and looked prosperous and happy. Mr. and Mrs. Stevinson treated them with every courtesy and seemed glad to have them as their guests. Billy Dalton was well liked and well treated by the best people in Merced County. No one would ever have dreamed that he was to become a bank or train robber.

It is well within the facts to state that in Merced County Bill Dalton was more respected than many of the officers who pursued him. This is best supported by the fact that his bondsmen included an ex-supervisor, the father of a Merced County deputy sheriff, and one of the most influential merchants in the county.

Lillian Collier said:

I knew a number of the Dalton brothers, Billy and Cole best of all. They worked a number of years for our neighbor, Mr. Turner. Often, in bad weather, Mr. Turner used to send one of them with a surrey to drive us girls to church, which was held in the little school house several miles distant.

In 1896 to 1898, Jane (Bliven) Dalton, widow of Billy Dalton, lived across the Merced River only a short distance from our home. She had married a neighbor named Adams. Her two children, Chub (Charles Coleman), and Gracie Dalton, attended the Fairview school, which I taught. They rode to and from school with me. I came to know them intimately and to dearly love them. Chub was a roly-poly blond, blue eyed boy, bubbling over with fun and talk. Gracie was quiet. She was a cripple. One of her hips had been injured in a fall.

On the drive in a cart to and from school, Chub used to entertain me with the most thrilling, fascinating stories about when the bad men broke into their home, took their money and jewels and killed their father, Billy Dalton.

The Dalton brothers I knew were as courteous and gentlemanly as any men I ever met. They didn't exhibit one rough characteristic of any kind, and I don't even yet believe one-tenth of the terrible things I have heard about them.

It has been the experience of the writer to interview many others of Bill Dalton's neighbors concerning the cause of Bill's "jumping the line." Their response has been almost unanimous: "Bill was no different from ninety per cent of us who are today occupying responsible positions in life and getting by rather successfully." Boiled down to a single statement, this is the essence of what most of these pioneers have said: "If it hadn't been for Bob and Emmett, Bill Dalton today would be a prosperous farmer, a good neighbor, and one of the finest fellows you ever met." Undoubtedly this is the truth about Bill Dalton.

As an introduction to the career of Bill Dalton, the outlaw, and his gang, let us consider what Littleton Dalton had to say, remembering always that Lit never referred to him as Bill, but always by his correct name, Mason:

When Mason went east after Grat's escape, he left his family at Livingston, California, with his wife's parents. After the three boys got together in the Cheyenne country, he sent for the family. They came to Kingfisher and soon located on a ranch about eight miles from that town.

I stayed with Mother at Kingfisher until after the Coffeyville raid. I didn't go to see Emmett until about a month after the raid. I talked with the sheriff at Kingfisher and he advised me not to go until things quieted down, that I probably would be involved in a shooting affray if I went.

Emmett was soon moved to the County Jail at Independence. I went up there to see him. The citizens there were surely angry and didn't look at me with any favor. In addition to the Coffeyville mixup, they knew I was a cousin to the Younger boys who had helped Quantrill raid Independence several times during the Civil War. The war was recent enough that some of them could remember it.

When I went to Independence, like everyone else at that time, I wore a six-shooter. The sheriff went in with me to see Emmett, but he had me take off my gun and leave it in his office. Emmett was very weak, but was then known to be out of danger. It was the last time I ever saw him. He lived here in California for more than twenty years, but he never came to see me. I guess he remembered that night at Clovis Cole's, when I told him and Bob that I never wanted to see them again.

When they found I was at Independence, the officers at Coffeyville, Kansas, wanted me to identify Bob, Grat, and Emmett's guns. I went down to Coffeyville and was taken to one of the banks, where they had the guns locked in a vault. They were the boys' guns all right, and I identified them for the bank officials. But they surely gave me a close looking over. I was never the subject of such close watching in my life. I didn't blame them for suspecting me. They had plenty of reason to suspect.

I stayed at Mother's for some time after the Coffeyville raid. I met several of the gang who had run with Bob and Emmett. I saw three of them: Bill Doolin, George Newcomb, and Charlie Pierce. They said they came to the house to console Mother, but when they found I was there they put up a proposition to me of joining up with them in order to even up scores for the boys up at Coffeyville. It was Doolin who propositioned me to go with them. I was too mad to laugh at him, but I guess that's what I should have done. As I have stated, Mason was then working on a ranch about eight miles from Kingfisher, and I was afraid all the time they would go to him. I had worried about his taking up with Riley Dean in California, and almost predicted what actually finally did happen to Mason.

After Grat's escape I didn't see my brother, Mason, again until I went to Kingfisher. I didn't attend his trial at Visalia, California.

Of course Mason had a plausible story about his association with Riley Dean, of Traver. He told me that Dean had simply been riding the horse until Grat could escape. Then Mason and Grat would have left for Indian

Territory, and Dean would have gone back to Paso Robles. The Ceres train robbery had interfered with their plans.

I wasn't satisfied with the story.

While I was at Mother's, I talked to Mason as soon as I could and tried to get him to go back to California with me. I also put Mother on his trail and she did all she could toward the same end. Mason would listen to us and laugh, and tell us he wouldn't have anything to do with any outlaw gang. I knew better. But I had to come back to California without him.

About two months after I went back to work at Clovis Cole's, Mother began to write me that she was afraid Mason was going to get into trouble. He had quit work and was running around with Doolin, Pierce, Newcomb, and some other outlaws. She thought he had been mixed up in several affairs, but wasn't sure. This went on for about a year, Mother getting more uneasy all the time. Then I read in the papers about the fight at Ingalls.

Ingalls was a little village in Payne County, Oklahoma, about sixty-five miles northeast of Kingfisher. I never knew much about Mason's trouble until after the Ingalls fight. The Gang was lucky at Ingalls. If the posse had been careful, the Gang would have been wiped out. As it was, every one of the Gang was wounded in the getaway. Several of the officers were killed. From then on it was all off with Mason. It was only a question of time until he would run into the same kind of a mess that the other boys had encountered up at Coffeyville. . . . .

> When Bill Dalton located near Kingfisher, what was left of the gang which had operated under the noted Cherokee Indian bandit, Henry Starr, was in hiding at the home of Ben Howell in the northeast portion of the Cherokee strip, about seventy-five miles northeast of Kingfisher. Bill Doolin, former member of the original Dalton Gang, had accompanied Starr on several raids. Doolin was delegated to bring Bill Dalton into the fold. Shortly after Littleton Dalton returned to California, Doolin was successful in his efforts. Bill Dalton soon aided in several robberies. Lit furnished the foregoing information, as well as the fact that by the last of August, 1893, Bill was accepted as leader of the Gang. Henry Starr had been arrested and was awaiting trial in the Federal Jail at Fort Smith. According to Lit, the Gang was known from then until the death of Bill Dalton as the Bill Dalton Gang.
>
> According to statements made by Littleton Dalton, the Indian Territory force of U.S. Deputy Marshals finally obtained reliable information regarding Bill's Gang. They were hidden in northeastern Payne

County, and were obtaining their ammunition, groceries, tobacco, and liquid refreshments at a little village known as Ingalls, about ten miles east of Stillwater. A raid was planned to catch them in Ingalls. This raid took place on a forenoon in September, 1893. From statements of Littleton Dalton and an article in a Stillwater newspaper, we have an accurate account of what took place that morning at Ingalls.

U.S. Deputy Marshals Dick Speed, T.J. Houston, and Lafe Shadley located the Gang in the O.K. Hotel in Ingalls. They were in an upstairs room, according to Lit, actually in the midst of planning a bank robbery. "Arkansas" Tom Jones was sick in bed. He looked out the window beside his bed, saw the marshals, and pointed them out to the rest of the Gang, which was composed of Bill Dalton, Bill Doolin, George Newcomb, and Tulsa Jack. Dalton, Doolin, and Newcomb crowded to the window and immediately opened fire, wounding Houston, and killing Speed and a young Ingalls man named Dell Simmons, who was mistaken for an officer.

The bandits had placed their saddled horses in a barn some distance from the O.K. Hotel. In order to reach this barn, it was necessary to cross an open space about a hundred yards wide. In the firing from the window, Shadley was not wounded. Houston was struck in the side by a bullet which glanced from the stock of his winchester, but he was not downed.

As the five bandits tumbled from the hotel entrance, the two officers poured into them a fire from winchesters that was hotter than some of them could stand. Dalton and Doolin ran through this fire to the barn, but Tulsa Jack and Newcomb dodged into the saloon, which was operated by N.D. Murry. From there they returned the fire.

The officers simply riddled the saloon, wounding everyone in it, including Murry. Houston continued firing into the saloon until he was brought down by another ball, this time through the body. Shadley mounted his horse and pursued Dalton and Doolin, reloading his winchester as he rode.

When Dalton and Doolin raced their horses from the barn, Shadley shot Dalton's horse. The horse fell, throwing Dalton flat on the ground, where he remained motionless. Thinking that Dalton was killed, Shadley dismounted and approached on foot, playing into the hand of tricky Bill, who, according to Lit, was "playing possum."

When Shadley had approached to within about thirty feet, Dalton opened fire with his winchester and shot the marshal three times, as

Shadley said before he died, "quicker than he could reload his gun." Dalton then caught Shadley's horse, and, although wounded, mounted and followed Doolin, who also had been wounded during the race from the barn.

When Shadley went down, the last of the marshals was out of action. Tulsa Jack and George Newcomb, both wounded, ran to the barn, secured their horses, and followed Doolin and Dalton.

According to Littleton Dalton, the entire Ingalls affair lasted less than three minutes. In this time four men had been killed outright or mortally wounded, four bandits had been wounded, and four bystanders struck by stray bullets. This would seem to indicate that either bystanders or stray bullets were quite numerous. In addition, five horses and two mules had been shot down. As it has become popular for writers to present a "bloodiest battle of western history," the Ingalls affair is hereby respectfully submitted.

"Arkansas" Tom Jones and an Ingalls man, thought to have aided the bandits at the time of the shooting, were captured and jailed. Jones stood trial, was convicted and sentenced to life imprisonment. George Newcomb and Bill Doolin took refuge near Guthrie in a hideout maintained by Newcomb. No one seems to know where Tulsa Jack holed up.

Bill Dalton fled to southern Oklahoma and took refuge at the log cabin retreat of Houston Wallace. When his wounds had healed, Bill moved his family to the Wallace place, which was near the present village of Poolville. From this headquarters a new series of robberies was planned.

Between the time of the battle at Ingalls and May 23, 1894, a period of eight months, the Bill Dalton Gang was credited with a number of robberies. But on the latter date, when the First National Bank of Longview, Texas, was robbed, we have the first undisputed evidence of their activities.

There have been few published accounts of the work of the Bill Dalton Gang. In fact, their activities have been avoided or treated briefly by most writers. This has been true of the questioned robbery of a bank at Southwest City, Missouri, the fight at Ingalls, the Longview Bank robbery, and the affair northwest of Ardmore, when Bill Dalton was killed. Such accounts as have been published do not agree with each other. It was some time after the death of Littleton Dalton in 1942 that complete details of these affairs were forthcoming.

Having Lit's account of how Bill inherited his gang from Bob and

Emmett Dalton and Henry Starr, we now are ready for the details of the trail leading to the roundup of the last outlaw Dalton, near the little village of Poolville.

By this time Bill Dalton had dropped those involved in the fight at Ingalls. Bill had taken in Jim and Houston Wallace, and Bill and Jim Jones, whose correct name is said to have been Knight. It was these five men who performed the Longview robbery.

Although the First National Bank of Longview was not held up until May of 1894, plans were being laid for the robbery several months in advance of that time.

About the first of April, two strange men came to the vicinity of Longview on horseback and worked for a while at a sawmill. This mill was owned by Brown and Flewellen and was located about seven miles north of town. According to a statement made by J.C. Lacy, resident of Longview at the time of the robbery, these two men were the Jones, or Knight brothers. They employed their spare time riding over the surrounding country and soon became familiar with all of the roads in the vicinity of Longview. Suddenly they disappeared, and no one knew where they had gone.

After an absence of several weeks the two men returned, accompanied by a third man, introduced by them as Mr. Bennett, but later identified as Jim Wallace. The three remained about Longview for several days and then all disappeared.

Some time after the three disappeared, they returned to the vicinity of Longview with a fourth man, identified as Bill Dalton. They had two of their saddle horses hitched to a hack and were leading two others. The party was well supplied with guns, and with camping and fishing equipment. They camped by Lake Merrill about nine miles west of Longview, remaining there hunting and fishing for several days.

Frank Fisher, who farmed near Longview, went to the lake to fish, saw the four strangers and talked to them for several hours. Later he was an important witness in the identification of Bill Dalton's body and at the trial of Jim Jones. On the day of the robbery the four men abandoned the hack and fishing equipment and went into Longview on saddle horses. Their plans were well laid and the robbery was under way before anyone knew what was going on.

According to Littleton Dalton, who had his information from Houston Wallace, Bill Jones (Knight) and Jim Wallace remained outside to cover the retreat. At four o'clock in the afternoon, Bill Dalton and Jim Jones entered the bank.

The bank force consisted at that time of Joe Clemons, President, and Tom Clemons, Cashier. A customer, M.L. Bartholomeu, was in the bank when Dalton and Jones entered. Tom Clemons was sitting at his desk in the bank and, being hard of hearing, knew nothing of the robbery until he got up from his desk and started to go out into the lobby. As he opened the door, Bill Dalton poked a revolver in his stomach and told him to get back inside.

According to J.C. Lacy, who has furnished these details of the robbery, Clemons grabbed the gun, catching it far enough back to push that portion of his hand between his thumb and forefinger under the hammer. Dalton yelled at Clemons to "let go". Clemons replied that he would if Dalton would promise not to shoot anyone. Bill promised. Clemons "let go" and was not shot.

Probably all would have gone according to plans, but for two things. The take was less than had been expected. Much of it was in sheets of new Longview banknotes of twenty dollar denomination. These had been received from Washington that morning, and had not been signed by the bank president, Joe Clemons, or separated from each other.

A thorough search was made and everything in the way of coin or currency was taken, including a collection of old coins owned by the bank. This delay inside the bank and the vigilance of citizens outside, turned the well planned robbery into a battle royal.

Court was in session in Longview. City Marshal Matt Muckelroy, and Charles Levan were in the court room. Jim Wallace was stationed as a guard on a vacant lot across the alley back of the bank in order to prevent the City Marshal from interfering with the robbery. Bill Jones remained on guard in front of the bank near the horses.

Thinking that two citizens, Walter McQueen and George Buckingham, were taking too much interest in the robbery, Bill Jones fired at them, downing both. The reports of his gun brought Muckelroy and Levan from the Court House. They were immediately shot down by Jim Wallace.

An unidentified citizen now entered the fray, downing Jim Wallace with his first shot, and sending Bill Jones running for his horse with his second. The three bandits remaining were able to mount their horses and ride from town on the run. A third shot was fired at them by another citizen as they rode out of town. This shot knocked a hat off the head of one of the bandits, but apparently did not injure him.

The shooting at the bank probably lasted not more than three minutes, and when it was over five men were on the ground. The bandit killed was unknown to Longview residents at the time, but was later identified as Jim Wallace. In the vicinity of Longview he had been going under the name of Bennett. It was learned that Wallace and his brother were living near a little placed then called Elk, now the village of Poolville, about thirty miles northwest of Ardmore, Oklahoma.

The Longview battle was high in casualties, as was the one at Ingalls. Besides Wallace, four citizens were shot down. According to the story told Littleton Dalton by Houston Wallace while he was in jail at Ardmore after the killing of Bill Dalton, all of the citizens were shot by Bill. From the statement made by Lacy it can be seen that Wallace was following the usual procedure of bandits, to pin all killings on any dead comrades.

Wallace stated that Bill ran from the bank with his winchester spewing flame, smoke, lead, and concussion in a solid blast. This description fits a dozen others related of Bill. It will be remembered that Marshal Shadley was shot by Bill three times, "faster than he could re-load his gun." Littleton Dalton stated that Bill could empty his winchester in this fashion at a row of small fruit cans, set fifty steps distant, and hit every one of them, something Bob Dalton could do only at a much slower rate of speed.

Bill Dalton claimed to be one of the best rifle shots in the United States. While in jail at Visalia, California, Bill wrote a statement which was printed in a Visalia paper in which he claimed that, given a loaded winchester, at a distance of a quarter mile he could kill any twelve expert rifle shots in the United States before they could down him. In spite of Bill's recognized vivid imagination, it is significant that this statement was never seriously questioned by any of the officers who were familiar with his skill with a winchester. In target exhibitions, Bill amazed some of the most experienced rifle shots. Sheriff Kay stated that when he took Bill from his home near Cholame, Bill showed what he could do with a 45-60, 1876 model winchester. He started a small fruit can rolling at close range and sent it to a distance of thirty yards, emptying the gun so quickly that the shots could scarcely be counted. Said Kay, "I never saw anything like it in my life and I never expect to see anything like it again. Detective Bill Smith was with us at the time. He said he would not have believed it if he hadn't seen it with his own eyes."

The story was told that Bill had rigged his winchester to fire automatically when the trigger safety was released as the lever closed. It has been impossible to verify this statement satisfactorily. Lit had heard it

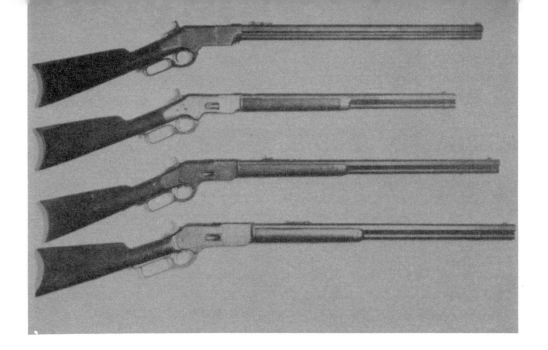

Four stages of development of the winchester rifle. Top: The Henry rifle, from which the winchester was developed, patented in 1860, and famous as the best repeating rifle of its time. It was so well known that some pioneers still call any early model winchester a Henry. The Henry had three serious faults. Firing sixteen shots, the one-piece barrel and magazine became too hot to hold. In addition, the cartridge follower often lodged against the left hand, relieved the pressure of the magazine spring and allowed a partially chambered cartridge to be deformed. This disabled the gun. It also was difficult to fill the magazine. The 44 caliber rimfire cartridge, known because of its flat pointed bullet as the 44 flat, and with only 20 grains of black powder, was not very effective at more than eighty yards. The Henry was fitted with a brass receiver and butt plate. The rifle pictured probably was used in the Civil War or the Indian Wars. Second from top: The 1866 model "King's Improvement" winchester, developed from the Henry. It corrected the defect in loading and added a wooden forestock for protection against the heat of the barrel. The short range cartridge, brass receiver and butt plate were retained from the Henry, and a brass forestock cap added. The rifle pictured was used by a stage robber who operated on the old Overland Stage road in Kern County, California, about 1868.

Third from top: The 1873 model winchester, finest repeating rifle of its time and the gun which decapitalized the name "Winchester." It was the first dependable rapid fire repeating rifle ever built, and was chambered to handle several centerfire cartridges of the same length, the 44-40 being most popular. With its 40 grains of black powder it had about twice the effective range of the Henry rimfire. The only brass used in this or later winchesters was in the carrier block and in the ramrod case cover in the butt plate. The rifle pictured was carried for more than forty years by John T. Allen, father-in-law of the writer.

Bottom: The 1876 model winchester, made in many common sizes from 22 caliber rimfire to 45-75 center fire and in several special sizes. Most common caliber was probably 45-60. The 1876 model winchester was used exclusively by the Daltons in California. The gun pictured was taken by Sheriff Kay from Bill Dalton at Cross Creek station in September of 1891 when he was arrested for the Ceres train robbery attempt.

from Riley Dean and from Bill's neighbors around Cholame, but had not actually seen that Bill's gun was rigged in that manner. Here is how Clark Bliven, brother-in-law of Bill, described Bill's shooting to Littleton: "Bill jammed his rifle between his cheek and shoulder with his left hand and slapped the lever up and down with his right fingers faster than you could see. His eyes were never off the sights and the rifle fired automatically when the lever closed. At night he could roll a five gallon kerosene can yards beyond his sight, shooting at the sound made by the can."

Regardless of Bill's method of shooting, it was deadly accurate and as rapid as the lever of a winchester could be worked. He and his three outlaw brothers had burned thousands of rounds of rifle and revolver ammunition in both night and day practice. Until Bill appeared on the scene in Oklahoma, Bob had borne the reputation of being the best rifle shot in the Nations. But before Bill was disposed of, he was recognized as being far better than Bob had ever been.

Reports have generally understated the casualties at Longview. As has been stated, City Marshal Matt Muckelroy was shot down. He eventually recovered. Walter McQueen was shot through the hips and suffered for more than two years before he died. George Buckingham was killed outright. Charles Levan was shot through the leg, the bone being carried away for a distance of several inches. The leg was amputated but Levan died two days later. Early news accounts did not carry information concerning the death of Levan or McQueen.

After the Longview robbery, several weeks passed with no definite clues being uncovered. At first it was only known that suspicious characters answering the description of the Longview robbers had been camped at Lake Merrill. The trail led northwest to Red River. In scouring the brush on the north side of Red River, it was learned that a covered wagon had been concealed there for more than a week and that, during this time, a man had camped beside it. About the second day after the robbery, this man had been joined by three others who were on horseback. The saddle horses were hitched to the wagon, and the outfit traveled west. Following the trail of the wagon, the officers were led to the little settlement of Elk, Carter County, Oklahoma. Being certain that Bill Dalton was one of the three men who had returned to the wagon on Red River, the officers avoided arousing the suspicions of the citizens near Elk, and made plans to go to the place with a posse and capture the entire band.

While plans for assembling a posse were under way, suspicions were confirmed when two women and a man entered Ardmore and began buying a large supply of ammunition and groceries. New banknotes were seen in their possession, and their actions further aroused the suspicions of both the merchant and the officers.

It is due to the kindness of Mr. Jack Snyder of the Daily Ardmoreite, that I am able to present from contemporary news items an account of the killing of Bill Dalton. Mr. Snyder interviewed local pioneers and searched the old files of his paper and dug out for me the following statement:

Just a few decayed logs are all that remain of the cabin near the town of Poolville, once known as Elk, in the northwestern part of Carter County, where Bill Dalton, last of the Dalton Gang of outlaws to meet a violent death, was killed on the morning of June 8th, 1894, when he tried to break through a ring of deputy United States marshals who had surrounded the cabin where he was staying. Bill Dalton had been identified as a member of the band that held up the bank at Longview, Texas. He had made his escape into Indian Territory with his share of the loot.

Officers who were constantly on the watch for Bill Dalton, for whom a large reward had been offered, dead or alive, were convinced that the bandit was in hiding between the old towns of Healdton and Elk. Their suspicions were further enhanced when Houston Wallace, a resident of Elk, and also bearing a very unsavory reputation, came to Ardmore with two women who gave their names as Mrs. Brown and Mrs. Pruitt. They began to spend money right and left. Among their purchases was a large amount of rifle and pistol ammunition, which further aroused the suspicions of officers trailing them.

The officers found no reason for arresting the women and so they might have left for the return trip to Elk if Houston Wallace had been a little more discreet. Wallace went to the express office and secured a package of suspicious appearance. The marshals decided to arrest him and investigate the package. The package was found to contain three gallons of whisky and Wallace was held for "introducing", a serious offense in the Territorial days.

The two women were detained at a hotel under guard and deputy U.S. Marshal S.T. Lindsey, summoned the following posse: Dave Hooker, Los Hart, J.H. Leatherman, C.R. Denton, J.M. Reynolds, W.B. Freeman, W.H. Glover and Ed. Roberts. They immediately set out for the Houston Wallace place near Elk, arriving there early next morning and immediately surrounding the place.

All seemed to be quiet. Two or three children were at play in the yard.

When within about two hundred yards of the house, a woman who had been out to drive up the cows came upon some of the officers. She maintained her composure, never letting on that she had discovered them. She went to the house and notified those within that the house was surrounded.

Bill Dalton had no desire to be captured and thought that by a quick move on his part he might get away. He opened a window in the rear of the house and jumped through, thinking that side of the house offered a better avenue to escape. In that he was mistaken. Los Hart, one of the posse, and a dead shot, called upon him to surrender, as he had him covered. Instead, Dalton started for the timber, close by. Hart called on him once more to surrender, but instead Dalton started to reach for his revolver. Hart fired and Dalton fell.

Dalton made but one move after he was hit. He turned over on his back and by the time the officers reached him he was dead. The officers cleared the house of women and children and a search of the place revealed money concealed in several places. A sack bearing the name of the Longview Bank was found.

The body of Dalton was placed in a wagon and the drive back to Ardmore began. Before leaving the Wallace place a search was made of Mrs. Brown's effects, revealing the probability that she was Dalton's wife. Some of his letters addressed to her at Fresno and Alameda, California, substantiated this belief.

Within a few miles of Ardmore the posse accompanying the body of Dalton met Mrs. Brown and Mrs. Pruitt and told them that Bill Dalton had been killed and that his body was in the wagon. At first Mrs. Brown denied knowing what they were talking about, but upon seeing the body, broke down and confessed that she was Bill Dalton's wife. She came back to Ardmore with the posse and ordered the undertaker to prepare the body for shipment to California.

The town of Ardmore was soon swamped with curiosity seekers. They tried to talk to Mrs. Dalton, but were barred. Identification of the body was confirmed by many who had known Dalton, and by relatives who came to Ardmore to make identification complete. Dalton was big news and the town was soon filled with newspaper men from the metropolitan centers. Mrs. Dalton was subjected to a severe test in standing off the news hounds. She finally paid all the bills and took her departure. The local interest soon subsided.

As soon as he was released from jail, Houston Wallace dropped completely from sight and was never heard of again by anyone in the vicinity of Ardmore. He could not be identified as one of the band that robbed the bank at

Longview, but officers and the public generally never doubted that he was one of them. The name of Elk was afterward changed to Poolville and the land upon which the log cabin stood was acquired as a ranch property. A bunch of brambles and vines now effectively hides the spot where one of the notorious Daltons came to his end.

The body of Bill Dalton was held at Ardmore for several days so that it could be identified by persons who had seen him near Longview. Gregg County Sheriff, J.C. Howard, took with him Frank Fisher, who had seen the bandits at Lake Merrill, and went to Ardmore. J.C. Lacy, who until 1944 lived in Longview, accompanied the sheriff and Fisher. He prepared the following statement about the trip to Ardmore:

I accompanied the Sheriff to Ardmore and saw the body of Bill Dalton. I also talked to Houston Wallace, brother of Jim Wallace, who was killed at Longview. I also heard the officers tell their story of how Bill was shot. It was quite different from the account given by Emmett Dalton in his book, *When the Daltons Rode*. I heard my story from the man who shot Bill.

According to the story I heard, shortly after daylight Bill Dalton jumped through a window in the back of the house and started running through a patch of corn and was shot and killed. He was shot with a winchester rifle. The officers searched the house. In the middle of the floor they found a trap-door, covered with a rug. They also opened a trunk and found in it eight hundred dollars, a part of it consisting of the old coins taken from the Longview bank. They found other articles, indicating that the house was occupied by Bill Dalton and his family. The officers put the dead man's body in their wagon and started back to Ardmore. Some of them rode in front of the wagon.

On the way the officers met the two women who had been released and were driving the team hauling their purchases. The officers stopped them and told the older woman that they had killed Bill Dalton. She replied that it made no difference to her, that she did not know him. When the wagon drove up and she saw the body she began crying. She turned her wagon around and followed the officers back to Ardmore Frank Fisher identified the body as that of the man he had seen at Lake Merrill. . . . .

The above account is given in full in order that the readers may see that separated sources agree about the death of Bill Dalton. Emmett

Dalton gave a different version, claiming that Bill was shot in the back while seated in a chair and playing with his two children, Chub and Gracie.

Poor Bill and his trap doors. Readers will remember that Bill took the first step "across the line" with a trap door in his house near Cholame, California, and that another trap door entered the story at the old Cross Creek Stage Station when Bill and Riley ean were arrested. It was Bill's fate to the last to be dependent on a trap door.

Before having the final word from Littleton Dalton about the death of Bill, J.C. Lacy tells us what became of the two Jones brothers, Jim and Bill:

Some time after Bill Dalton was killed, officers located Bill and Jim Jones in a camp in south Texas. These officers were looking for them because of some charge other than robbing the Longview bank. In the fight that followed, Bill was killed and Jim was severely wounded, captured and placed in jail.

In the newspapers the Gregg County Sheriff read the account of the fight with the Jones brothers. He took with him a man named Willey Pillen, who had worked at the sawmill near Longview with the Jones boys, and went to South Texas to see the wounded man. Pillen identified him as the man who had worked at the mill. Jones was brought to Longview and placed in jail here, where he remained until he recovered. He was indicted by the Grand Jury. When his case was called his lawyer asked that it be transferred elsewhere. This request was granted, the case being transferred to Tyler, Texas. He was tried, convicted and given a long prison sentence. His lawyer then asked for a new trial and this request was granted. While Jones was in the Tyler jail waiting the next term of court, he escaped and was not seen for several months.

A New Mexico sheriff with a posse was on the trail of some law breakers. They ran on their men and several were killed and one captured. The one captured was identified as Jim Jones. A reward had been offered for the arrest of Jones. The New Mexico sheriff brought him to Texas and delivered him to the officers at the Texas State Penitentiary. He finally began serving a sentence of thirty-five years. After several years Jones was made a trusty and was finally released. I learned that after his release he went to Oklahoma and was killed by someone in one of the oil fields. That was the finish of the Bill Dalton Gang. . . .

The old Bliven home at Livingston, California. Bill Dalton was buried at the left front corner of the old home for many years.
Photo by Frank F. Latta in 1940 and now in Bear State Library.

In view of the previous accounts of the killing of Bill Dalton, we are fortunate to have a statement by Littleton, who was at both Ardmore and Elk the day after the killing. His statement in many respects supports the newspaper account and the statement of J.C. Lacy:

After the fight at Ingalls, Mother wrote me repeatedly, asking me to come home. When the Longview bank was robbed and Mason was wanted for that robbery, I had to go to her and see what I could do to help. There was really little I could do, except wait. Mason wasundoubtedly guilty and it looked to me like he would surely be run down and killed. It didn't take long.

While I was with Mother we received word that what we expected had happened. I immediately took the train to Ardmore. I heard and saw everything within forty-eight hours after Mason was killed. He heard that the officers were coming and was sneaking out through a field of young corn when he was shot in the back, probably with a rifle, the ball going in low and coming out of his chest. He had his revolver on, and had a pocketful of revolver cartridges, but was without a rifle. He fell about a hundred and fifty yards from the house. He had about a thousand dollars on him when he was killed.

I talked with everyone concerned: the officers, including the man who shot Mason; the boy who was working on the ranch and who saw the shooting; and to Charlie and Gracie, Mason's children. In his book Emmett stated that Mason was shot at the house while he was playing with Gracie. I don't believe that. No one told me any such story when I was there the day after Mason was killed. I saw the spot where he fell and bled in the cornfield, and the tracks of the wagon that carried his body away. The ground was soaked with blood where Mason fell. If he had been shot at the house and carried there as a blind, I am certain he would never have bled so much out in the cornfield.

Mason had three thousand five hundred dollars left from the Longview robbery. Twenty-five hundred dollars of it was hidden in a dirty dress of Gracie's, hanging on the wall. The officers found the thousand dollars on Mason, but they searched the house from one end to the other and missed the twenty-five hundred. They even took the dress down and threw it on the floor. When Mason's wife was released and returned to the place, she found the money, still in the dress.

Mason's companions, Jim and Bill Jones, left the ranch the evening before the killing and wanted Mason to go with them. He decided to wait until his wife returned with the supplies. Then he intended to take the family down into Texas.

I had Mason's body embalmed and shipped to Kingfisher, and then from Kingfisher to Livingston, California. Mason's wife was afraid to use the new money from the Longview robbery, so I paid the embalming and shipping charges out of my own pocket. It took almost every cent I had. I had just money enough to buy a ticket back to Kingfisher.

Littleton Dalton and Clovis Cole in 1938.
Photo by Frank F. Latta and now in Bear State Library.

CHAPTER FIFTEEN

Holing Up

While visiting through the San Joaquin Valley with pioneers who had known Littleton Dalton during the '80s and '90s, many of them expressed surprise at the news that he had hidden himself in Northern California. When he disappeared from Fresno County his old friends supposed he had returned to Oklahoma. Clovis Cole was the closest friend Lit had in California. No one was more surprised than Cole to learn that Lit had been hidden away in California for more than forty-two years. Cole supposed that Lit had been dead for many years. He had talked with no one who had seen Lit since 1896, when they had returned together from a vacation in San Francisco. In 1937 this writer was able to bring Clovis Cole and Lit Dalton together after their forty-two year separation. That experience is one of the most pleasant remembrances of more than sixty years of such work.

It is difficult to imagine the effect of Lit's story on readers of *Dalton Gang Days* who didn't know him and hear him tell it. In some respects he was extremely bitter. As I analyzed this bitterness, it grew largely from the fact that Lit as a young man had been possessed of intense family pride. His great ambition was to have a family of his own and to raise them in the way he saw his own father hadn't done. It was Lit's urge to correct a family wrong, to administer justice, if you will.

The disgrace of the Dalton Gang weighed on Lit as heavily as anything could weigh on anyone. During our discussions he continually came back to the disintegration of the family and the formation of the Gang. As we were waiting for the stage to take him back to his home in Broderick he again went back to the three brothers who first brought disgrace on the Daltons. Here is what he last contributed:

The last time I ever saw Bob or Grat was just before the Coffeyville raid, when the three boys came to Mother's home near Kingfisher. They had been running and hiding for months. Their clothes were worn out. I gave them about all the clothes I had, a good Stetson hat, which Bob had on when he was killed, and a good coat and overcoat. They scarcely thanked me. They expected me to keep on putting up for them indefinitely.

After the raid I heard that Mason claimed the three boys had more than nine hundred dollars on them when they were shot to pieces. I don't believe it. They showed me their money before they left Mother's and, if they told me the truth, they didn't have seventy-five dollars among them. I know they didn't offer me money so I could replace the clothing I gave them.

I put up at least a thousand dollars for Grat, Bob, and Emmett. If you want to put it that way, you might say that I financed the Dalton Gang. I furnished Father at least three hundred dollars. I spent six hundred dollars running back and forth between California and Indian Territory because of the Gang, not counting my lost time. It cost me three hundred dollars to have Mason embalmed and shipped to California. All of this money I earned skinning a string of mules for a net wage of about seventy-five cents a day. The money I was out was equal to my entire earnings for eight years. It actually kept me broke for fifteen years.

Grat was a heavy drinker. He would later have gone completely to pieces from drink, just as Cole finally did. Both would drink a quart of bad whisky in a day and work at the same time. But it made fools of them and it killed Cole. Mason drank too much, too. He always had a jug of whisky with him when he was at work and got into his first serious trouble at a saloon in Ingalls, Oklahoma, when he had been drinking, and when Deputy U.S. Marshals Houston, Speed, and Shadley were killed in an attempt to arrest him, Doolin, Pierce, and Newcomb. It was also a shipment of whisky that put the officers on his trail when he was killed in 1894 near Poolville, Oklahoma.

Together with gambling, it was drink that ruined Grat. This was partly true of Emmett and absolutely true of Bob, in spite of the fact that Emmett has claimed that Bob didn't drink to excess. None of the gang would work. All they wanted was money, money, money. I couldn't have shoveled it at them fast enough to suit them.

If I feel bitter toward them it is because they ruined my entire life. I had several opportunities to marry well, but had to give them up because I couldn't get enough money ahead to support a wife.

I could never get shut of the boys. They never came near me except when they wanted money. They would promise absolutely that they would go straight. I would help them out of a jam and they would go away. Then they would go right ahead with another job of law breaking. Back they would come for more help; money, a horse, a riding rig, guns, and ammunition. I got so I never wanted to see any of them again. . . . .

As the Dalton family disintegrated and Lit saw his mother with nothing left of her heritage, and the Dalton Gang going headlong from one tragedy to another, he had to give up all thought of his lifelong dreams. He said, "I decided to hole up until I could figure my way out of the mess. And I never figured it out."

Here is Lit's story of the manner in which he left Fresno County and of his life in Northern California:

Almost every time there was a robbery anywhere all of us boys were under suspicion. Probably Ben and I were bothered least of all. The last two times I was home, just before the Coffeyville raid and just after the Longview bank robbery, were worst of all. There must have been at least a dozen detectives snooping around me for two weeks each time.

At the time of the Ceres train robbery attempt, Cole Dalton and I were working near where the town of Clovis is now located, northeast of Fresno, California. Several days after the robbery, a deputy sheriff drove out there and questioned everybody on the place, except me. He talked to Cole for at least two hours, but didn't say a word to me. In fact, I was never questioned by a detective or an officer in my life. The officers suspected that Cole and I had robbed the train. A day or so later, Mason and Riley Dean were arrested for the Ceres job.

Cole was as angry as he could be about the stories told about the rest of us after the Ceres robbery, and wrote a letter to the Fresno newspapers about it. I remember reading it in the paper at the time. . . . .

A search was made of the old *Fresno Republican* newspaper files, and this letter was found. Here is a portion of it:

The Dalton Boys.
Cole Dalton, who is the oldest of the boys, sends the following open letter:
Livingston, Cal., Sept. 6, 1891.
J.A. Fellmore: Dear Sir: Reading for several days the account of the Ceres attempted train robbery, and finding myself and brothers (those in this state) so criticized and misrepresented, I beg leave to inform you that those in this state are wholly innocent of any and all attempts made against either railroads or Express companies. Furthermore, that we submitted to an arrest and that I vindicated myself honorably before the grand jury of Tulare County, when if guilty it was possible to have made a successful resistance.

I claim allegiance and stand loyal to this government and find no fault with the abrogation of a crime. But I do find fault with an accusation so base and written for the purpose of prejudicing the commonwealth to the injury of myself and other brothers equally innocent. As for Robert and Emmett Dalton, they are not and never have been in this state except a few months from last October to about January 25, when I last saw them. For the present, dear sir, I am respectfully, Cole Dalton.

There is more of the above letter in which Cole Dalton stated that Dean and Middleton had been in a shooting scrape at Hanford, and that Dean was hiding out because of a warrant Bill Hall had for him and Middleton. Cole stated that Dean had bought the rifle and ammunition to hunt coyotes, and that Scott Camp of Hanford had furnished him more ammunition for the same purpose.

Littleton Dalton continues with his account of the persecution he suffered due to the activities of his brothers:

As late as 1896, when an attempt was made to rob the train at Tagus Switch south of Goshen, in Tulare County, Cole and I were again suspected. Dan McCall was killed while he was trying to rob the train. I don't know what they thought we had to do with it. But a Fresno County deputy came out and snooped around us for the best part of two days.

In July of 1896, Clovis, Ora and Bert Cole, and I went to San Francisco on a vacation. We had Cole Dalton with us, but he drank heavily and we had to ditch him. We all had plug hats and swallow-tailed coats, and a hundred and fifty dollars apiece. We didn't go second class. We put up at the best places in town. We felt like twenty dollar pieces and had the finest time of our lives. Once a day one of us would treat the gang. Generally we went to the nearest saloon, but I always managed to treat in the bar at the Palace Hotel. Drinks were higher there, but whenever I had any business, I always wanted to conduct it in the best place I could find. I am sure none of us ever forgot that trip. We were eating the frosting off our cake and didn't know it.

On that trip to San Francisco I got a taste of the first freedom and real enjoyment I had known in almost twenty years. So, just after the Cole brothers and I returned from our visit to the city, I decided to leave the Fresno country and go back to Glenn County. I was so persecuted by people who insisted that I had been one of the Dalton Gang of outlaws that I simply couldn't

Littleton Dalton at the time of his vacation in San Francisco, in 1896, in company with Cole Dalton and the Cole brothers. You see here what Lit meant when he said, "We felt like twenty dollar pieces — we were eating the frosting off our cake and didn't know it."

Photo courtesy Mrs. Bolton and now in Bear State Library.

stand it. I believe I would have got into trouble if I had stayed there any longer. Stories were told about my robbing trains and holding up people, and I was pointed out on every occasion. I couldn't visit Fresno without being embarassed, getting mad, and going home.

So I collected my pay from Clovis Cole, got on my horse one Sunday morning, and rode north. I rode to the Turner ranch on the San Joaquin River, west of Livingston. Cole Dalton was working for Turner. I visited with him for about a week. He wanted me to stay there. Turner offered me a job, but I wanted to make a new start where I wasn't known at all, so I rode to the Willows, in Glenn County.

I have never been sorry that I made the change.

At the Willows I drove a mule team for Jim and Wash Snowden until they both died. They were the finest kind of people in the world. But mule skinning was a poor occupation. We were laid off during the winter so much because of rain that during the driest winters we only cleared at most six bits a day. In the summer we could lay around on the ranches after harvest and haul straw for awhile, then work for our board until fall plowing time.

At the Willows I got along very well until after the Spanish-American War. My youngest brother, Simon Noel Dalton, served in the Army in the Philippines. When he was discharged at the Presidio in San Francisco he came up to the Willows to see me. I was working for Stoval at the time, skinning mules for thirty dollars a month.

After Simon had visited with me for a few days he asked me for some money, saying he needed some clothes. I gave him a note to Stoval, asking him to write a ten dollar order for Simon. This money would be held out of my pay by Stoval. When Simon got the order he started out by raising it to twenty dollars. Then he went to the Willows, got into a poker game and began drinking. Soon he was drunk, had lost most of the money, and was in a free-for-all fight.

Cole Dalton was working near me and was in the Willows soon after Simon arrived. He came in and stopped the fight, spent the rest of the night sobering Simon up, bought him a ticket for Kingfisher, Oklahoma, and put him on the train. The money for the ticket Cole borrowed from a Willows saloon man and I later had to settle with him, as Cole never had any money. It cost me an even hundred dollars to square up after Simon: almost four months of hard work.

When he found that the order had been raised, Stoval wanted to get out a warrant and bring Simon back. But I knew that would only cost me more money. I said, "I'll make it good. We are rid of him now, let's just let him stay away."

Simon was one of a pair of twins. His twin sister died in infancy. He was about five feet nine inches tall and weighed about a hundred and seventy pounds. He knew nothing but to drink and fight and wasn't much good at either.

When the Snowden boys died and after Simon had cut up so at the Willows, I had a hard time of it for a while. You have no idea how a person in my position can be persecuted. The same thing started that I had left at Fresno. Every fool in the country began pointing me out as one of the Dalton Gang and told the most impossible stories you ever heard. I decided to leave that country, cut out mule skinning and get a job out in the hills by myself, running sheep.

At Red Bluff I got a job running sheep for Douglas Cove. I was with him five years and enjoyed every day of it. It was the best change I could have made. I had my entire time to myself and I never lost a day's pay. The sheep had to be tended every day, rain or shine. I could save from three hundred to three hundred and fifty dollars a year and be well dressed. Most of the summers I was in the cool Sierra. I also had all the good grub I could eat and no one to bother me. The sheep didn't care whether I was related to the Dalton Gang or not. During the last fifteen years I worked with sheep I got fifty dollars a month. I was then an experienced man at that work and had supervision over several bands.

My last work with sheep was for Miller & Lux at Firebaugh, in Merced County. I went to work there on the Poso Farm in 1922 and stayed three years without losing a day. Then I went to Yolo County and have lived there ever since.

During all of this time I was working at a disadvantage. About 1900 I had all the toes cut off my right foot. I was working on the old Stanford ranch at Vina, but had been in the Sierra all summer with sheep. I went to Chico on the train and bought a good suit of tailored clothes and an outfit to wear to a dance at Vina. In getting off the moving train at Vina the soles of my new shoes were slick and my foot slipped and went under the wheels of the train.

The conductor of the train telegraphed to the railroad doctor at Red Bluff and took me there to meet him. I wasn't in any shape to go to a dance that night. I was in the hospital at Red Bluff for more than three months. The railroad company paid all of my expenses. Then I went back to the Stanford ranch, where they made it easy for me until my foot got strong. I have worked ever since at walking jobs with a crippled foot.

As I have said before, Cole worked in Glenn County near me for several years. I want to tell what finally happened to Cole. It will give some idea of how stubborn the boys were when they got started in the wrong direction.

About 1908, Cole appeared to me to be about ready to die from stomach ulcers, caused by constant, heavy whisky drinking. I decided to take him back to Kingfisher. I thought Mother might be able to straighten him out.

Six months or so before we started to Kingfisher, I broke completely with Cole. I came out from Redding with about half a quart of whisky. I always took a drink of whisky when I thought I needed it, but I always tried to be moderate about it. I have been in and around saloons all of my life and no one can say that he ever saw me in the slightest way under the influence of liquor. I asked Cole if he would *like* a drink of whisky. That was what I always asked everyone. I have never asked a man to *take* a drink of liquor in my life. I thought it was his *own* business whether he took it or not.

Well, I handed Cole that bottle half-full of whisky and the fool turned it up and emptied it without taking it from his lips. He thought it was smart to show that he could drink a pint of whisky without stopping. At that time he was already suffering extremely from stomach ulcers and was living on milk and whisky. I got as angry as a man can get. I said, "Cole, if we live to be a thousand years old, that is the last chance you'll ever have to take a drink with me. I like a hog, but you please me too well." And I kept my word.

When we left Glenn County, Cole was almost skin and bones. At Sacramento we took the train for Kingfisher. On that whole trip Cole didn't eat a bite of solid food. He just drank milk and whisky: a little milk and a lot of whisky. He wouldn't eat a bite and I couldn't keep him from drinking whisky. At Denver the train was late — held up by a washout. Cole walked up and down the track and swore at me because were delayed. I told him I wasn't running the railroad and that when they got the washout fixed they would send down a train. But Cole kept on swearing at me because I didn't get the train for him.

At Kingfisher both Mother and I talked to Cole for several days and tried to straighten him out. But he wouldn't listen to either of us. I told him to go his way. He hadn't long to go anyway. So I left him there. He went down into western Kansas and took up a claim and died there. His body was shipped back to Kingfisher for burial.

The best that can be said about Cole is that he took no part in any of the train robberies.

It is unfortunate if an unjust picture has been given of Emmett Dalton. There was much to admire in Emmett. It has been the opinion of all persons interviewed that he was largely a victim of circumstances. Most important of these circumstances was the fact that he was next to Bob in age.

Bob and Emmett ran together from the time Emmett could run. Bob was of a dominating, decisive nature, the one who furnished almost all the ideas ever presented to the Dalton Gang. Bob was perhaps the most handsome of all the Dalton boys. At least Emmett thought so. But Lit thought that Emmett was the finest looking of them all. Bob was about six feet tall, straight as an arrow, and as particular about his person and dress as Littleton, which is saying a lot.

Even with the domination of Bob, Emmett is known to have taken exception to Bob's ideas on several occasions. First of these was in the planning of the Alila robbery. This came out when Bob and Emmett called on Lit at the Clovis Cole ranch, when they wanted a horse and riding rig for the ride to Indian Territory. Lit went for them unmercifully in an attempt to learn the truth about the holdup. It was then that Emmett agreed that he had killed the fireman in the Alila holdup attempt, but stated that he had been against the robbery from the start. Bob had agreed to Emmett's contention.

The other serious difference of opinion between Bob and Emmett came just before the Coffeyville raid, but was not as important as that preceeding the Alila affair, because by then the two had run too long a course for the difference of opinion to have made much change in their future. If they had been successful at Coffeyville, they would have become more bold and would have been killed at some other place.

But Emmett did disagree about Coffeyville. He discussed this disagreement fully with me. It is one of the few important contributions made by Emmett toward the story of *Dalton Gang Days*.

Were walking along the street near Emmett's North Hollywood home, discussing various phases of Dalton Gang activities, when the Coffeyville raid entered our conversation. Said Emmett concerning the affair:

I was against going into Coffeyville. I had gone to school at Robbins Corners near there and knew several hundred Coffeyville people as well as I knew anyone. I had more friends there than anywhere. I was afraid some of them would be injured if there was any hitch in Bob's plans. But Bob was positive that there would be no hitch. He said, "It will all be over before they know what's happening."

Then, I wanted to ride in and see if there had been any change in Coffeyville that would interfere with the plans Bob had made. This was on the evening prior to the raid. Bob thumbed this down because he was afraid I would be recognized. If we had known the hitching racks were down, we could have made other plans while we were going over the program the night before. As it was, Bob had only a few seconds in which to figure what to do when he saw we couldn't tie our horses in front of the Opera House, where they would have been shielded from all of the shooting by brick walls. There was no worse place in Coffeyville than the place Bob picked. It would have been better to have ridden to the bank doors and have left the horses standing while we were inside.

Then I wanted Bob to let Grat go with him, and let me go with Powers and Broadwell. I was afraid that Grat would make a mess of it, which he finally did, but Bob wouldn't agree to that either.

This disagreement about Coffeyville was the first serious difference we ever had. It was in the air as we rode into Coffeyville. We all felt it.

When we started to ride to Coffeyville it was cold. Bob was tying the collar of his coat up around his neck with a handkerchief and complained about the cold. I was irritated about the whole affair and said, "Just wait 'till we get into Coffeyville. You won't need any coat, brother. It's going to be hotter than hell up there."

I had this difference of opinion in the back of my head when I rode back to take Bob up on my horse when he was shot that morning in Coffeyville. I couldn't bear to go away with him thinking I had cut loose from him. . . . .

> Emmett had been a fine looking man, but was wrecked by poison from the old arm wound received at Coffeyville. This wound had never healed and Emmett never would have the arm amputated. He had been told repeatedly by medical specialists that to save his life its removal was absolutely necessary.
>
> I protested to Emmett about the arm, stating that, in justice to everyone, it should be removed. Emmett's attention was called to the fact that Mrs. Dalton had labored beside him since he came out of prison and that she should be considered in such a matter. Here was his answer:

At the end of the Coffeyville raid, when I was lying on the table in old Doctor Wells' office, he said, "Emmett, this arm will have to come off." I drew my left forefinger across my throat and said, "Doc, when you begin cutting, start right here. When I go to the grave I am going in one piece." I have never changed my mind about it.

> The reader will find in the above another instance of the determina-

tion characteristic of the Daltons. After all, wasn't much of their fate just happenstance? Both Cole and Lit early had taken the stand that they would have no part in any outlawry. Both were just as determined as any of the four who went bad. Nothing ever was said more characteristic of Lit than the statement by Arch Turner: "When Lit said no, his jaws stuck out farther than his ears."

Sober, clean-living, clear-headed Lit would have made a more resourceful bandit than any of the other Dalton boys.

It was obvious to me that Emmett was not a drinking man. No one who had been acquainted with him since he left prison knew of him doing any drinking. Lit has shown that both Emmett and Bob drank heavily for several years before the Alila job. Emmett was just past twenty when the Alila affair took place. So he began drinking quite young. Undoubtedly Bob's influence had something to do with this.

Each succeeding visit to Emmett found him weaker. The last found him sitting propped in a chair and clad in pajamas. An effort was made to have him make some definite statements for publication. These were concerning the discrepancies in his book, *When the Daltons Rode*. He freely admitted to me that he was the William McElhanie who had been represented as being in California with Bob. But he didn't want anything published about it while he was living.

There was none of the suspicious, circumspect attitude about Emmett. He talked freely or he talked not at all. I don't believe anyone would have taken advantage of anything Emmett said. Anyone would have hesitated to break faith with him. One interesting thing happened during discussion of the statement made by Eugene Kay and to which Emmett was considering adding his own.

Mrs. Dalton said, "Emmett, why don't you loosen up and talk to this man. He can tell your story better than you can." Emmett's reply was, "Well, I guess the trouble is that I spent a long time where they told me when to talk."

But Emmett did say, "I know what you want, and, before I get ready to kick off, I will write something for you." This never was done, simply because no one ever "gets ready."

It was with definite regret that the account of Emmett's death was read, not long after the last interview with him. He was an attractive, likable sort of fellow. One could not help but regret that he had been denied the chance of success that might have been his if he never had run with the Dalton Gang.

The experience of an interviewer of pioneers is one of constantly broken ties. Rapidly as one contracts new characters, the older ones are as rapidly passing away. In assembling and checking data for *Dalton Gang Days*, the statements of no less than one hundred pioneers were consulted. Of these none are known now to be alive.

One of the most touching pioneer losses I have experienced came when newspapers told of the death of "Gene" Kay. True, his passing had been expected for a year, but our family had not realized what his loss would mean. Gene cashed his chips in San Francisco in 1941 and with him the last of the true-blue, old-time western sheriffs passed from the earth.

As has been stated before, Littleton Dalton was a fascinating old fellow. Keen as a child, but appearing to be oblivious to everything around him, he missed nothing. During the time he was in our home we became so attached to him that it was like losing one of the family when he left. I put him on the stage at Lerdo to travel alone back to Broderick. He was past eighty-one years of age at the time, but was capable of traveling alone anywhere. We talked until the stage was ready to leave.

"Some difference between this outfit and the first stage I ever rode on, an old rockaway drawn by four horses. I rode from Harrisonville, Missouri, up to Independence." This was the last statement made by Lit to me.

The stage driver finished transferring some packages at the station. He told us he was ready to leave. Silently Lit shook hands and climbed aboard. Stopping with one foot on the lower step, cane hooked over his left arm, he took off his broadbrimmed Stetson hat, showing his clear, rugged face and snow-white hair. The roar of the motor was strange and far away. The outlines of the stage were blurred and wavy to my vision.

This is the picture that will always remain of Lit. With him, January 3, 1942, passed from the life of today an irreplacable bit of pioneer America.

Littleton Dalton in 1938 when he was being interviewed concerning *Dalton Gang Days.*
Photo by Frank F. Latta and now in Bear State Library.

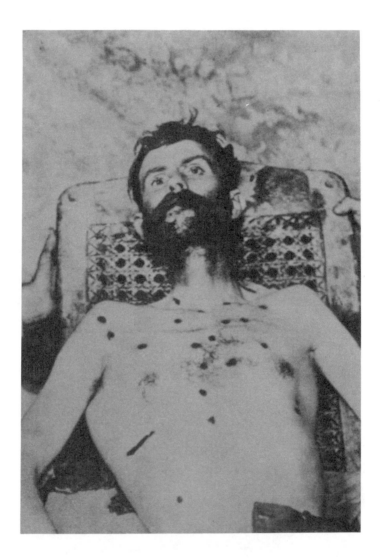

Bill Doolin, leader of the famous Doolin outlaw gang, Okla.
This photo disproves the statement that Bill Doolin was treacherously shot in the back.
Photo courtesy N.H. Rose and now in Bear State Library.

Bill Dalton, in death, illustrating the fact that the bullet did not emerge from the front of Bill Dalton's body.

Photo courtesy N.H. Rose and now in Bear State Library.

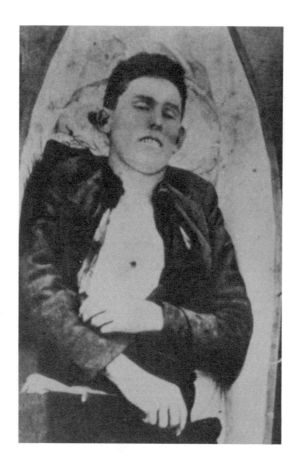

Bob Dalton just before burial, corroborating the statements that Bob Dalton was shot through the head as well as the heart. Note the blood under his right ear.

Photo courtesy N.H. Rose and now in Bear State Library.

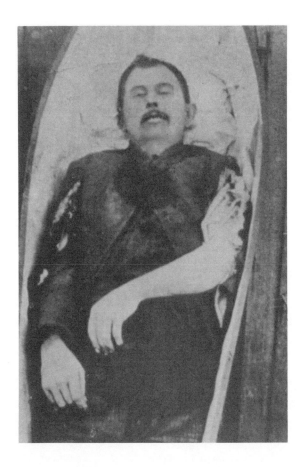

Grat Dalton just before burial, corroborating the statement that Grattan Dalton was shot squarely through the neck.

Photo courtesy N.H. Rose and now in Bear State Library.

Bob Dalton (left) and Grat Dalton (right), photographed after their death.
Photo courtesy N.H. Rose, and now in Bear State Library.

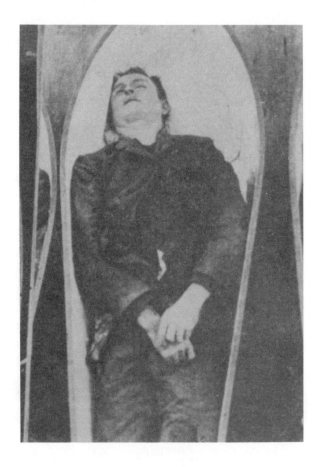

Dick Broadwell just before burial.
Photo courtesy N.H. Rose, and now in Bear State Library.

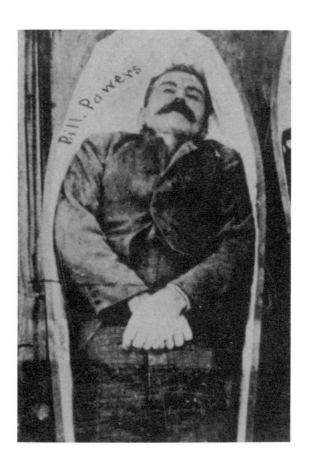

Bill Powers just before burial.
Photo courtesy N.H. Rose, and now in Bear State Library.

Left to right: Bill Powers, Bob Dalton, Grat Dalton, Dick Broadwell, four of the five men killed when they attempted to rob two banks at Coffeyville, Kansas, Oct., 5, 1892. Emmett Dalton who was with them survived 21 bullet wounds, served time in the penitentiary until pardoned.

Photo courtesy of N.H. Rose and now in Bear State Library.

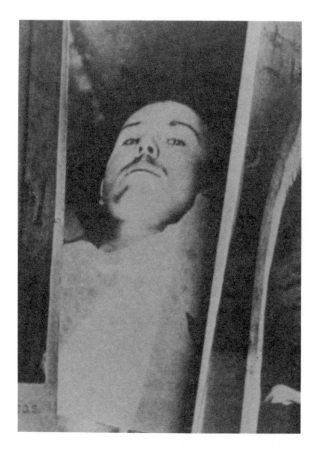

Emmett Dalton as he lay in Dr. Well's office just after the Coffeyville battle.

Photo courtesy N.H. Rose and now in Bear State Library.

INDEX

Index

A

Adair robbery, Okla., 184, 205, 206, 212
Ahern, Jack, 123
Álamo Mocho, Cal., 71, 92, 142
Álamo Solo, Cal., 9, 58, 93
Alila robbery (Earlimart), Cal., xiii, xiv, 8, 53, 57–74, 79, 84, 93, 99, 103, 118, 124, 125, 128, 129, 131, 132, 148, 181, 186, 231, 263, 265
Alila robbery clues, 59, 63, 72, 87, 93, 96, 97, 131, 149
Alila Prohibitionists, 82
Allens' Hill, Kan., 213
Allen, Stony and Mrs., 44, 49
Andy Neff Special, 84, 87, 88
Antelope Valley, Cal., 181
Ardel, Charlie, xv
Ardmore, Okla., 241, 244, 246, 248–250
Arkansas City, Kan., 199, 200, 201
Armbruster, Dan, 123
Armona, Cal., 89
Avenal ranch, Cal., 93
Ayres, Bert, 215
Ayres, Thomas G., 215, 217

B

Babb, Tom, 215
Bakersfield, Cal., xiii, 130
Baldonabro, Mustang Ed, 124
Baldwin, Lucius, 215
Ball, Charles M., 213, 215
Barnett, 49
Barfield Family, Hills Ferry, Cal., 236
Barstow, Cal., 105, 106
Bartholomeu, M.L., 243
Bartlesville, Okla., 202
"Battle of the Banks", Coffeyville, Kan., 207
Baxter Springs, Kan., 48, 50, 51, 56
Bealsville, Cal., 105
Beaver, Oscar, xv

Beck, Arvil, 133, 135, 139, 144–147, 154–157, 159
Bellota, Cal., 158
Belton, Mo., 6, 12, 13, 22–24, 44, 212
Belt Family, Hills Ferry, Cal., 236
Benedict, Ed, 8, 14, 17, 18, 21, 24, 99
Bennett (alias of Jim Wallace), 244
Beyond The Law, Emmett Dalton, 73, 74, 229
Biddison, A.J., 223
Biggs, Major, 29
Bitter Creek (Bob Yokum and/or George Newcomb), 188
Bitter Creek ranch, Okla., 189
Bitter Water Valley, Cal., 102, 103
Black Bear robbery, Okla., 198, 202
Bliven, Clark, 44, 49, 56, 72, 102, 109, 231, 246
Blue Cut, Mo., 3
Boone, Justice, 154
Border Ruffian Trail (Old Whiskey Trail) Mo., 23
Boswell Hardware, Coffeyville, Kan., 215
Braden, 33
Breckenridge, J.C., 128
Breckenridge, John W., 122, 123, 126, 128–130
Breckenridge, Mrs. John, 180
Brewer, 33
Brewer, Billy, 146
Brewster, 221
Broadwell, Dick, 187, 196, 205, 207, 213, 217, 220, 222, 264
Broderick, Cal., 13, 255, 266
Borgwart, Sheriff, 88
Brown (Longview Mill), Texas, 242
Brown, Charles, 217
Brown, Mrs. (alias of Jane Dalton), 247, 248
Brush Creek Hill, Mo., 24
Bryant, Charlie, 188, 190, 194, 195

Buckingham, George, 243, 246
Buford, Judge, 202, 203
Burland, Cal., 163
Buttonwillow, Cal., 103, 105
Buzzard's Roost (Waukena) Cal., 84, 99
Byrd, Perry, 84, 87, 88, 138, 144, 163, 168

C

Calcroft, Marshal, 129
Caldwell Hotel, Centerville, Cal., 171
Caldwell, Kan., 192
Camp, Scott, 258
Cantonment, Okla., 183
Cantúa, Cal., 180
Carpenter, Charles, 210, 212, 220–223
Carrizo Plains, Cal., 102
Carroll, Jo P., 106
Carter Co., Okla., 246, 247
Casey Boys, 198
Cattle King of the Joaquin, 235
Centerville, Cal., 163, 171, 175
Ceres robbery, Cal., 84, 131, 147–149, 151, 154, 186, 194, 231, 239, 257, 258
Chalk Level, Mo., 23
Chapman, Amos, 204
Chappel, 197
Charters, Harry, xvi, 77, 79, 82, 101, 141, 144, 145, 150, 151
Cherokee Advocate, 189
Cherokee Indian Bandit (Henry Starr), 239
Cherokee Strip (Neutral area) Okla., 184, 185, 190, 204
Chico, Cal., 109, 110, 261
Cholame, Cal., 57, 71–73, 94, 183, 224, 244, 250
Christian Brothers, 198, 202
Cimarron R., Okla., 204
Civil War, 9, 12, 13, 22, 24, 28, 181, 238
Claremore, Okla., 48
Clark, 33
Clemons, Joe, 243
Clemons, Tom, 243
Cleveland, Wash., 155
Clifton, Dick, 188
Clovis, Cal., 179, 257
Coalinga, Cal., 88, 89
Coffee, Nora, 234
Coffeyville, Kan., xviii, 1, 27, 51, 184, 186, 187, 189, raid: 207–220; acc'ts: 221–229; 238, 239, 255, 257, 263, 264
Coffeyville telegram, 224, 226
Cole, Bert, 258
Cole, Clovis, 47, 50, 51, 57, 58, 102, 121, 122, 126, 180, 182, 238, 239, 255, 258, 260, 263
Cole, Jim, 27
Cole, Ora, 258
Collier, Carroll, 47
Collier, Lillian, 235, 237
Collier, Mary, 235
Collier ranch, Cal., 235
Collier, Sarah, 235
Collier, Sierra Nevada Summit (Emma Summit Collier) 235
Collier, W.G., 235
Collins, Jim, 195
Collis robbery (Kerman), Cal., 98, 138, 186
Colorado State Prison, 202
Columbia Building, Coffeyville, Kan., 213
Columbus, Kan., 48
Commodore (Grat's getaway horse), 181, 182
Condon Bank, Coffeyville, Kan., 207, 208, 213, 215, 217, 221, 223
Connelly, City Mar., 210, 217, 220
Cotton ranch, Cal., 49, 92, 102
Cottonwood Pass, Cal., 71, 93
Court House Park, Stockton, Cal., 4
Cove, Douglas, 261
Cowboy Flat, Okla., 204, 226
Cox, 215
Crawford Co. Bank, Van Buren, Ark., 224
Crawford, Johnnie, 124
Crawford's Visalia Bar, 124
Cross Creek, Cal., 131, 149, 154, 231, 232, 250
Cross Creek Stage Station, 250
Crossmore, George, 99
Crow, Walter, 30, 32–34, 36
Crow's Landing, Cal., 32
Cubine, George, 210, 217, 229
Cuningham, Sheriff, 147, 148
Cunningham, Tom, 4
Cutler, Cal., 111

D

Daggett, Alfred, 130

INDEX

Daily Ardmoreite, Ardmore, Okla., 247

Dalton, Adeline Lee, née Younger, 1, 4, 9, 11–13, 17, 23, 24, 27, 44, 45, 54, 115, 122–124, 182, 183, 207, 237–239, 252, 255, 256, 262

Dalton Alley (Death Alley), Coffeyville, Kan., 210, 215, 217, 220, 221, 223

Dalton, Charles Benjamin (Ben), xi, 2, 8, 11, 17, 27, 28, 43, 44, 99, 122, 183, 207, 231, 232, 236, 257

Dalton, Charles Coleman (Chub), 44, 236, 237, 250, 252

Dalton, Cole letter (Ceres robbery), 258

Dalton-Doolin gang, 196

Dalton, Emmett, xiii, xvi, xvii, 5, 14, 22, 46, with The Nations, horse stealing: 47–51; 53, 54, 56, Alila robbery: 57–67; 69, 70, getaway: 71–73; alias McElhanie: 74; 95–101, escape to Ind. Terr.: 102–119; 124, 125, 128, 134, 142, 148, 149, 161, 169, 170, 177, 180, 182–185, Okla. robberies: 188–206; Coffeyville raid: 207–229; imprisonment, books, death: 229; 235, 238, 249, 250, 252, 258, 263, Coffeyville: 263, 264; death: 265

Dalton, Frank, 2, 8, 17, 18, 24, 27, 99, 212, 223, 236

Dalton Gang members, Okla., 187, 188, Bob's gang: 189, 205, 207; Bill's gang: 239, 240

Dalton, Gracie, 237, 250, 252

Dalton, Gratton Hanley (Grat), xi, xiii, 8, 9, 22, 27, 31, 36, 41, 47, 51, 54, 56, Alila robbery: 58–62; 64–69, jailed: 70; 93, 95, 98, 99, 101, 105, 118, trial: 121–132; jail escape: 133–148; chased by Kay: 147, 152, 153, 154, 157, 159; Dalton Mt. hideout, battle: 161, 162, 168, 169–174; escape: 174–179; hideout: 180; to Ind. Terr.: 181–184; 185, 187, 202, Okla. robberies: 188, 195, 202, 205; Coffeyville raid: 207, 210, 213, 215, 217; death: 219; 223, 224, 231, 232, 236–238, 255, 256, 264

Dalton, Henry Coleman (Cole), xi, xv, xvi, 2, 6, 17, 22, 24, 30, 41, 51, 54, 71, 108, 109, 121, 122, 124, 148, 180–184, 188, 231, 234–236, 255–257, Ceres robbery letter: 258; 260, 261, death: 262; 265

Dalton, James Louis, 1, 3, 4, 6, 12, 17, 19, 21–24, 40, 41, 44, 45, 256

Dalton, Jane, née Bliven, 204, 236, 247, 248, 253

Dalton, Julia, née Johnson, 198, 202, 229, 264, 265

Dalton, Littleton, Younger, xv, xvii, xviii, family, Belton: 1, 3, 4, 6, 8, 9, 11–14, 17–19, 21–24, 27, 28; 29, Mussel Slough: 30–36; 38, 39, family, Kingfisher: 41, 43–45; 46–56, Alila robbery: 57–66; Grat's arrest, release: 67–70; Bob, Emmett escape: 71–73; McElainie: 74; Bob, Emmett to Ind. Terr.: 102–105; Grat's trial: 121–126; Grat's escape tools: 134; Ind. Terr.: 180–184; 185, Okla. gang: 187, 188; Coffeyville raid: 207, 208; Mason: 238, 239, 241, 242, 244, 246, 252, 253; bitterness: 255–257; refuge: 258–261; Simon, Cole: 260, 262; 265, 266

Dalton, Louis Kossuth, 2, 22, 41

Dalton, Mason Frakes (Bill), xiii, xv, 2, 21, 27, 44, 47, Estrella ranch: 49; 51, 53, 54, 56, Alila robbery: 57, 58; escape aid to Bob, Emmett: 71–73, 96–99; aiding brothers to Ind. Terr., his arrests, release on bond, freedom: 101–103, 105, 108, 112, 121, 122, 123–126, 128, 129–131, 141, 144, 145, 147–154; 180, Okla. robberies: 185, 187, 188, 195, 202, 203–205; Coffeyville raid: 222, 226; "jumping the line", family: 231–234; 236–238, his gang: 196, 239; robberies: 240–246; death: 247–253; 256, 257

Dalton Mt. battle, 164–177

Dalton Mt. hideout, Cal., 137, 162–164, 170, 171, 176, 177, 179

Dalton, Nancy, 19, 22

Dalton, Robert Rennick (Bob), xi, xiii, 2, 22, 27, 41, U.S. Dep., with The Nations, horse stealing: 47–51; 53, 54, 56, Alila robbery: 58–67; 69, 70, getaway: 71–73; 95, 96, 98, 101, to Ind. Terr.: 102–119; 125, 128, 137, 142, 143, 148, 149, 151–154, 161, 169, 180, 182, 185, his gang, robberies: 188, 190, 191, 194, 204–206; Coffeyville raid: 207–217; death: 219; 220–223, 226, 229, 231,

236-238, 244, 246, 255, 256, 258, 263-265
Dalton School, Mo., 24, 44
Dalton, Simon Noel, 2, 17, 183, 207, 236, 260, 261
Dalton sisters, 122
Darby (Grat's getaway horse), 176
Davis, 56
Dean, Riley, xiii, 110, 111, 130, 136, 145, 147, 150, 153, 162, 163, 167-169, 171, 172, 174, 176, 177, 231, 232, 238, 239, 244, 246, 250, 257, 258
Dearing, Kan., 46
Death Alley (Dalton Alley), Coffeyville, Kan., 210, 215, 217, 220, 221, 223
Deep Water, Mo., 12
De Hart Family, Hills Ferry, Cal., 236
Delano, Cal., xiii, 59, 62, 69, 97, 98, 102, 123
Denny, Co. Recorder, Visalia, Cal., 143, 145
Denton, C.R., 247
Diets, Lew, 219
Dixon, 27
Dodge, Fred, 203
Doolin, Bill, 187, 188, 196, 201, 205, 226, 238-241, 256
Dudley, Cal., 71, 93, 97
Duncan, Okla., 188
Dynamite Dick (Dick Clifton and/or George Newcomb) 188

E

Earlimart (Alila), Cal., 62, 79
Eaton, James, 129
Eighth Street, Coffeyville, Kan., 208, 213, 217, 221, 222,
Elite Saloon, Fresno, Cal., 123
Elk (Poolville), Okla., 187, 241, 244, 246, 249, 252, 256
Elmwood Cemetery, Coffeyville, Kan., 27, 212, 229
El Reno, Okla., 189, 195, 197, 200
Elwood, Judson, 167, 169, 170, 171, 174-176
Elwood, Leonard, 170, 174-177
Elwood, Mrs., 164, 171, 175, 180
Elwood ranch, Cal., 163, 164, 167, 170, 179, 180

Estancia in Argentina, 185
Estrella ranch, Cal., 49, 53, 56, 57, 71, 73, 100, 102, 125, 149, 152
Evans, Chris, xv, 8, 31, 84, 106, 137-139, 147, 148, 172, 187
Evans, Tom, 187

F

Fairview School, Merced, Cal., 237
Famosa (Poso), Cal., 89
Farmington, Cal., 158
Fellmore, J.A., 257
Fightmaster, Sheriff, 197
Finley, Jessie, 198
Firebaugh, Cal., 58, 261
First National Bank, Coffeyville, Kan., 207, 208, 210, 213, 215, 217, 220
Fisher, Frank, 242, 249
Fitzgerald's Place, Okla., 226
Flewellen, Caleb, 36
Flewellen (Longview Mill), Texas, 242
Ford, Bob, 110, 212
Ford, Jim, 84, Alila robbery clues: 87-98 cross country chase with Kay: 108-119; 129, 163, 186, 190, 231
Fort Reno, Kan., 192
Fort Smith, Ark., 24, 48, 49, 139, 192, 224, 239
Fort Supply & Indian Agencies, Ind. Terr. Okla., 204
Fowler, Tom, 102, 103
Frakes, Mason, 22
Freeman, W.B., 247
French Camp, Cal., 131
Fresno, Cal., xiii, 68, 69, 125, 148, 159, 162, 169, 170, 174, 229, 257, 261
Fresno Republican, 257

G

Gibbons, Mary née Younger, 9
Gila Bend, Ariz., 182, 183
Gilroy, Cal., 32
Glazer, Conductor, 198, 199
Glenn, Old Doc, 29, 30
Glen ranch, Cal., 29, 51
Glover, W.H., 247
Gorham Family, Hills Ferry, Cal., 236

INDEX

Gorman Station, Cal., 181
Goshen, Cal., 27, 32, 70, 89, 92, 149
Goshen robbery, xiii, 84, 95, 129, 138, 139, 141, 148
Grand Central Hotel, Fresno, Cal., 68, 128
Grangers' Union, Pixley, Cal., 139
Granite Mt., Wichita Res., Kan., 190
Gray, Judge, 123, 129
Gray, W.W., 179, 180-182
Gray, Mrs. W.W., 180
Greenland, Ark., 223
Greyhounds at Alila School, 79, 81
Griffith, Frank, 70, 162
Grimes, U.S. Dep. Mar., 118, 129, 190, 194, 195, 199, 224
Gump, Charles, 210, 212, 220-223
Guthrie, Okla., 101, 115-118, 124, 190, 192, 193, 197, 199, 201, 204, 208, 226, 241
Guthrie Telegram, 129

H

Hall, Bill, 143, 144, 163, 167, 258
Hall, Fred, 163, 167, 175
Halsell, 201
Halter, Frank, 56, 63, 102
Hanford, Cal., xiii, 8, 14, 18, 20, 32, 70, 99, 157, 162
Hanford Rd., Tulare, Cal., 157
Hanford Sentinel, 14
Harris, Jim, 33, 34
Harris, John, 69
Harris, Len, 147
Harrisonville, Mo., 12, 23, 266
Hart, Los, 247, 248
Hartman, Mrs., née Collier, 235
Hart, M.J., 32-34, 36
Haswell, C.C., 54, 64-68, 125, 128
Hawkins Family, Hills Ferry, Cal., 236
Haymaker, 34, 36
Hazen, Bill, 101
Hazen John, 34, 134
Healdton, Okla., 247
Henderson, 34, 36
Hennessey, Okla., 194, 195
Hensley, Claud E., 189
Hensley, Sheriff, 162, 163, 168, 170-174, 179

Herrick, Manuel, 198, 199
Hickey, Detective, 63, 69
Hills Ferry, Cal., 181, 234-236
Hinnery, L.L., 206
Hockett, Bob, 84, 89, 141, 142, 163, 167, 168
Hooker, Dave, 247
Hope robbery, Ark., xiv
Houston, T.J., U.S. Dep. Mar., 131, 256
Howard, J.C., 249
Hughes Hotel, Fresno, Cal., 123
Hughston, Old Billy, 221
Hume, Detective, 88, 89, 148, 154
Huron, Cal., 32, 89, 92, 94, 142
Hutchinson Family, 212
Hutchison, Kan., 187
Hyde, R.E., Banker, 164-166

I

Independence Co. jail, Kan., 238
Independence, Kan., 210, 238, 266
Indian Terr. (The Nations incl. among others: Sac and Fox, Cheyenne, Arapaho, Osage, Chicasaw), Okla., 12, 24, 47, 101, 103, 105, 108, 115, 116, 137, 152, 161, 180-182, 185, 186, 190, 198, 202, 207, 208, 212, 239, 247, 256, 263
Ingalls fight, Okla., 201, 239-241, 244, 252, 256
Irish Boy, 234
Isham Hardware, Coffeyville, Kan., 210, 215, 217, 219, 221, 222
Isham, Henry, 219

J

Jail breaking tools (Grat), 134, 135, 145
James Boys, 3, 8, 9, 187, 212
James, D.E., 215
James, Frank, 23, 212, 213
James, Jessie, 3, 23, 110, 212, 213
Joaquin, 124
Johnson, Charles F., 135
Johnson, Julia (husbands: Lewis, Emmett Dalton), 198, 202, 229
Johnson, Sid., U.S. Dep. Mar., 206
Jo, Ling and Mary, 39
Jones, Arkansas Tom, 188, 240, 241
Jones, Bill (Knight), 242, 243, 250, 252
Jones, City Mar., Okla. City, Okla., 198

Jones, Jim (Knight), 242, 243, 250, 252
"Jumping the line" (Bill Dalton), 231, 237

K

Kansas City, Mo., 18, 23, 24
Katy (M.K.&T. R.R.), 184, 205, 212
Kay, Eugene, xvii, xviii, 38, 53, 59, 65, 67, 69, 72, 73, Alila electioneering: 79-83; 84; "little dinkey train": 87, 91, 92; Alila robbery clues: 87-98; 99, 106, cross country chase of Bob, Emmett, Cole: 108-119; 125, 126, Grat conviction: 128; 131, 135, Grat escape: 136-141; 144, 145, 147, arrests of Bill Dalton, Dean, Beck, Smith: 147-159; 161, 162, R.E. Hyde: 164-166; Dalton Mt. battle: 167, 168; Grat escape: 169, 170; 171-175, 179, 180, 186, 190, capture of Bill Dalton, Dean: 231, 232, 234; 244, 265, death: 266
Kelly, 34, 36
Kettleman Hills, Cal., 89, 142
Kettleman Plains, Cal., 89, 92, 142
Killian, Lee, 188
Kingfisher, Okla., 45, 49, 54, 101, 105, 114, 118, 122, 126, 181-183, 187, 195, 202, 207, 212, 226, 238, 239, 253, 255, 260, 262
Kirkpatrick, 11, 23
Kirkpatrick, Sofronia, née Younger, 9, 11, 23
Kloher, John, 217, 219
Knight (Jim and Bill Jones), 242
Knights of Pythias sword, 198
Knudsen, Ivar, 34, 36
Kress Building, Coffeyville, Kan., 213

L

Lacy, J.C., 242-244, 249, 250, 252
Lake House ranch, Cal., 102
Lake Merrill, Longview, Texas, 246, 248, 249
Lamberson, C.C., 130, 144
Landers, Al, 47
Lansing Prison (Emmett), 229
Lathrop, Cal., 131
Latta, F.F., interviews with principal informants: *Littleton Dalton*—The Dalton Clan: 2, 3, 6, 8, 14, 17, 20; Mussel Slough Tragedy: 21, 30, 31, 36, 38; Playing With Fire: 39, 46; Alila Robbery: 57, 66, 67, 70, 73, 74; Six Thousand Mile Manhunt: 101; Grat Dalton's Trial: 121, 126; Grat Dalton's Escape: 134; Grat Dalton's Ride: 180; Okla. Train Robberies: 185, 186, 189; Battle Of The Banks: 207; Bill Dalton's Gang: 237; Holing Up: 255, 257, 258. *Eugene Kay*—Andy Neff Special: 77, 79, 81, 82; Six Thousand Mile Manhunt: 106; Grat Dalton's Escape: 126, 135, 141; Captured: Bill Dalton, Dean, Beck, Smith: 147, 150; Dalton Mt. Battle: 161; Bill Dalton's Gang: 231. *Chris Madsen*—Six Thousand Mile Manhunt: 101; Okla. Train Robberies: 192; Battle Of The Banks: 224. *Jim Wagy*—Grat Dalton's Escape: 141. *Ed McCardle*—Dalton Mt. Battle: 170. *Leonard Elwood*—Dalton Mt. Battle: 174. *Roy Owen*—Grat Dalton's Ride: 179. *Claud Hensley*—Okla. Train Robberies: 189. *Emmett Dalton*—Battle Of The Banks: 208, Holing Up: 263, 264. *Charles Carpenter*—Battle Of The Banks: 212. *Charles Gump*—Battle Of The Banks: 220. *Jacob Yoes*—Battle Of The Banks: 223. *Arch Turner*—Bill Dalton's Gang: 234. *Sarah Collier*—Bill Dalton's Gang: 236. *Lillian Collier*—Bill Dalton's Gang: 236. *Jack Snyder*—Bill Dalton's Gang: 247. *J.C. Lacy*—Bill Dalton's Gang: 249, 250, 252

Latta narration—xi-xviii; The Dalton Clan: 4, 5; Mussel Slough Tragedy: 31; Playing With Fire: 39; Alila Robbery: 66, 67, 74; Andy Neff Special: 77, 79; Grat Dalton's Trial: 129, 131; Grat Dalton's Escape: 133, 134; Okla. Train Robberies: 185, 186, 189-192; Battle of the Banks: 208-212, 229; Bill Dalton's Gang: 235, 236, 239-247; Holing Up: 263, 265; End of an era: 266
Lawrence, Kan., 9, 11, 12, 22, 24
Leatherman, J.H., 247
Lee, Gen. Robert E., 9
Le Flore, Charlie, 206

INDEX

Leg o' mutton (gun), 110
Lelietta (Wagoner) robbery, Okla., 196, 203, 205
Lemoore, Cal., 89
Lerdo, Cal., 266
Levan, Charles, 246
Levan, John D., 215
Lewis, Ernest, 198, 200-202
Liberty, Mo., 11, 22
Light, Din, 71
Linders, Tulare, Cal., xiv
Lindsey, S.T., U.S. Dep. Mar., 247
Lipscomb, Duke, 164, 165
"little dinkey train", 87, 89, 92, 144
Livingston, Cal., 106, 149, 179, 180, 183, 234, 237, 257, 260
Lobergrub, Ky., 41
Loco, Okla., 205
Logan Co., Okla., 197
Long-Bell Lumber Co., Coffeyville, Kan., 213
Longview, First Nat'l Bank robbery, Texas, 244, 246, 248, 250, 252
Longview, Texas, 247, 248, 250
Lost Hills (The Bubbles), Cal., 71
Louis, Tillie, 13, 41
Lovern, Si, xv
Ludlow, Cal., 101, 105, 106, 108, 183

M

Maddox, Ben, xvi, 186
Madera, Cal., 122
Madsen, Chris, 101, 188, 191-206, 224-229
Magala, Cal., 57-59, 68, 69, 123
Mahoney, 124
Maple St., Coffeyville, Kan., 210, 213
Maricopa, Cal., 121
Martin, Mrs., 92
Maxwell, Bud, 47
Mayes Co., Okla., 205
McAdams, 102
McCall, Dan, xv, 258
McCardle, Ed, 163, 167, 170-175, 177
McCarty, 159
McDonald Brothers, xvi
McDonald, Loftis, 124, 125
McElhanie, William (alias of Emmett) 46, 47, 73, 74

McGee College, Ky., 41
McGregor, Archibald, 33, 34, 36
McKenna, Alec, 210
McKinley's Place, 204
McQueen, Walter, 243, 246
Mead, Jim, 163, 175
Mendoza Family, Hills Ferry, Cal., 236
Merced, Cal., 28, 106, 122, 123, 149, 157, 159, 179, 180
Merced Law Firm (Breckenridge & Peck), 130
Merrill, Louis, 93
Mexican War, 38, 60
Middlton, 258
Middleton, Joe, 102, 157, 161-163, 167, 171, 175, 177
Miller, Doc, 234
Miller, Henry, 105, 235
Miller & Lux Buttonwillow ranch, Cal., 56, 103, 235, 261
Minturn, Cal., 157
Missouri, Kan., 12
M.K. & T. R.R. (Katy), 184, 205, 212
Modesto, Cal., 147, 148
Mojave, Cal., 105, 106
Monroe, Cal., 105
Montegaw Springs, Mo., 23
Montgomery, Charlie, 47
Moore, Eugenia, 190, 193, 196
Moore, George, 170
Morena Family, Hills Ferry, Cal., 236
Morgan, 200
Morgan, Martha, née Younger, 9
Mrs. Mundays (alias Tom King), 193, 196-198, 200, 202
Muckelroy, Matt, 243, 246
Mulhall, Okla., 194
Munn, Charles, 213
Murderer's Bar, Coloma, Cal., 29
Murray, Pat, 89, 142
Murry, N.D., 240
Musgrove, Frank, 48
Mussel Slough battle, 20, 21, 30-32

N

Needles, Cal., 105, 112
Neff, Andy, 84, 89, 92
Negro Trusty (Tulare Co. jail), 134, 137

Neutral Strip (Cherokee land), Okla., 184, 185, 190, 204
Newcomb, George, 188–190, 194, 196, 205, 238–241, 256
Newsome Family, Hills Ferry, Cal., 236
Nicholaus, Cal., 28
Noel, Robert and Nancy Emaline, 28, 41
North Canadian Riv., Okla., 186, 190, 192
North Hollywood home (Emmett), Cal., 263

O

O.K. Hotel, Ingalls, Okla., 240
Oklahoma City, Okla., 197, 200
Oklahoma Co. jail, 198, 202
Old Columbia ranch, Firebaugh, Cal., 56, 57
"Old Liddy", 1, 6, 9, 17
Old Whiskey Trail (Border Ruffian Trail), Mo., 23
O'Neal, Sheriff, 71–73, 96, 98, 101
Opera House, Coffeyville, Kan., 208, 264
Orr, Tom, 87, 89
Osage Nation, Ind. Terr., Okla., 47, 48, 200, 201, 204
Overall, Dan, 88, 89, 97, 138, 141, 142
Overland Stage Rd., 149
Owen, Charlie, 45–47, 50, 51, 54, 59, 68, 103, 179, 180
Owen, Roy, 179, 180
Owen, Tom, 180

P

Pacheco Pass, Cal., 181
Palace Hotel, San Francisco, Cal., 258
Parker, Jack, 124
Parker, Isaac C., the hanging Judge, 178
Paso Robles, Cal., 88, 94, 95, 97, 98, 102, 105, 108, 112, 124, 131, 149, 239
Patrick, Cornelius, 33
Pawhuska, Okla., 198, 201, 204
Payne Co., Okla., 238, 239
Peach Tree ranch, Cal., 56
Peck, James, 122, 123, 126, 130
Perkins, Luther, 215, 223
Petit, Charley, 201
Phillips, Perry, 29
Pickering, George, 217, 221, 222

Pierce, Charlie (Cockeye Charlie), 188, 196, 204, 238, 239, 256
Pierson Dude ranch, Cal., 171, 179
Pillen, Willey, 250
Pixley: *A Full Account Of A Train Robbery*, 129, 130
Pixley robbery, Cal., xii, 53, 54, 88, 129, 138, 139, 141, 148
Plaza, Coffeyville, Kan., 217
Poole, A.W., U.S. Dep. Mar., 32, 33
Poolville (Elk), Okla., 187, 241, 244, 246, 247, 249, 252, 256
Pope, W.B., 224
Porterville, Cal., xii, 141
Poso farm, Cal., 261
Power, Maurice E., 79, 81, 122, 123, 125, 128, 130
Powers, Bill, 187, 196, 205, 207, 210, 213, 215, 220, 264
Price, General, 24
Prohibitionists, Alila, Cal., 82
Pruitt, Mrs., 247, 248
Pryor Creek, Okla., 205, 212
Purcell, Okla., 203

Q

Quantrill (Guerilla), 3, 11, 22, 24, 28, 238

R

Radcliff, George, 63–68, 87, 125, 128
Raider, Bill, 188
Ragan, Sophia, née Younger, 9
Rammel's Drugstore, Coffeyville, Kan., 217
Reception Saloon, Fresno, Cal., 68, 69, 123
Red bird dog (Grat's), 172, 176, 177
Red Bluff, Cal., 261
Redding, Cal., 262
Red River, Okla., 246
Red Rock, Okla., 184, 203–205
Reynolds, Art, 219
Reynolds, J.M., 247
Rhoades, Dan, 32
Richmond, Joe, 14
Riley, 118
Riley, Jim, 192, 194
Robbin's Cemetery, Coffeyville, Kan., 46
Robbin's Corner, Kan., 27, 263

INDEX

Roberts, Ed, 247
Roeding Park, Fresno, Cal., 4
Rogers, Bob, 48, 49
Rucker, Maggie, 150, 152, 153
Ruddle Family, Hills Ferry, Cal., 236
Russell, Billy, 101, 134, 135, 138, 149, 154, 165

S

Sac and Fox Ind. Res., Okla., 118, 129, 192
San Emigdio ranch, Cal., 181
San Francisco Chronicle, 129
Sanger, Cal., 157, 162
San Joaquin Co. jail, Stockton, Cal., 159
San Luis Gonzaga, Cal., 181
San Luis Obispo, Cal., 98, 131
San Miguel, Cal., 49, 51, 56, 72, 74, 88, 98
San Quentin Prison, 142, 162
Santa Margarita, Cal., 98
Saunders, B.F., 123
Sawyer Bank, El Reno, Okla., 189
Sawyer, E.J., 189
Sawyer, Mrs., 189, 190
Sawyer, S.W., 189
Scott, 48, 56
Seaman, Cary, 220, 229
Shadley, Lafe, U.S. Dep. Mar., 198, 201, 240, 241, 256
Shelby, General Jo, 22
Shepard, Will, 215
Short, Ed, 194, 195
Silver Dollar Saloon, Guthrie, Okla., 205
Simmons, Dell, 240
Six Shooter Jack, 188
Slaughter Kid (Dick Clifton and/or George Newcomb), 188
Smith, Bill, 8, 27, 63, 69, 71–73, 96, 98, 125, 126, 128, 147, 148, 244
Smith, W.B., 133, 135, 139, 144–148, 154, 156–159
Snelling, Cal., 157
Snowden, Jim, 260, 261
Snowden, Wash, 260, 261
Snyder, Jack, 247
Sol Sweet's Store, Visalia, Cal., 138
Sontag Brothers, 137, 147
Sontag, John, 84, 106, 138, 147, 148, 172
Southern Pacific pay car, 59, 97, 130

Southern Pacific R.R., xiii, 21, 31, 32, 122, 128, 158, 183
Southern Pacific R.R. vs Settlers' League, 31, 32
Southwest City robbery, Mo., 241
Spanish land grants, 32
Speed, Dick, U.S. Dep. Mar., 240, 256
Speed, Horace, U.S. Atty., 202
Stanford, Gov., 32
Stanford ranch, Vina, Cal., 261
Starr, Henry, 185, 196, 200, 239, 242
Steinberg Family, Hills Ferry, Cal., 236
Stevinson, J.J., Col., 236
Stevinson, Louise Jane (Cox), 235, 236
Stevinson ranch, Cal., 28, 235
Stevinson (town), Cal., 235
Stillwater, Okla., 226, 240
St. Joseph, Mo., 212
St. Louis, Mo., 124
Stockbird, Ed, 157, 158, 233
Stockton, Cal., 159
Stokes Boys, 141
Storer, 33
Stoval, 260
Sunflower Valley, Cal., 92
Sycamore Creek, Kan., 222
Sylvia, Nate, 188

T

Taft, Cal., 121
Tagus Switch robbery, Cal., xv, 258
Taloga, Okla., 192
Tampa, Fla., 183, 184
Tehachapi Pass, Mts., 103, 184
Terr. Capital (Guthrie), Okla., 197
Terry, Judge, 32
Texarkana, Texas, xiv
Thacker, Detective, 88
The Bubbles (Lost Hills), Cal., 71
Thomas, Old Heck, 200, 201
Thorne, Joe, 63–67
Three-Fingered Jack, 200
Tilton, George, 62
Timber Culturalists, 79
Timber Hill, Okla., 47
Tipton, Cal., 8, 139
Tishomingo, Okla., 129
Toll House Grade, Fresno, Cal., 51

Tombstone, Ariz., 202
Tom King (Mrs. Mundays), 193, 197, 198, 200, 202
Towerly, 27
Tranquility, Cal., 57
Traver, Cal., 59, 62, 97, 98, 149, 152
Traver Saloon., 153
Tres Pinos, Cal., 32
Tulare, Cal., xiii, 69, 92, 97, 98, 123, 157, 158, 169
Tulare Co., Cal., 133, 137, 146, 147, 156, 162, 164, 231, 258
Tulare Co. jail, Visalia, Cal., 36, 69, 98, 99, 107, 136, 137, 139, 141, 146, 147, 156-158, 161
Tulare County Times, 129, 186
Tulsa Jack, 188, 240, 241
Turlock, Cal., 44, 180, 181, 235
Turlock Cemetery, 44
Turner, Arch, 4, 180, 231, 234, 265
Turner, Ellie, 180
Turner ranch, 28, 30, 234, 236, 260
Tyler, Texas, 250

U

Uncapher, Joe, 215
Union St., Coffeyville, Kan., 208, 213, 215

V

Van Buren, Ark., 224
Vance, 157, 159
Vann, Emmett, 48, 49
Vinita, Okla., 190
Visalia, Cal., 17, 71, 93, 95, 97-99, 105, 110, 118, 122, 124, 129, 131, 133, 136, 141, 142, 144, 147, 148, 150, 158, 159, 163, 164, 169, 183, 186, 190, 205, 232, 238, 244
Visalia Delta, 131
Visalia Saloon, 153

W

Wagoner (Lelietta) robbery, Okla., 184, 196, 203, 205
Wagy, Jim, 89, 141-146
Wagy, Milt, 89
Wallace, Jim, 242-244, 249
Wallace, Houston, 242, 244, 247-249

Wallace Place, Okla., 241
Walnut St., Coffeyville, Kan., 213, 215, 217
Ward, John, 188
Waucomis, Okla., 194, 195
Waukena (Buzzard's Roost), Cal., 84, 99
Wells, Dr. Walter, 220, 222, 223, 264
Wells Fargo Express, xiii, 200
When The Daltons Rode, by Emmett Dalton, 73, 74, 107, 134, 177, 192-194, 202, 203, 205, 206, 229, 249, 265
Whipple, Mrs., née Dalton, 132
White, Mike, 34
Whitworth, Mrs., née Collier, 235
Whorton, (Perry), Okla., 53, 119, 184, 190, 193, 198, 201, 203, 205
Wichita, Kan., 194, 199, 204
Wilcox, Cond. S.F. train, 201
Wilcox, J.H., 215
Williams, Jailor, 84, 132, 139, 143, 144, 146, 150, 152, 233
Williams, Shelby, U.S. Mar., 205
Willows, Cal., 260
Wilson, Floyd, U.S. Mar., 47
Wilson, John (alias of Grat), 62
Winchester rifle, 18, 21, 103, 109, 125, 134, 137, 153, 173, 175, 210, 212, 213, 215, 217, 220, 222, 224, 232, 240, 241, photo caption: 245; 151, 244, 246
Winfield, Kan., 204
Witty, George, 84, 89, 97, 108, 131, 138, 147, 148, 150, 151, 152, 162, 163, 167, 232
Woodward, Okla., 196, 203, 204
Worth, Charlie, 123

Y

Yoes, Col. Jacob, U.S. Dep. Mar., 192, 223, 224
Yoes, George A., Ex U.S. Mar., 188, 192, 223, 224
Yokum, Bob, 188
"You'll Never Miss My Brother 'Till He's Gone", by Bill Dalton, 145
Young, Felix, 288
Younger, Bob, 28
Younger Boys (part of Quantrill's gang), 8, 9, 11, 28, 207, 212, 238
Younger, Bruce, 9

INDEX

Younger, Coleman, 9, 11, 12, 23, 27, 28, 187
Younger, Charles, 6, 8, 9, 17, 22, 23, 28, 41
Younger, Frank, 9
Younger, Henry, 9, 11, 23
Younger, Jim, 9, 23, 28
Younger, John, 11–13
Younger, Littleton, 9, 22

Younger, Thomas Jefferson, 9
Yukon, Okla., 197
Yuma, Ariz., 181

Z

Zirker, Adolph, A., 154
Zumwalt, Cicero, 14, 144

Frank F. Latta was born near the mouth of Orestimba Creek in Stanislaus County, September 18, 1892, son of Cumberland Presbyterian minister, Eli C. Latta and schoolteacher Harmonia (Campbell) Latta. In 1919 while in the U.S. army, he married Jeanette M. Allen born in Oakland, September 3, 1897. Frank and Jean with their four children have shared equally in the efforts and sacrifices made to gather, prepare, and publish these data.

In 1906 Occidental Elementary teacher, Edith V. Hollingsworth, encouraged him to gather the history of the school district by interviewing the original settlers, many of whom then were still living. Latta started with James Hitchcock who came to California before the discovery of gold by James Marshall. He came with the first wagons to cross the Sierra Nevada, lead by Captain Elijah Stevens, and was scalped by the Indians on the way.

To date, Latta has gathered more than 17,000 stories of San Joaquin Valley pioneers. His combined books, newspaper and magazine articles total more than 3000 publications, some of which are listed at the beginning of this edition.

Latta's 1976 books; DALTON GANG DAYS, SAGA OF EL TEJÓN, TAILHOLT TALES, and JOAQUÍN MURRIETA AND HIS HORSE GANGS, published by the Latta family press, Bear State Books, honor 1976 with the Bear State Books Bicentennial seal.

Joe Rodriquez was born in Yuma, Arizona in 1913. His father had been a miner in the Picacho gold fields around 1900. Both parents had migrated from the Parral presidio country in Mexico, where his mother's people had operated an hacienda for many generations.

To provide schooling for the elder youngsters, Joe's father acquired work with the railway in Yuma. The family moved to Winslow in 1918. Joe completed twelve years of public school there, art being his principle interest from the very early years of his life.

In the atmosphere of most early western towns; wagons, buggies, with packhorse and saddlehorse activity, and aided and abetted by his own heritage, our artist was influenced by what he observed and his own involvement.

He says, "Northern Arizona was cattle and sheep country and many of us kids learned to ride on donkeys and graduated to horses. You can sum it up that I have been something of a horseman and something of an artist all my life."

Joe Rodriquez' work has appeared in books and many magazines. In 1976 he was selected as library poster artist for National Library Week for Arizona, April 1-10. The posters and bookmarks featuring two of his oil paintings were displayed in libraries in Arizona and received national distribution during the event.